Direct Foreign Investment in the United States

Harvey A. Poniachek

Bank of America

Lexington Books

D.C. Heath and Company/Lexington, Massachusetts/Toronto

Library of Congress Cataloging-in-Publication Data

Poniachek, Harvey A.
  Direct foreign investment in the United States

  Bibliography: p.
  Includes index.
    1. Investments, Foreign—Unites States.   2. International business
enterprises—United States.   3. United States—Economic
conditions—1981-   . I. Title.
HG4910.P66   1986   332.6'73'0973   85-40457
ISBN 0-669-11076-0 (alk. paper)

Published simultaneously in Canada
Printed in the United States of America
International Standard Book Number: 0-669-11076-0
Library of Congress Catalog Card Number: 85-40457

The paper used in this publication meets the minimum requirements of American
National Standard for Information Sciences—Permanence of Paper for Printed
Library Materials, ANSI Z39.48-1984.
  ∞ ™

The last numbers on the right below indicate the number and date of printing.

10 9 8 7 6 5 4 3 2 1

95 94 93 92 91 90 89 88 87 86

To Judith,
  Shelley,
  and
  Dana

Contents

List of Figures

List of Tables

Introduction

Although direct foreign investment (DFI) in the United States dates back to the preindependence era, impressive growth in such investments did not begin until the 1970s. According to the U.S. Department of Commerce's definition, DFI involves the establishment of a new firm, the expansion of an existing firm, or the acquisition of a business enterprise or real property in which a foreign person or company obtains direct or indirect ownership of at least ten percent of controlling equity. By the end of 1984, DFI in the United States reached $160 billion, almost ten times the 1970 total. If present trends continue, investments could reach $300–400 billion by the end of this decade.

In the United States, most investments are made by multinational companies (MNCs). Over 10,000 MNCs are headquartered in the free world, and they control over 90,000 foreign affiliates. The largest 500 companies account for about 80 percent of international investment, production and trade.[1] Of these 90,000 foreign affiliates, 22,000 are in the United States. Their estimated total assets are $473 billion; they have $515 billion in sales, $4 billion in profits, and employ 2.4 million people.[2] The major investments have been made by companies from Canada, the United Kingdom, the Netherlands, Switzerland, West Germany, and Japan, with the latter two experiencing the highest growth.

The U.S. provides foreign investors with an attractive economic, financial, and political environment and with the opportunity to benefit from the largest and most affluent free market in the world. The government conducts an "open door" policy toward foreign investment, treating foreign and domestic companies equally under the law. Although there is some concern in the United States about the extent of foreign ownership of U.S. industry and natural resources, the government is likely to continue to admit and treat foreign capital equally. Thus, foreign-controlled domestic corporations are on an equal footing with U.S. citizens and corporations in this country.

There are some minor restrictions on participation in certain businesses, however, and restrictions and surveillance of foreign investment in real estate, particularly in agricultural lands, are likely to increase.

The federal government offers no special incentives to attract new foreign investors, and this policy is not likely to change in the future. But individually, the fifty states, Puerto Rico, the Virgin Islands, and American Samoa have a variety of programs to encourage investment by both domestic and foreign concerns. Because DFI generates substantial benefits in employment and capital formation, state and local governments compete vigorously by offering various incentives to attract investment. These consist primarily of tax incentives and financial assistance.

The United States doesn't have a federal corporate law, rather, each state and the Commonwealth of Puerto Rico have its own corporate laws and tax system. Thus, much of the jurisdiction over doing business in the United States rests with state and local governments. While companies are subject to the federal laws that do exist, considerable differences in state and local business laws and taxation create certain attractive incorporation and operation sites.

Population growth, income, and economic activity and opportunity differ widely among the regions and states in the United States. The South and West, in particular, have become increasingly attractive in the past decade and have drawn a large amount of foreign investment. Investors should consider regional differences when selecting a location. The most popular states for DFI companies are California, Texas, New York, Florida, and Illinois.

Foreign companies can enter the U.S. market through the acquisition of an existing corporation or the formation of a new company. These alternatives present different costs and benefits, which must be carefully considered by investors. The form and structure of a U.S. company can have significant financial and tax ramifications. Careful analysis should be performed before adopting any legal entity.

This book can serve as a reference for prospective foreign corporations interested in investing in the United States, for foreign corporations already doing business in the United States, and for U.S. corporations seeking to expand in their own country. The book alerts readers to new trends and their implications for doing business in the United States. It also highlights those conditions to which foreign investors or U.S. corporations may be subject. It provides background information to assist investors in deciding whether to invest, in choosing a location, in organizing financing and taxes, and in operating a business in the United States. It contains sections on operating, financing, taxes, employment practices, and imports and exports.

Careful planning is required for entry in the U.S. market. Once the investment objectives have been set, the investor should identify potential sites, assess competing investment modes, review financing sources, and prepare a business plan. It is often necessary to consult government officials, tax advisors, and attorneys for specific information. Further assistance is available from banks—for example, Bank of America's Direct Foreign Investment Section and investment banks—whose specialists can help investors establish or expand businesses in this country.

1
Worldwide Trends in and Motives for Investing Abroad

Global Trends in Direct Foreign Investment

The expansion of global trade and investment in the post-World War II era has largely been made possible by rapid economic growth and liberal trade and investment policies pursued by most industrial countries. The internationalization of production and financial markets has been a major feature of the global economy since the 1960s. However, pressures for protectionism in trade have recently emerged because of slow economic growth and high unemployment. Furthermore, the rapid growth of direct foreign investment and the expanding role of multinational corporations have become increasingly controversial, particularly in the less developed countries (LDCs) where inward-looking nationalistic policies are widespread.

Direct foreign investment by multinational corporations continued to expand in the 1970s. The global book-value of the stock of direct investment reached an estimated $600 billion in 1984 (see tables 1-1 and 1-2). The average annual cumulative growth of investment was about 22% in the 1970s and 7% in the early 1980s. This growth exceeded the aggregate gross national product (GNP) of the OECD countries. About three-fourths of total investment is located in industrial countries, while the remainder is in LDCs.

The phenomenon of DFI abroad is closely associated with the expanding role of MNCs in the world economy, which has become enormously significant. These companies have a major impact on trade, technology, and finance. Foreign products of multinationals account for about 20 percent of world production, and the intracompany trade of these companies is 25 to 40 percent of international trade of manufactured goods.[3] Table 1-3 contains a breakdown of MNCs by country.

Table 1-1
Stock of Direct Investment Abroad of Industrialized Countries

Country of Origin	Percentage Distribution							Billions of dollars, end of						
	1967	1971	1980	1981	1982	1983	1984	1967	1971	1980	1981	1982	1983	1984
U.S.	53.8	52.3	45.93	43.77	41.80	40.15	38.74	56.5	82.8	215.6	226.4	221.3	226.1	230.9
U.K.	16.6	15.0	11.42	12.38	12.84	12.82	12.79	17.5	23.7	53.6	63.9	68.5	72.2	76.2
Germany	2.8	4.6	8.71	8.85	9.24	9.27	9.13	3.0	7.3	40.9	45.7	49.3	52.2	54.4
Japan	1.4	2.8	6.84	7.17	7.78	8.01	8.64	1.5	4.4	32.1	37.0	41.5	45.1	51.5
Switzerland	4.8	6.0	6.67	6.39	6.56	6.68	6.80	5.0	9.5	31.3	33.0	35.0	37.6	40.5
France	5.7	4.6	4.22	4.73	5.10	5.15	5.17	6.0	7.3	19.8	24.4	27.2	29.0	30.8
Canada	3.5	4.1	4.13	4.36	4.18	4.33	4.51	3.7	6.5	19.4	22.5	22.3	24.4	26.9
Netherlands	2.1	2.5	6.11	6.18	6.39	6.32	6.36	2.2	4.0	28.7	31.9	34.1	35.6	37.9
Sweden	1.6	1.5	1.53	1.45	1.50	1.55	1.63	1.7	2.4	7.2	7.5	8.0	8.7	9.7
Belgium-Lux.	1.9	1.5	1.53	1.36	1.41	1.44	1.46	2.0	2.4	6.3	7.0	7.5	8.1	8.7
Italy	2.0	1.9	0.96	1.14	1.29	1.62	1.86	2.1	3.0	4.5	5.9	6.9	9.1	11.1
Total above	96.2	96.8	97.87	98.06	97.75	97.34	97.48	101.3	153.3	459.4	505.2	522.6	548.1	581.0
All other	3.8	3.2	2.13	1.94	2.25	2.66	2.52	4.0	5.1	10.0	11.0	12.0	15.0	15.0
Grand total	100.0	100.0	100.00	100.00	100.00	100.00	100.00	105.3	158.4	469.4	516.2	533.6	563.1	596.0

Source: United Nations Economic and Social Council, Transnational Corporations in World Development, Third Survey, United Nations Center on Transnational Corporations, U.N., New York, 1983.

Note: Data for 1981–84 are estimates by the author.

Table 1-2
Direct Investment Abroad: Net Capital Flows
(millions of U.S. dollars)

Year	Total	U.S.	France	West Germany	Italy	Netherlands	U.K.	Japan	Canada
Net Capital Outflows									
1970	11,463	7,590	374	873	109	551	1,310	355	301
1977	22,795	11,890	990	2,206	551	1,518	3,290	1,645	696
1978	32,933	16,056	1,891	3,605	168	1,755	5,202	2,371	1,885
1979	45,515	25,222	1,983	4,440	544	2,402	5,892	2,898	2,134
1980	43,464	19,222	3,099	4,083	744	3,258	7,979	2,385	2,694
1981	43,473	9,860	4,583	4,470	1,383	3,194	10,348	4,894	4,921
1982	13,849	-4,756	2,844	3,584	960	2,228	4,611	4,540	-162
1983	22,600	4,881	1,760	2,908	2,205	1,529	3,656	3,612	2,049
1984	23,381	2,249	1,877	2,174	1,960	2,220	3,996	6,373	2,532
Net Capital Inflows									
1970	5,652	1,464	622	595	606	536	871	94	864
1977	10,728	3,728	1,890	831	1,138	358	2,315	21	447
1978	15,592	7,897	2,454	1,558	510	670	2,420	8	75
1979	22,381	11,877	2,588	1,650	360	1,287	3,804	239	576
1980	29,673	16,892	3,290	239	584	1,904	5,986	278	500
1981	27,527	23,148	2,457	1,215	1,130	1,396	1,829	189	-3,837
1982	20,192	14,865	1,596	1,264	643	532	2,008	439	-1,155
1983	21,448	11,299	1,795	1,130	1,229	648	4,769	416	162
1984	31,613	20,708	2,094	941	1,654	703	3,833	-136	1,816

Source: U.S. Department of Commerce, International Trade Administration, *International Economic Indicators* March 1985, p. 54-55.
Note: Data for 1984 are estimates by the author.

Table 1-3
Worldwide MNCs

Name of Country	Number of Parents	Percentage of Total
United States	2,185	21.3
West Germany	1,443	14.0
United Kingdom	1,398	13.6
Switzerland	723	7.0
France	596	5.8
Japan	572	5.6
Netherlands	571	5.6
Canada	407	4.0
Others[a]	2,380	23.2
Of which		
Singapore	133	1.3
Hong Kong	97	0.9
Malaysia	74	0.7
Taiwan	18	0.2
Thailand	12	0.1
Philippines	10	0.1
Portugal	8	0.1
Indonesia	6	0.1
South Korea	6	0.1
Total	10,275	100.0
Of which		
Developed countries	9,911	96.5
Developing countries[a]	364	3.5

Source: John M. Stopford and John H. Dunning, *Multinationals: Company Performance and Global Trends,* (London: MacMillan Publishers, 1983), p. 4. Reprinted with permission.

Note: Parent companies which are subsidiaries of others were excluded to prevent double counting.

[a]Excluding firms based in the Indian sub-continent, Central or Southern America, Africa, the Middle East, and the Comecon countries. Our best estimate of these, drawn from a variety of sources, is 850.

During the 1970s MNCs from the industrial countries—especially the United States and Japan—tended to concentrate their direct foreign investment activities in other developed countries. However, during that period major shifts occurred in the source and the direction of investments. Sources of direct investment became more diversified and less dominated by U.S. corporations, and a two-way investment flow between the industrial countries emerged. More countries became homes and hosts; more companies became participants. The Japanese and Europeans, particularly the West Germans, emerged as important foreign investors as they accelerated their growth and investment activities abroad. In addition, some

OPEC countries, beginning with the 1973-74 oil price increase, embarked on direct investment abroad. Moreover, companies in some large developing countries are now expanding their investments abroad, particularly in their own geographic regions. Estimates in table 1-1 show that in 1984, the United States owned about 39% of DFI stock in the industrialized world, compared with 52% in 1971 and 54% in 1967.

Domestic political stability and the degree of country risk are significant factors affecting the selection of locations for direct foreign investment. Historically, companies have located manufacturing facilities in areas where labor costs are low and natural resources are plentiful, characteristics found in many LDCs. However, severe local antagonism coupled with political uncertainty has weakened the flow of foreign investment to LDCs. Furthermore, investment in primary sectors, especially in petroleum and mining, has diminished as a percentage of the outstanding stock of direct investment largely because of several sizable disinvestments. Accordingly, the level of investment activity in these areas has been reconsidered, causing the direction of DFI flows to shift.

The developing countries now act as hosts to about one-fourth of DFI, a share that has declined continuously since the 1960s. Foreign investment is heavily concentrated in about two dozen middle-income, oil-exporting countries that are reasonably industrialized and endowed with natural resources. Of the $140 billion invested in the LDCs, about 50% is from the United States, and it is primarily invested in Central and South America. The U.K. accounts for more than 10%, located primarily in Africa, while West Germany, with 6.9%, and Japan, with 6.7%, have invested primarily in Asia.[4]

The bulk (57%) of DFI flowing to developing countries has gone to Latin America and the Caribbean, with Brazil and Mexico being the prime recipients. Asia accounts for 30% of DFI and Africa for 13%.[5] A few newly industrialized countries outside the OECD area have become major recipients of direct foreign investment. Foreign investment flowing to Latin America has declined in the past few years because of the poor economic conditions there. Asia is now the developing region receiving the largest flow of foreign investment.

Despite recent acceleration in European and Japanese direct foreign investment, the United States remains the principal foreign investor in most countries, accounting for about half of all new investments (see tables 1-1 and 1-2). This can be partly attributed to the accumulative effect of high U.S. investment throughout the postwar period. However, the very high level of U.S. investment in Europe in the late 1950s and the 1960s—described by Servan-Schreiber in *The American Challenge*—has diminished, mainly because of increased European investment in the United States and around the world since the 1970s.

The preeminence of the United States has not only been challenged but in many cases has been reversed. Still, the U.S. is the major player in the direct foreign investment market, both as a home and host country, even though its share has somewhat diminished in recent years. A narrowing of the technological gap between the United States and the other industrial countries, along with the emergence of the newly industrialized countries, has affected the international competitive positions and the flow of trade, investment, and capital. Particularly important has been the emergence of large European and Japanese MNCs. Currently, European and Japanese market shares are growing rapidly in industries formerly dominated by U.S. corporations. European and Japanese corporate investment in the United States is growing, mostly through acquisitions. These foreign corporations are optimistic about the United States and view it as a safe haven for growth and success. Their level of investment will probably continue to rise as many established European and Japanese MNCs expand operations in the United States and as medium-sized European firms penetrate the U.S. market.

The European Economic Community (EEC) ranks second in global DFI, with more than one-third of the world's total investments. By far, intra-EEC investment activities are the largest component of European DFI. Among the EEC members the United Kingdom is the main investor, followed by Germany and the Netherlands.

Japan's direct foreign investment has increased sharply in recent years. It accounted for about 9% of DFI in 1984, compared with about 3% in 1970.

Recently, European- and Japanese-based MNCs have vigorously shifted their investment preferences toward the high-income, rapid-growth markets of the EEC and the United States. The U.S. in particular has become the central attraction and has increased its importance relative to Europe and the LDCs as a recipient of DFI.

About one-fourth of the assets of MNCs in major industrial countries, both home and host, are in extractive industries. Another one-fourth are in services, and one-half are in manufacturing.[6] A decline in the U.S. and U.K.'s share of the extractive sector in investment stock abroad occurred in the 1970s because of some nationalization of petroleum and mining assets by LDCs.

In summary, global direct investment abroad over the past few years has slowed down because of cyclical and structural factors. Lower global economic growth and improved opportunities in the U.S. have reduced operations of MNCs abroad.

The high growth rate of MNCs and international transactions between the mid-1960s and mid-1970s has now subsided. Apparently, most U.S. corporations had already positioned themselves abroad in the 1960s and 1970s, and their growth is now in terms of continuous adjustment but not in terms of major shifts. Price stability has substantially deflated trade flow, and country risk and portfolio balance considerations suggest more subdued expansion (8% per annum to 1990, compared with 13.7% p.a. from 1966 to 1977 and 11.8% p.a. from 1977 to 1983.

The outlook for DFI activities will be heavily influenced by global economic conditions. Current economic conditions suggest that direct investment is unlikely to regain the dynamism it displayed in the 1960s and 1970s, although investment in certain attractive sectors may expand rapidly.

Motives for Investing Abroad

In assessing the foreign investments and strategies of MNCs, we usually try to answer such questions as Why firms invest overseas, where do they locate their foreign operations, and what determines the amount and composition of international production. However, since international direct investment has become a heterogeneous phenomenon, there is no unique theory that addresses all these issues.[7] Instead there are several complex theories—including micro, macro, and location theory or eclectic theories—which attempt to explain this phenomenon. The latter includes a checklist of company surveys on motives for investing abroad.

Obviously, motivations behind foreign investment and location selection vary according to the type of industry and its maturity as well as the host country and its corporate strategy. Different types of companies, such as those in mining and petroleum, are apparently affected by various factors and for that reason are attracted to different locations.

Micro Explanations

The micro-oriented theories of international direct investment analyze firms that invest abroad and recognize MNCs as the vehicle for these investments. Some theories are based on the industrial organization of a firm, while others stress asset allocation determinants and processes. In this context the theory of capital budgeting provides an appropriate framework for assessing investment, whether domestic or international, and gives insight into how organizations allocate scarce resources.

Budgeting Methods. Domestic and international investment decisions, or capital budgeting, can be based on one of the following five methods, some of which are reconcilable:

1. Net present value
2. Payback period
3. Average return on book value
4. Internal rate of return
5. Profitability index[8]

The internal rate of return (IRR) is defined as the rate of discount, which equates:

$$\text{NPV} = C_0 + \sum_{t=0}^{t} \frac{C_t}{(1 + \text{IRR})^t}$$

The profitability index, or the cost—benefit ratio, is the present value of expected cash flows divided by the initial investment:

$$\text{Profitability index} = \frac{\text{PV}}{-C_0}$$

The profitability index recommends that all projects with an index greater than 1 be accepted. Such an index implies that the present value of the cash flow is greater than the initial investment. The profitability index leads the decision maker in the same direction as the net present value method.

Companies often require that the initial investment on a project be recoverable within a specified time period, commonly referred to as the pay-back period. The pay-back period is determined by the number of years it takes for cumulative cash flows from the project to equal the initial investment. It suggests how rapidly a project can recover that initial investment. In practice, the pay-back period approach requires a corporation to decide on an appropriate cutoff date. Some analysts and companies determine the present value of the cash flow before computing the pay-back period.

Although international budgeting uses this basic theoretical framework, actual analysis can be considerably more complex because of:

Different tax systems, constraints on financial flow, and differences in financial markets and institutions

Foreign exchange rate changes modify the competitive position of a foreign affiliate and the value of its cash flow to the parent

Political risk often reduces the value of a foreign investment by blocking anticipated cash flow.[9]

Since the same capital budgeting framework is used to choose between competing foreign and domestic projects, all foreign complexities must be quantified as modifications of either expected cash flow or the discount rate. Risks peculiar to foreign operations—such as political or foreign exchange risks—can be best accounted for by adjusting the project's cash flow rather than the project's discount rate.

Since capital budgeting for foreign projects involves complex factors that are nonexistent in domestic projects, when assessing a foreign project, one should take a parent company's point of view rather than a project's point of view. A foreign project should be assessed on its net present value (NPV), considering whether funds can be freely remitted to the parent. Use of NPV based on local cash flow is inappropriate for capital allocation.

The Group of Thirty, an independent international research organization headquartered in New York, suggests that the target pay-back period for new foreign direct investment in both industrial countries and less developed countries has been shortened over time. The target pay-back period varies between industries. For instance, in mining that period is five to six years and in manufacturing, four to five years.[10] The required pay-back period is shorter, however, for LDCs. U.S. companies consistently look for a much shorter pay-back than Europeans, 3.5 to 4 years versus 5.5 years. The higher cost of capital, increased political and financial risk, and need for earnings all shorten the required pay-back period.

The capital budgeting process within the corporation considers the world as a single market composed of many countries. Although each country market has a distinct character, it can be summarized in the project's cash flow or discount rate. This framework encompasses all the environmental variables that affect earnings, such as cost of production, tax, foreign exchange movements, and country risk. In accordance with the global perspectives of the MNCs, the budgeting method suggests that resource allocation within the company, in terms of projects and their location, is done on a competitive basis. This method could determine whether firms invest abroad, and if so, where and how much.

Macro Interpretation

Macro theories of international direct investment are derivations of international trade theory. For instance, the product-cycle theory describes the investment process as the end result of a cycle, which begins with innovation, export, direct marketing, and servicing abroad. The cycle ends with the setting up of a manufacturing facility. The investment, in the context of this theory, is undertaken to protect the company's market share, since innovation or similar products threaten its export market.

Furthermore, the decision process motivating international direct investment is derived from various considerations, including strategic, economic, and behavioral.[11] Strategic motives include market seekers, raw material seekers, and technology and efficiency seekers. Economic motives are based on such market imperfections as economies of scale, technology, and financial resources.

Location Theory

Choosing a corporate location is one of the most critical and complex decisions management must make. It may affect the profitability, growth, and even survival of the firm. There is no unique approach to selecting a location. Some methods are highly quantified, while others are judgmental. Various location theories, are used in an ad hoc fashion.[12]

Selecting an operating location, say, in the U.S. involves many factors, including the cost and availability of labor, transportation, and utilities. One must also consider economic and business regulations, zoning, availability of state and local incentives, proximity to the source of input, and customers. These factors vary substantially with location, and they will have a major impact on the company's performance and success. Variations in these costs can make a major difference in the company's competitive position.

The Checklist Approach

A simple checklist of factors that induce investment abroad clarifies the motives behind DFI and how locations and industrial organizations are selected. A U.S. Department of Commerce study of foreign direct investment identified several typical motives for international investment by multinational corporations.[13] The Conference Board publishes *Worldbusiness Perspectives, Foreign Capital Expenditures by U.S. companies,* a semiannual survey of U.S. companies' expenditures and reasons for investing abroad. Recently, the Group of Thirty published *Foreign Direct Investment 1973-87*, the results of a survey of major MNCs around the world and the factors affecting their decisions to invest abroad. These surveys are quite consistent and could add significant insight into the investment decisionmaking process. The Commerce Department findings are more thoroughly discussed below, while the Conference Board's findings are summarized in figure 1–1 and the Group of Thirty's in table 1–4.

According to the U.S. Department of Commerce Survey cited above, motives behind international direct investment are:

1. To open up new markets, to ensure access to export markets, and to protect or expand one's market share in the face of high tariff walls and growing protectionism. Increased protectionism requires exporting countries and companies to secure access to

Table 1-4
Main Influences on DFI Decisions
(percent of respondents)

	In Industrial Countries		In Less Developed Countries	
	1970	1983	1970	1983
Access to host country's domestic market	89	67	82	87
Access to markets in host country's region	41	37	29	34
Avoidance of existing or anticipated tariff barriers	24	16	51	43
Avoidance of existing or anticipated nontariff trade barriers	13	18	29	28
Integration with company's existing investments	26	37	4	17
Changes in industry structure	20	22	11	9
Slower growth of home market	17	18	11	11
Access to raw materials	13	10	13	11
Inducements offered by host country	11	12	16	13
Integration with other companies' investments	4	8	4	4
Comparative labor cost advantages	4	6	11	13
Comparative material cost advantages	4	6	2	4
Shifts of political and social stability	2	8	9	8
Tax advantages	6	4	7	0
Market presence	6	5	3	0
Distribution of risk	0	5	0	3
Return on investment in R&D	3	3	3	3
Development of local market	3	3	3	0
Acquisition opportunities	3	3	0	0
Exchange-rate movements on siting (not financing) investment	0	2	0	0

Source: Foreign Direct Investment 1973–87 (New York: Group of Thirty, 1984), p. 30. Reprinted with permission.

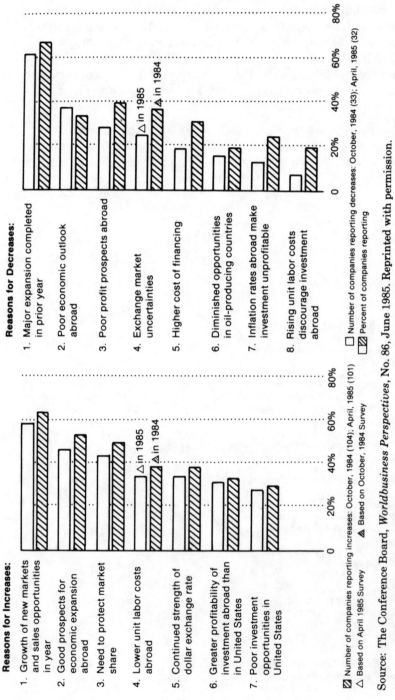

Reasons for Decreases:

1. Major expansion completed in prior year
2. Poor economic outlook abroad
3. Poor profit prospects abroad
4. Exchange market uncertainties
5. Higher cost of financing
6. Diminished opportunities in oil-producing countries
7. Inflation rates abroad make investment unprofitable
8. Rising unit labor costs discourage investment abroad

△ in 1985
△ in 1984

☐ Number of companies reporting decreases: October, 1984 (33); April, 1985 (32)
🔲 Percent of companies reporting

Reasons for Increases:

1. Growth of new markets and sales opportunities in year
2. Good prospects for economic expansion abroad
3. Need to protect market share
4. Lower unit labor costs abroad
5. Continued strength of dollar exchange rate
6. Greater profitability of investment abroad than in United States
7. Poor investment opportunities in United States

△ in 1985
△ in 1984

🔲 Number of companies reporting increases: October, 1984 (104); April, 1985 (101)
△ Based on April 1985 Survey   △ Based on October, 1984 Survey

Source: The Conference Board, *Worldbusiness Perspectives*, No. 86, June 1985. Reprinted with permission.

Figure 1-1. Reasons for Plant and Equipment Expenditures Outside the United States— All Manufacturing

their markets by establishing manufacturing facilities there. In fact, getting behind the EEC tariff wall was a major consideration for U.S. companies investing abroad during the past twenty-five years.

2. To gain greater market efficiency by producing goods and services in the local market. Products can thereby be supplied and serviced more quickly and can be tailored to local tastes, all at minimum cost.

3. To benefit from relatively abundant factor inputs, particularly labor and natural resources, which are relatively inexpensive, thereby reducing production costs. In addition, high domestic taxes, labor strikes, overvalued currencies, and high domestic inflation have been among the major factors affecting DFI.

   A rapid decline in the price competitiveness of domestically manufactured products, caused by the continued appreciation of home currencies, has provided further impetus to establish direct manufacturing facilities abroad. Generally, trends in the long-term exchange rate affect the flow of foreign direct investment, while short-term exchange-rate fluctuations stimulate the flow of intracompany finance. Fluctuations in the exchange rate are considered in a company's budget process, but they are only one of many factors evaluated, and by themselves often have little impact. Many companies suggest that the main effect of foreign-exchange movements is not on the direction or level of DFI, but rather on its financing and timing.[14] Some MNCs maintain that the uncertainty created by wide movements of currencies may make companies reluctant to contemplate large projects in countries affected by such swings. The strong dollar makes DFI more attractive for some U.S. corporations but less attractive for investment in the United States.

4. To prevent market preemption by a competitor or to keep market outlets and sources of supply open. A firm may fear that competitors going abroad may capture a lucrative foreign market or may, by acquiring less expensive sources of supply, threaten the company's position in the domestic market. Direct foreign investment is often influenced by offensive strategies as well. The most crucial factors are the quest for profit, the expectation of profit, and the desire to maintain one's market share through access to the host country's domestic market by avoiding tariff barriers.

5. To diversify product lines, country risk, and currency risk and to avoid fluctuations in earnings. Diversification can also serve as

a defensive motive and can shield a company from cyclical movements, strikes, or threats to its supply sources.

6. To assist a licensee abroad who needs capital to expand operations.

7. To avoid home country regulations, such as U.S. antitrust laws.

8. To exploit raw materials abroad and to safeguard their supply at a reasonable cost.

In summary, direct foreign investment expanded very rapidly in the past four decades, and it has proliferated among the major industrial countries. Its expansion in the years ahead might be somewhat selective, as the major companies have already positioned themselves. There are various motives for going abroad, and the phenomenon of investment is therefore interpreted by various theories. Yet, in assessing the possibility of investing abroad, the capital budgeting criteria must be satisfied to yield the optimum results.

2
Why Invest in the United States?

The United States has recently become the central attraction for European and Japanese companies emerging as important foreign investors. Motivations behind foreign investment in the United States vary according to the industry and its maturity, the country of origin, and the corporation's strategy. Foreign investors are attracted by the following benefits of the U.S. market:

1. growth potential and accessibility to the immense U.S. market
2. availability of high technology and a highly skilled and stable labor force
3. relatively easy access to financial markets in the United States
4. undervaluation of some companies' common stocks
5. the proximity of resources and the efficient distribution system in the United States
6. lower production costs in the United States brought about by rising real wages, falling productivity, and increased taxes abroad
7. relatively limited government intervention in industry
8. political stability in the United States. The poor political climate in some home countries, coupled with an expanding public sector and the threat of nationalization, has stimulated foreign investment activity.
9. currency fluctuations
10. the need to secure access to the United States market in light of growing protectionism and the desire to increase vertical integration.

The Size of the U.S. Market

The United States has more buying power per capita than any other country.[15] Personal consumption spending, which accounts for about two-thirds of the gross national product was $2,342 billion in 1984. The U.S. population also exhibits an unusually low propensity to save. Gross savings averaged under 15% of GNP over the past ten years, while personal savings were 6.1% of GNP in 1984, down from 8.5% a decade ago. The U.S. population is expected to spend about $3,500 billion in current dollars on personal consumption by the year 1990.

Since consumption patterns in the rest of the industrialized world are not as strong, foreign companies are extremely interested in operating in the United States, if only to cash in on the benefits of this spending bonanza. Furthermore, although the United States is geographically one of the largest countries in the world, its highly developed distribution system ensures that competitors have access to the whole market rather than just isolated regions of it.

Markets: Breadth and Scope

A foreign investor deciding whether or not to establish or join an operating entity in the United States must take into account the extraordinary size and diversity of the U.S. market. The country's vast physical size; its wide ranging climate and physical character; the uneven geographic distribution of its population; and the diverse regional, ethnic, racial, and religious backgrounds of the people make the United States a heterogeneous market. Thus location becomes an immediate concern, as does the definition of the business. Fortunately, the United States has extensive systems for collecting data and reporting on sales activity, population, investment, and other categories of information that a potential investor would want to analyze for the development of market profiles.

One highly significant consideration in choosing a market area is whether the investor wants to compete nationally or within one or more regional markets. Each regional market is unique in its wages, population, and income growth and in its availability and cost of raw materials. Companies confining investment activities to one or two regional markets can usually proceed with less capital than companies with national ambitions.

Smaller businesses play a major role in the U.S. economy—96% of U.S. companies have fewer than 250 employees, and these companies employ 43% of the work force in the manufacturing sector.[16]

In addition, the United States has the most extensive system of subcontracting in the world. For example, half of the 1983 production in the $350 billion plant-and-equipment industry was subcontracted on a private-bid basis by the major contractors. Furthermore, most subcontracting companies fall into the middle-market range in size, with annual sales of between $5 million and $100 million. This system, which operates both regionally and nationally, provides opportunities for small- and medium-size companies to complement rather than compete with very large firms.

Regionally and nationally, the United States has one of the world's most extensive transportation networks. There are: (1) 25 major railroad companies operating 69,000 miles of track; (2) about 33 million trucks and buses using 3.9 million miles of highway; (3) more than 420,000 miles of oil and gas pipeline; (4) thirty-two scheduled passenger and cargo airlines, which have flown 5.8 billion ton-miles; and (5) an ocean shipping system, which has moved 2 billion tons of cargo through the nation's deepwater ports.[17]

Other advantages of investing in the United States include: (1) the availability of electrical power through an extensive though increasingly costly system of power grids; (2) the nation's communications network, which permits virtually instant contact between facilities anywhere in the country; and (3) the proximity of Canada, Mexico, the Caribbean, and the Pacific, creating an even wider market which can be served with relative ease.

Competitive Strength

Over the past two decades, the domestic economies of Europe and Japan have grown substantially. As a result, European and Japanese companies achieved markedly higher growth rates than their U.S. counterparts while increasing both their profit and asset bases. Competitiveness was further enhanced by widespread mergers and acquisitions in both European and Japanese industry in the late 1960s and early 1970s. Accordingly, their capacity to compete with their U.S. counterparts, both locally and in the United States, improved. For instance, according to *Fortune* magazine, twenty-one of the world's fifty largest industrial corporations are U.S.-owned, and they account for 53% of total sales. Compare these figures with those of 1974, when twenty-four were U.S.-owned and accounted for 60% of total sales.[18] Since company size is a major factor in determining competitive strength, U.S. corporations will continue to face increasing competition both within the United States and abroad.

Production Costs and Productivity

Labor costs, measured in U.S. dollars, increased more slowly in the United States than in any other major industrial country in the world during the 1970s and 1980s. However, hourly compensation costs and direct pay to production workers in manufacturing is higher in the United States than in other major industrial countries.

Although growth in productivity lagged behind that of other major industrial countries from 1960 to 1982, it has since accelerated. The improved performance should continue, bolstered by the increased purchase of productivity-enhancing equipment and by the slower growth and consequent maturing of the labor force.

Several characteristics of the U.S. environment will help keep costs down:

1. Relatively low levels of labor unrest in the U.S., in contrast to Europe—a factor significant to European investors who foresee increasing labor problems in their home countries
2. Greater expected labor productivity because of U.S. attitudes toward job mobility, technology, and automation
3. Less U.S. government intervention in the economy than in Europe and Japan
4. Reduced international transportation costs. With the ever-increasing cost of energy, transportation costs are expected to escalate. Therefore, it becomes less expensive to manufacture in the United States than to export to it
5. Proximity to technological development. The United States is a prime innovator in product, process, and marketing technology. Investors realize that long-term competitiveness can only be retained by operating in markets where such innovation is taking place.

Political Stability

The United States offers exceptional political stability. Generally, foreign investment involves country and political risks. It also entails a higher degree of commercial risk than domestic investment, given the greater capital expenditures usually required, the tougher competition, and the unfamiliar business environment. Traditionally, many nations have turned to the less-developed countries, where local government incentives guaranteed them a competitive edge. However, political conditions in these countries are becoming less attractive to foreign companies because of rising nationalism, government demands for greater control, and increasingly stringent restrictions on repatriation of earnings. These developments have led foreign companies toward more stable areas in the industrial world.

Many senior managers are also growing disenchanted with the economic and political conditions in their home countries. This is particularly true among Europeans, where the rising militancy of labor unions, government intervention in the economy, and the low return on capital, coupled with some nations' political shift toward the left, have caused business conditions that discourage new investment. In the view of many foreign managers, the United States is the last bastion of capitalism, where political and economic stability are conducive to free enterprise.

The Dollar Exchange Rate

The 1970s witnessed a sharp decline in the value of the U.S. dollar. This decline was largely because of account deficits, high inflation, loss of faith in U.S. policy, and the end of the Bretton Woods exchange system, which encouraged international currency diversification. For instance, the German mark appreciated by 50% from 1970 to 1979, and the Japanese yen gained about 40%. The dollar's depreciation brought increased purchasing power to foreigners. Foreign corporations therefore considered dollar assets undervalued. This undervaluation, combined with relatively low U.S. stock prices, induced foreign acquisitions in the United States.

Conditions in the foreign exchange markets have dramatically changed since the latter half of 1980. The dollar has experienced substantial gains against the major currencies, thereby reversing the trend in previous years. New fundamental factors and foreign exchange intervention by the Group of 5 countries (U.S., U.K., West Germany, Japan, and France) since September 1985 have substantially modified the exchange rate structure among the industrial countries. Market participants suggest that the dollar could remain relatively strong through the 1980s. Such a strong dollar, combined with relatively high common-stock prices, will make foreign acquisitions and direct investment in the United States more costly (See appendix F for further implications of a strong dollar).

Inflation

The inflationary bias in many western economies played a significant role in the growth of DFI in the United States in the past decade. The mid-1970s was a period when inflation in Britain was more than 20%; in Japan about 12%. This situation induced many foreign investors to turn to the United States, where fairly low inflation rates were initially found. However, for several years U.S. inflation rates were in double digits, while western European economies, such as Germany and Switzerland, experienced inflation rates of around 5%. The inflation rate in the United States has declined under the Reagan administration to under 5%, which should be attractive to direct foreign investors.

Protectionism

Many foreign companies export finished products to the United States because of its large market. However, with slower economic growth and higher inflation and unemployment, many western economies may periodically resort to some protectionist measures to insulate domestic markets from foreign penetration, despite the successful completion of the Tokyo Round of Multilateral Trade Negotiations.

The United States, which has traditionally provided the most accessible markets, may react to deteriorating balance of payments and economic conditions by imposing protectionist measures. As a defensive measure against such an occurrence, foreign-based MNCs are setting up manufacturing operations in the United States. Some of these companies have attempted to vertically integrate themselves by setting up both wholesale and retail outlets in the U.S. This, in fact, has been a major contributor to the sharp rise in DFI in recent years.

3

Patterns of Direct Foreign Investment in the United States

Definition, Size, Trends, and Outlook

Direct foreign investment is defined, according to the U.S. Department of Commerce, as the movement of long-term capital to finance business activities abroad, whereby investors control at least 10% of the enterprise. Any foreign investment with less than a 10% controlling interest is considered a portfolio investment. More specifically, direct foreign investment includes several activities:

1. Financial outlays to establish a new enterprise, to expand an existing business enterprise, or to acquire real property whose operation is controlled by the foreign investor

2. Financial outlays to acquire an existing enterprise—or part of it, either through direct purchase or through purchase of equities; to increase the equity interest in an existing affiliate, with a controlling interest by the foreign investor of at least 10% of the enterprises value; or to a joint venture with local interest. Direct investment refers to ownership by an individual, not to the combined ownership of all people in a country. If one person owns 11% and another owns 9%, the 11% interest is included, but the 9% interest is excluded. Use of the single-owner criterion excludes investment in publicly held companies, where ownership is dispersed, so that no one person has an interest of 10% or more, and the owners do not, or cannot, act in concert to influence management

3. Intercompany, long-term loans between a parent and affiliate, including the flow of cash or other liquid assets, and account receivables

This chapter draws on data published by the U.S. Department of Commerce, in *Survey of Current Business, Foreign Direct Investment in the United States*, various issues.

4. Reinvested earnings by the parent company of its share of foreign affiliate earnings.

There has been steady but increasing interest by foreign-based multinational corporations in the United States. Although this initially resulted during the 1960s in relatively small capital inflows ($7 billion from 1960 to 1970), activities have rapidly increased. From 1971 to 1984, the industrialized world's direct foreign investment in the United States expanded at an average nominal-growth rate of 66% annually, and reached about $160 billion at the end of 1984. Of that amount, about $150 billion was invested between 1971 and 1984 (see table 3–1 and figure 3–1).

According to the U.S. Department of Commerce, there were about 22,000 U.S. affiliates of foreign companies in the United States in 1982. Their total assets were $473 billion; sales, $516 billion; and profits, about $4.3 billion.[19] A U.S. affiliate of a foreign company is defined as a U.S. business enterprise in which a foreign person owns or controls, directly or indirectly, at least 10% of the voting securities or an equivalent interest (see tables 3–2, 3–3 and 3–4, and figure 3–2).

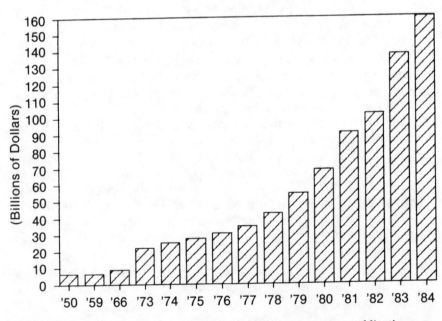

Source: Data compiled from various U.S. Department of Commerce publications.

Figure 3–1. Growth of DFI in the United States, 1950–1984

Table 3-1
Direct Foreign Investment in the United States, 1977-1984
(millions of dollars)

	Position Year-End							
	1977	*1978*	*1979*	*1980*	*1981*	*1982*	*1983*	*1984*
Areas	34,595	42,471	54,462	68,351	107,590	123,313	135,313	159,571
Petroleum	6,573	7,762	9,906	12,363	15,193	17,619	18,458	24,916
Manufacturing	14,030	17,202	20,876	25,159	40,334	44,100	47,803	50,664
Trade	7,237	9,161	11,562	14,269	15,501	17,699	20,006	24,042
Insurance	2,318	2,773	4,148	5,365	NA	NA	NA	NA
Other	4,437	5,573	7,971	11,168	36,563	44,172	49,047	59,949
Canada	5,650	6,180	7,154	10,074	11,870	11,435	11,115	14,001
Petroleum	710	734	943	1,308	1,744	1,509	1,374	1,419
Manufacturing	3,077	3,213	3,615	5,199	3,263	3,428	3,337	3,888
Trade	758	907	911	1,141	1,099	1,067	984	1,120
Insurance	207	209	278	452	NA	NA	NA	NA
Other	898	1,116	1,406	1,973	5,764	5,432	5,420	7,573
Europe	23,754	29,180	37,403	45,731	71,945	82,767	92,481	106,567
Petroleum	5,523	6,569	8,010	9,766	12,854	15,062	16,565	22,897
Manufacturing	9,267	11,717	13,952	16,064	30,852	33,146	36,983	36,684
Trade	5,120	6,023	7,838	9,312	7,927	8,671	9,769	11,396
Insurance	1,787	2,261	3,449	4,307	NA	NA	NA	NA
Other	2,056	2,611	4,154	6,282	20,313	25,889	29,163	33,590
Japan	1,755	2,749	3,493	4,225	7,688	9,679	11,145	14,817
Petroleum	48	(D)	160	58	-78	121	-325	-178
Manufacturing	332	474	696	837	1,320	1,636	1,682	2,262
Trade	811	1,522	1,767	2,307	4,975	6,089	7,625	9,696
Insurance	38	(D)	61	142	NA	NA	NA	NA
Other	527	627	808	881	1,471	1,833	2,163	3,037
Other	3,436	4,362	6,412	8,322	16,087	19,709	20,573	24,187
Petroleum	292	(D)	793	1,230	673	927	844	778
Manufacturing	1,354	1,798	2,612	3,059	4,899	5,891	5,801	5,830
Trade	548	709	1,045	1,536	1,500	1,872	1,627	1,829
Insurance	285	(D)	359	465	NA	NA	NA	NA
Other	956	1,219	1,603	2,031	9,016	11,019	12,301	15,750

Source: U.S. Department of Commerce, Bureau of Economic Analysis, *Survey of Current Business*, various issues and August 1985.
DSuppressed to avoid disclosure of individual companies.

Table 3-2
Nonbank U.S. Affiliates, 1982, by Country

	Millions of dollars					Thousands of acres		Millions of dollars			
	Total assets	Sales	Net income	Employee compensation	Number of employees	Land owned	Mineral rights owned and leased	Gross book value of property, plant, and equipment	Expenditures for new plant and equipment	U.S. exports shipped by affiliates	U.S. imports shipped to affiliates
All countries, all industries	472,989	515,722	4,332	62,013	2,435,143	14,164	73,951	223,265	28,835	59,744	84,831
By country											
Canada	91,786	64,934	−490	13,396	457,989	2,943	32,066	57,040	7,763	4,262	6,179
Europe	259,229	302,216	3,479	39,595	1,626,478	9,157	35,011	136,293	15,448	27,119	32,321
European Communities (10)	210,277	261,256	3,761	33,531	1,382,848	6,321	34,021	122,662	13,876	23,164	27,402
Belgium	4,762	6,119	151	589	29,350	123	(*)	3,064	264	150	583
Denmark	785	1,051	−14	299	17,074	5	(*)	445	128	42	260
France	33,135	43,413	−374	5,280	191,428	581	2,109	15,005	1,624	11,021	3,878
Germany	37,950	53,081	−137	8,480	350,987	764	1,791	19,913	2,278	4,750	8,312
Greece	241		−18	1	46	(P)		210	43	0	(P)
Ireland	1,209	26	−11	209	13,014	(P)	1	690	165	2	(P)
Italy	3,645	3,345	−113	374	14,448	122	19	1,751	197	1,133	588
Luxembourg	1,012		−15	195	7,672	24	19	506	61	170	310
Netherlands	47,854	47,505	1,695	6,167	222,974	2,485	(P)	38,951	3,546	2,259	5,190
United Kingdom	79,683	101,326	2,597	11,987	535,855	2,081	9,381	42,127	5,569	3,637	8,243
Other Europe	48,952	40,961	−282	6,064	243,630	2,836	990	13,631	1,572	3,955	4,918
Austria	810	393	−13	67	2,678	30	0	383	76	92	155
Finland	494	206	−55	55	1,824	1	0	267	37	8	36
Liechtenstein	1,369	1,165	−34	(P)	10,302	(P)	0	984	81	87	95
Norway	613	610	−48	129	3,926	7	16	270	20	29	117
Spain	616	528	−13	108	4,351	173	(P)	420	65	29	41
Sweden	5,634	9,748	−48	1,163	45,221	9	(P)	1,961	357	329	1,913
Switzerland	39,084	27,741	−66	4,114	173,232	(P)	330	9,262	924	3,294	2,164
Other	333	570	−6	(P)	2,096	4	0	83	12	(P)	397
Japan	35,615	106,644	456	3,229	138,935	105	2	8,664	1,830	22,250	36,145
Australia, New Zealand, and South Africa	43,063	16,165	630	1,715	52,269	194	924	3,786	472	(P)	(P)
Latin America	14,529	11,689	−53	2,174	79,656	932	4,289	7,186	1,386	(P)	(P)
South and Central America	5,143	4,726	−73	573	21,674	688	7	2,919	506	493	981
Argentina	200	101	2	4	258	32	0	104	13	6	(P)
Brazil	204	394	−4	9	346	8	0	30	5	137	73
Mexico	999	877	−39	118	4,535	145	1	576	112	77	466
Panama	2,525	1,820	−7	361	12,753	(P)	2	1,409	280	145	304
Venezuela	687	1,032	−6	23	1,398	92	5	1,461	66	9	12
Other	528	502	−19	58	2,384	(P)	0	340	30	118	(P)

	1	2	3	4	5	6	7	8	9	10	11
Other Western Hemisphere	9,386	6,963	20	1,601	57,982	244	4,281	4,267	880	(D)	(D)
Bahamas	1,108	1,257	-20	187	13,563	42	(*)	687	98	85	87
Bermuda	1,269	1,416	-38	(D)	(D)	56	4,066	549	95	27	82
Netherlands Antilles	4,557	3,619	75	247	6,451	117	210	2,798	653	4	(D)
U.K. Islands, Caribbean	2,434	658	5	5	159	26	5	219	28	4	1
Other	18	12	-1			3	0	14	5	2	2
Middle East	17,553	5,508	-60	902	28,923	379	1,620	7,069	1,440	1,336	523
Israel	906	409	43	42	1,873	2	0	51	7	272	(D)
Other	16,647	5,099	-103	860	27,050	377	1,620	7,018	1,432	1,064	(D)
Kuwait	7,004	1,510	-20	389	10,171	(D)	1,579	4,013	847	(D)	4
Lebanon	981	672	-17	121	5,079	20	(D)	560	78	(D)	2
Saudi Arabia	7,880	2,787	-64	342	11,055	(D)	(D)	1,803	274	0	(D)
United Arab Emirates	475	66	-2	3	220	2	0	425	172	0	0
Other	306	65	1	5	525	5	0	217	61	9	0
Other Africa, Asia, and Pacific	4,194	3,537	-54	374	16,425	422	33	2,061	367	530	1,379
Other Africa	103	34	-6	6	353	33	(D)	88	15	1	4
Other Asia and Pacific	4,092	3,503	-49	368	16,072	389	(D)	1,973	352	529	1,375
Hong Kong	2,104	1,318	(*)	220	9,854	352	12	1,334	275	161	335
Philippines	323	529	-35	53	1,747	(*)	0	207	25	26	(D)
South Korea	1,137	1,300	-13	36	1,481	32	0	80	8	304	638
Other	528	356		59	2,990			352	44	38	(D)
United States	7,020	5,029	425	629	34,468	31	6	1,167	129	246	132
Addendum—OPEC[1]	16,315	5,530	-92	771	23,621	454	1,593	6,858	1,381	873	(D)
By industry											
Government	22,975	13,795	-363	2,972	86,633	736	3,842	13,311	1,884	2,610	2,615
Individuals, estates, and trusts	60,602	61,835	166	8,961	382,415	7,095	2,928	32,983	4,216	9,008	4,245
Agriculture	58,615	55,016	3,575	4,345	117,637	1,005	47,245	55,903	6,011	1,863	7,847
Mining	812	2,560	-20	109	6,754	(*)	(*)	365	58	(D)	(D)
Petroleum	46,403	16,458	348	2,047	56,661	476	(*)	6,746	683	2,780	(D)
Construction	3,308	5,452	-43	980	36,087	26	3,964	1,332	113	107	69
Manufacturing	118,155	144,978	408	27,000	1,029,025	2,196	(*)	66,993	7,757	11,422	32,403
Transportation, communication, and public utilities	6,367	8,499	-71	1,544	60,262	(D)	(*)	3,834	884	450	(D)
Wholesale and retail trade	24,675	104,368	446	3,916	218,924	97	(*)	6,022	1,125	22,912	26,351
Banking	15,120	33,441	35	463	16,181	84	(*)	606	95	(D)	388
Holding companies	33,601	40,310	-264	6,579	266,235	731	2,686	16,125	2,315	7,364	2,322
Other finance and insurance	60,324	20,814	505	1,707	67,349	53	(*)	3,722	692	88	138
Real estate	18,263	4,583	-348	385	19,641	428	2	14,111	2,806	(D)	(D)
Services	3,770	3,613	-42	1,005	71,339	16	(D)	1,213	197	291	216

ᴰ Suppressed to avoid disclosure of data of individual companies.
*Less than $500,000 (±) or 500 acres.
1. OPEC is the Organization of Petroleum Exporting Countries. Its members are Algeria, Ecuador, Gabon, Indonesia, Iran, Iraq, Kuwait, Libya, Nigeria, Qatar, Saudi Arabia, Venezuela, and the United Arab Emirates.

Source: Ned G. Howenstein, "U.S. Affiliates of Foreign Companies: Operations in 1984," U.S. Department of Commerce, BEA, *Survey of Current Business* (Dec. 1984):33.

Table 3-3
Nonbank U.S. Affiliates, 1982, by Industry

	Millions of dollars				Number of employees	Thousands of acres		Gross book value of property, plant, and equipment	Millions of dollars		
	Total assets	Sales	Net income	Employee compensation		Land owned	Mineral rights owned and leased		Expenditures for new plant and equipment	U.S. exports shipped by affiliates	U.S. imports shipped to affiliates
All industries	472,989	515,722	4,332	62,013	2,435,143	14,164	73,951	223,265	28,835	59,744	84,831
Mining	13,885	5,928	-247	1,507	38,927	(D)	4,492	11,748	868	1,234	132
Petroleum	59,952	72,228	3,537	4,299	122,865	(D)	51,545	57,680	6,780	1,497	8,415
Manufacturing	129,505	141,219	195	34,321	1,238,884	6,286	14,161	84,376	9,584	13,170	12,593
Food and kindred products	12,446	14,942	468	2,568	125,822	77	2	4,421	539	604	1,396
Chemicals and allied products	51,444	54,264	1,129	12,197	390,088	925	(D)	42,638	4,394	4,831	2,813
Industrial chemicals and synthetics	38,308	39,828	739	8,715	241,479	757	0	33,895	3,438	4,008	2,152
Drugs	3,162	3,014	-70	1,010	36,642	13	0	1,996	206	277	228
Soap, cleaners, and toilet goods	3,355	4,654	148	899	30,582	(D)	0	1,335	157	227	128
Agricultural chemicals	5,659	5,689	(D)	(D)	(D)	(D)	(D)	4,924	533	266	229
Other	960	1,079	(D)	(D)	(D)	(D)	5	489	60	52	77
Primary and fabricated metals	12,165	13,442	-247	2,983	103,807	74	(D)	8,035	924	1,169	1,472
Primary metal industries	9,508	10,406	-307	2,078	69,800	70	(D)	6,735	772	893	1,254
Fabricated metal products	2,657	3,036	60	905	34,007	4	0	1,300	151	276	218
Machinery	24,249	25,796	-620	7,733	286,266	164	(D)	10,242	1,552	3,624	3,298
Machinery, except electrical	13,139	12,484	-687	3,818	130,272	148	(D)	5,383	570	1,938	1,468
Electric and electronic equipment	11,110	13,311	67	3,916	155,994	16	0	4,859	983	1,686	1,830
Other manufacturing	29,201	32,775	-534	8,840	332,901	5,046	320	19,040	2,175	2,942	3,614
Textile products and apparel	1,613	2,208	69	633	37,207	11	0	935	90	74	105
Lumber, wood, furniture, and fixtures	554	569	-13	103	7,065	(D)	(D)	276	28	106	146
Paper and allied products	7,132	6,254	101	1,664	51,031	4,663	(D)	6,643	798	607	572
Printing and publishing	2,988	3,763	94	1,057	45,216	7	0	1,461	143	89	237
Rubber and plastics products	1,429	2,098	-13	526	25,643	4	0	939	103	75	177
Stone, clay, and glass products	5,404	4,944	-277	1,419	46,621	130	33	4,467	202	194	107
Transportation equipment	6,189	9,002	-355	2,320	68,088	29	0	2,948	614	1,422	1,692
Instruments and related products	1,691	2,018	-111	567	24,822	(D)	0	645	91	236	369
Other	1,600	1,920	-30	550	27,208	(D)	(D)	725	107	137	210

Wholesale trade	93,324	209,523	444	7,306	279,602	404	(ᴰ)	13,460	2,506	42,554	62,114
Motor vehicles and equipment	13,824	42,333	482	1,437	52,031	10	(*)	3,730	1,065	3,307	20,825
Metals and minerals, except petroleum	48,284	56,094	463	1,429	37,896	27	349	2,017	208	13,361	17,802
Other durable goods	17,850	55,963	−373	2,814	117,756	192	(ᴰ)	3,684	766	2,610	13,118
Farm product raw materials	7,126	39,863	(*)	725	32,004	(ᴰ)	(ᴰ)	1,740	220	21,735	5,781
Other nondurable goods	6,240	15,270	−128	901	39,915	(ᴰ)	(ᴰ)	2,289	247	1,540	4,588
Retail trade	14,794	31,633	402	5,307	389,992	10	(*)	7,698	1,060	627	1,020
Food stores and eating and drinking places	5,572	18,846	140	2,858	211,913	4	0	3,637	449	12	57
Retail trade, nec	9,222	12,788	262	2,449	178,079	6	(*)	4,062	612	615	963
Finance, except banking	51,611	7,980	294	1,135	24,607	15	(ᴰ)	1,130	305	133	(ᴰ)
Insurance	47,974	23,060	573	1,558	70,640	18	0	1,884	283	(*)	1
Real estate	40,226	6,882	−486	483	25,152	2,566	98	32,841	5,575	(*)	4
Other industries	21,718	17,268	−378	6,098	244,474	3,055	(ᴰ)	12,448	1,874	522	(ᴰ)
Agriculture	2,474	905	−107	188	12,058	1,505	3	2,084	300	50	3
Forestry and fishing	155	37	2	3	96	1,328	21	132	9	4	(ᴰ)
Construction	7,533	7,212	−61	1,558	51,158	39	(ᴰ)	2,705	436	393	89
Transportation	2,965	3,144	−42	1,273	50,102	104	(ᴰ)	2,318	133	(ᴰ)	13
Communication and public utilities	1,654	417	(*)	130	6,849	52	2	1,231	395	(ᴰ)	(ᴰ)
Services	6,938	5,552	−169	2,946	124,211	27	(ᴰ)	3,978	601	67	49

ᴰ Suppressed to avoid disclosure of data of individual companies.
* Less than $500,000 (±) or 500 acres.

Source: Ned G. Howenstein, "U.S. Affiliates of Foreign Companies: Operations in 1984," U.S. Department of Commerce, BEA, *Survey of Current Business* (Dec. 1984):31.

Table 3-4
Total Assets of Nonbank U.S. Affiliates, 1982, by Industry and Country
(millions of dollars)

Industry	All countries	Canada	Europe — Total	Of which — France	Germany	Netherlands	United Kingdom	Switzerland	Japan	Australia, New Zealand, and South Africa	Latin America	Middle East	Other Africa, Asia, and Pacific	United States	Addendum— OPEC [1]
All industries	472,989	91,786	259,229	33,135	37,950	47,854	79,683	39,084	35,615	43,063	14,529	17,553	4,194	7,020	16,315
Mining	13,885	2,877	10,217	(D)	1,229	(D)	(D)	(D)	5	(D)	10	(D)	3	15	0
Petroleum	59,952	5,979	49,927	1,110	601	(D)	21,173	303	830	197	2,411	(D)	25	(D)	509
Manufacturing	129,505	40,237	74,955	9,865	19,625	9,603	19,331	8,520	5,410	(D)	3,709	369	259	(D)	195
Food and kindred products	12,446	(D)	(D)	462	109	130	4,048	(D)	404	90	212	(D)	147	0	(D)
Chemicals and allied products	51,444	(D)	(D)	1,336	11,631	3,112	6,112	3,808	443	22	(D)	3	(D)	0	3
Industrial chemicals and synthetics	38,308	(D)	2,667	(D)	5,594	14	4,913	(D)	280	0	1	0	0	0	0
Drugs	3,162	(D)	3,216	(D)	102	(D)	380	(D)	(D)	0	(D)	0	0	0	0
Soap, cleaners, and toilet goods	3,355	(D)	(D)	8	622	0	499	224	49	(D)	5	3	(D)	0	3
Agricultural chemicals	5,659	(D)	(D)	(D)	(D)	0	59	2	(D)	(D)	0	0	0	0	0
Other	960	110	846	37	(D)	20	261	19	(D)	(D)	0	0	0	0	0
Primary and fabricated metals	12,165	2,809	6,728	1,047	709	514	1,523	(D)	1,332	923	229	132	12	1	5
Primary metal industries	9,508	2,375	4,888	992	457	(D)	227	(D)	(D)	832	87	(D)	0	0	5
Fabricated metal products	2,657	434	1,840	55	252	(D)	1,296	82	(D)	91	142	(D)	12	1	0
Machinery	24,249	4,377	12,990	587	3,198	2,551	3,436	1,016	1,714	(D)	227	(D)	13	(D)	4
Machinery, except electrical	13,139	3,100	6,105	292	1,308	(D)	2,065	501	(D)	(D)	(D)	(D)	6	(D)	(D)
Electric and electronic equipment	11,110	1,278	6,885	294	1,889	(D)	1,371	515	(D)	0	(D)	(D)	7	12	(D)
Other manufacturing	29,201	4,841	21,667	6,434	3,979	3,296	4,212	981	1,517	366	227	94	(D)	467	17
Textile products and apparel	1,613	194	920	30	175	0	461	85	140	0	(D)	0	1	0	0
Lumber, wood, furniture, and fixtures	554	132	331	(D)	196	0	0	(D)	(D)	18	0	12	0	0	0
Paper and allied products	7,132	778	5,667	11	48	36	(D)	0	(D)	0	0	(D)	0	0	0
Printing and publishing	2,988	1,816	897	(D)	(D)	(D)	523	0	29	(D)	0	(D)	2	0	2
Rubber and plastics products	1,429	181	1,146	28	383	4	488	79	71	9	9	0	0	0	0
Stone, clay, and glass products	5,404	1,398	3,892	1,896	407	33	1,001	(D)	31	0	0	0	17	0	0
Transportation equipment	6,789	(D)	6,334	4,032	(D)	(D)	32	230	(D)	0	0	0	0	0	0
Instruments and related products	1,691	204	1,185	58	488	5	538	90	210	(D)	(D)	2	1	0	0
Other	1,600	(D)	1,296	359	51	(D)	(D)	(D)	(D)	(D)	(D)	(D)	(D)	0	0

Wholesale trade	93,324	(P)	25,042	4,944	7,040	654	6,323	2,155	23,648	(P)	969	492	1,313	(P)	402
Motor vehicles and equipment	13,824	(P)	6,336	1,617	3,152	20	649	1	6,953	(P)	53	(P)	254	(P)	(P)
Metals and minerals, except petroleum	48,284	1,156	120	(P)	848	(P)	1,744	10	6,027	79	(P)	(P)	72	0	0
Other durable goods	17,850	1,318	7,625	269	2,345	160	2,646	611	7,770	0	277	(P)	(P)	4	4
Farm product raw materials	7,126	62	(P)	(P)	43	76	493	1,306	2,360	0	124	0	(P)	0	0
Other nondurable goods	6,240	2,097	2,512	306	652	(P)	790	227	538	146	(P)	5	479	5	5
Retail trade	14,794	2,162	11,075	(P)	2,290	1,514	(P)	313	218	262	595	(P)	359	(P)	0
Food stores and eating and drinking places	5,572	989	4,399	(P)	(P)	(P)	(P)	80	83	0	0	0	(P)	(P)	0
Retail trade, nec	9,222	1,173	6,676	70	(P)	(P)	(P)	233	135	262	595	(P)	(P)	3	0
Finance, except banking	51,611	(P)	36,420	8,398	733	1,710	6,631	(P)	2,719	(P)	2,428	6,299	250	(P)	(P)
Insurance	47,974	13,148	28,839	310	3,103	5,602	12,459	1,367	364	(P)	(P)	0	7	(P)	0
Real estate	40,226	16,971	12,786	681	1,700	3,157	4,360	1,618	1,116	160	(P)	5,152	1,456	(P)	5,086
Other industries	21,718	3,129	9,969	2,817	1,630	(P)	(P)	(P)	1,305	332	1,753	4,639	522	70	(P)
Agriculture	2,474	(P)	1,462	2	372	35	215	500	90	2	495	81	12	(P)	118
Forestry	155	9	120	27	38	(P)	14	7	0	1	12	0	(P)	0	0
Construction	7,533	(P)	3,016	1,297	762	230	475	(P)	211	15	88	6	(P)	(P)	(P)
Transportation	2,965	1,304	1,192	61	93	(P)	338	211	(P)	(P)	0	(P)	7	7	4
Communication and public utilities	1,654	690	579	(P)	0	1	(P)	0	(P)	(P)	0	0	0	0	0
Services	6,938	709	3,600	752	365	416	1,086	419	698	64	1,151	194	194	(P)	240

P Suppressed to avoid disclosure of data of individual companies.

*Less than $500,000 (±) or 500 acres.

1. OPEC is the Organization of Petroleum Exporting Countries. Its members are Algeria, Ecuador, Gabon, Indonesia, Iran, Iraq, Kuwait, Libya, Nigeria, Qatar, Saudi Arabia, Venezuela, and the United Arab Emirates.

Source: Ned G. Howenstein, "U.S. Affiliates of Foreign Companies: Operations in 1984," U.S. Department of Commerce, BEA, *Survey of Current Business* (Dec. 1984):37.

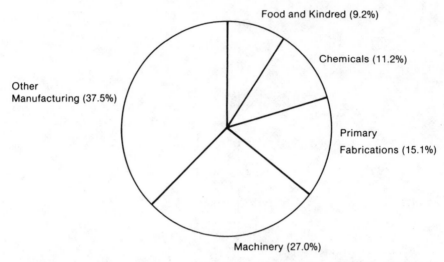

Food and Kindred (9.2%)

Chemicals (11.2%)

Other
Manufacturing (37.5%)

Primary
Fabrications (15.1%)

Machinery (27.0%)

Source: U.S. Department of Commerce, Bureau of Economic Analysis, *Foreign Direct Investment in the U.S.*, Preliminary 1982 estimates, December 1984.

Figure 3-2. U.S. Affiliates of Foreign Companies, by Manufacturing Industry and Number of Affiliates

The outlook for direct foreign investment in the United States is affected by the business cycle, the economic conditions of the investing countries, energy costs and availability, exchange rates, and portfolio considerations of the investing companies. If recent trends continue, total DFI in the United States could exceed $350 billion by 1990, more than a four-fold increase over the 1980 level.[20]

Composition of DFI by Investor Countries

Traditionally, the U.K., the Netherlands, and Canada were the largest investors in the United States, accounting for more than half of total DFI. However, their dominance will likely be eroded in the near future by Japan, which currently accounts for 10.8%, and Germany, with 8.7%. Both countries are benefiting from huge balance of payment surpluses, and DFI is just a natural means of recycling these balances. The United Kingdom with $38.1 billion, or about 28% of all DFI in the United States, was the largest single investor in 1984, followed by the Netherlands, with $32.6 billion, or 23.8%; Japan with $14.8 billion, or 10.8%; and by Canada, with $14.0 billion, or 10.2% (see tables 3-5 and 3-6 and figure 3-3).

The overall country compostion of DFI is undergoing rapid change. The vigorous foreign investment policies of Germany and Japan have yielded average annual nominal growth rates of more than 73.0% and 80.0%, respectively, from 1978 to 84. If these countries' investments in the United States continue to expand at these rates, by 1990 their DFI will account for $20 to 30 billion and $30 to 40 billion, respectively. Their combined total could account for 17 to 23% of DFI in the U.S.[21]

DFI Position by Industry

Foreign companies in the United States operate in almost all major sectors in which they are legally allowed. In particular, investment is heavily concentrated in manufacturing (31.8% of total DFI in the U.S., trade (19.1%), and petroleum (15.6%), which together account for two-thirds of total DFI. In recent years, above-average growth rates were experienced in trade, finance, machinery, and chemicals. The trade and finance sectors are growing at a significantly higher rate than the average DFI growth in the past decade.

In 1984 investment in the manufacturing sector was over $50 billion, or 31.8% of total DFI. Chemicals, machinery, food, and primary and fabricated metals, the four major sectors, accounted for some $40 billion, or about 25%, of that total. Foreign investment in the manufacturing sector expanded at an annual average nominal rate of 27.4% from 1977 to 1984. Total DFI expanded at a rate of 48.5% during this time.

Wholesale and retail trade account for $30.5 billion, or 19.1%, of all DFI. From 1977 to 1984 the average annual nominal increase for this sector was over 40%, the second-fastest growth rate among all sectors. This growth rate is particularly remarkable considering the large investment base. The petroleum sector experienced substantial growth in 1984, and from 1977 to 1984 its growth averaged about 40% per annum.

For the balance of this decade, the composition of direct foreign investment is expected to remain essentially unchanged. The manufacturing sector will continue to expand rapidly and dominate the DFI scene. The machinery sector will grow at a slightly faster rate as investing countries establish local manufacturing facilities in the United States. These facilities will substitute for the direct export of finished products. The petroleum sector, which experienced the slowest growth among the DFI sectors in the late

Table 3-5
Direct Foreign Investment in the United States, 1983
(millions of dollars)

	All industries	Mining	Petroleum	Manufacturing						Wholesale trade	Retail trade	Banking	Finance, except banking	Insurance	Real estate	Other industries
				Total	Food and kindred products	Chemicals and allied products	Primary and fabricated metals	Machinery	Other manufacturing							
All countries	137,061	1,928	18,209	47,665	7,447	15,766	5,322	8,608	10,522	21,031	5,482	8,697	2,269	8,665	14,636	8,478
Canada	11,434	613	1,391	3,313	74	100	1,255	1,016	867	1,040	323	492	304	757	2,274	927
Europe	92,936	1,256	16,326	36,866	6,796	13,506	2,415	5,772	8,377	10,124	4,360	5,577	1,236	7,214	6,835	3,141
European Communities (10)	82,286	1,100	15,906	31,479	5,891	11,732	1,956	4,599	7,301	8,818	4,247	5,172	1,009	5,429	6,419	2,707
Belgium	2,261	(D)	(D)	514	(D)	(D)	(D)	(D)	141	141	(D)	(D)	(D)	(D)	10	6
France	5,726	239	79	5,487	266	2,970	584	110	1,556	664	(D)	460	-1,476	71	24	10
Germany	10,845	515	-11	4,487	30	2,190	200	1,079	986	2,559	509	259	281	1,135	893	310
Italy	1,238	(D)	(D)	359	(D)	0	4	85	104	130	1	237	(D)	(D)	6	493
Luxembourg	297	(D)	(D)	79	(D)	(D)	(D)	(D)	2	50	(D)	(D)	79	0	24	2
Netherlands	29,182	113	8,646	11,222	2,094	2,923	628	1,879	2,611	1,435	745	1,537	981	1,354	2,254	956
United Kingdom	32,152	96	5,955	9,221	(D)	3,201	(D)	1,416	1,882	3,685	2,876	2,390	956	2,821	3,196	884
Denmark, Greece, and Ireland	584	0	(D)	110	1	(D)	(D)	18	(D)	153	(D)	(D)	1	(D)	12	31
Other Europe	10,650	156	420	5,388	905	1,774	459	1,173	1,076	1,306	113	405	227	1,785	416	434
Sweden	2,124	(*)	361	1,051	(D)	85	(D)	579	195	517	2	2	-21	0	0	40
Switzerland	7,464	(D)	57	4,165	(D)	1,694	(D)	539	812	494	75	198	230	1,600	328	323
Other	1,061	(D)	3	171	6	-4	44	56	69	295	36	205	19	185	88	71
Japan	11,336	(D)	-408	1,605	186	283	140	466	530	7,823	234	1,384	(D)	182	515	430
Australia, New Zealand, and South Africa	999	9	67	392	8	6	261	9	107	169	25	40	(D)	(D)	70	164
Latin America	15,035	47	829	5,225	274	1,876	1,250	1,335	490	1,691	477	511	960	507	4,068	720
South and Central America	2,747	0	142	1,069	8	178	(D)	(D)	(D)	54	-4	51	125	(D)	331	150
Panama	2,073	0	(D)	(D)	3	(D)	(D)	(D)	48	4	34	(D)	(D)	(D)	224	8
Other	674	0	(D)	(D)	5	(D)	(D)	-69	6	17	(D)	420	(D)	(D)	107	142
Other Western Hemisphere	12,289	47	686	4,156	266	1,697	(D)	(D)	436	1,695	426	(D)	835	(D)	3,738	570
Bermuda	1,168	5	167	296	(D)	(D)	(D)	(D)	7	526	1	(D)	1	(D)	90	61
Netherlands Antilles	9,948	-2	423	3,754	(D)	1,629	(D)	10	346	968	393	(D)	567	20	3,244	486
U.K. Islands, Caribbean	985	44	62	94	1	(D)	(D)	22	(D)	175	13	(D)	280	(D)	335	21
Other	188	0	35	12	-2	11	-2	(D)	(D)	26	14	(*)	-13	0	69	2
Middle East	4,446	0	14	99	(D)	(D)	(D)	4	91	(D)	4	429	(D)	(D)	602	(D)
Israel	449	0	6	96	(D)	0	(D)	1	94	(D)	0	280	(D)	0	0	(D)
Other	3,997	(D)	8	3	(D)	(D)	(D)	3	-3	(D)	4	150	(D)	0	602	(D)
Other Africa, Asia, and Pacific	875	(D)	-9	164	(D)	-5	8	6	59	139	58	263	6	(D)	273	(D)
Memorandum—OPEC [1]	4,039	0	10	-22	6	-3	8	-28	-5	139	(D)	205	6	0	614	(D)

Source: U.S. Department of Commerce, BEA, *Survey of Current Business*, (Aug. 1985):52.

Table 3-6
Direct Foreign Investment in the United States, 1984
(millions of dollars)

	All industries	Mining	Petroleum	Manufacturing: Total	Food and kindred products	Chemicals and allied products	Primary and fabricated metals	Machinery	Other manufacturing	Wholesale trade	Retail trade	Banking	Finance, except banking	Insurance	Real estate	Other industries
All countries	159,571	4,049	24,916	50,664	8,141	16,749	5,725	8,950	11,100	24,042	6,452	10,203	4,246	8,819	16,899	9,279
Canada	14,001	785	1,419	3,888	89	103	1,402	1,201	1,093	1,120	531	1,093	547	982	2,717	917
Europe	106,567	1,409	22,897	38,684	7,482	14,494	2,476	5,773	8,459	11,396	5,080	5,891	2,890	7,131	7,888	3,301
European Communities (10)	94,850	1,213	22,557	32,697	6,387	12,376	2,037	4,553	7,343	9,784	4,961	5,488	2,528	5,439	7,375	2,808
Belgium	2,559	(D)	495	495	(D)	69	(D)	(D)	43	503	105	418	(D)	(D)	10	-2
France	6,502	(D)	-1	5,402	338	2,849	590	141	1,484	135	121	272	-560	61	26	341
Germany	11,956	243	(D)	4,431	27	2,346	210	922	927	3,453	513	321	335	1,287	969	455
Italy	1,614	505	(D)	340	(D)	(D)	2	49	84	88	(D)	(D)	(D)	(D)	(D)	-1
Luxembourg	751	-3	(D)	74	(D)	0	(D)	(D)	47	(D)	(D)	(D)	98	0	0	15
Netherlands	32,643	160	9,878	12,470	2,193	3,340	717	1,942	2,985	1,620	1,065	1,418	1,377	1,473	2,308	873
United Kingdom	38,099	168	10,917	9,347	3	3,302	2	1,467	1,668	3,580	3,128	2,337	943	2,573	4,008	1,100
Denmark, Greece, and Ireland	725	0	(D)	138	(D)	10	(D)	18	106	216	0	214	(D)	(D)	12	27
Other Europe	11,718	197	340	5,988	1,095	2,118	439	1,219	1,116	1,612	119	404	361	1,691	513	493
Sweden	2,222	(D)	316	1,008	(D)	60	(D)	553	229	664	2	(D)	(D)	99	0	45
Switzerland	8,349	(D)	22	4,782	(D)	2,056	(D)	614	813	726	79	(D)	331	1,538	391	375
Other	1,147	(D)	3	198	3	(D)	68	52	73	222	38	267	(D)	54	121	73
Japan	14,817	7	-178	2,262	197	267	535	539	724	9,696	244	1,778	-312	175	663	481
Australia, New Zealand, and South Africa	2,366	(D)	43	317	8	-5	221	8	85	132	(D)	42	(D)	(D)	72	141
Latin America	15,516	272	695	5,287	271	1,898	1,098	1,435	586	1,394	504	651	924	530	4,482	778
South and Central America	2,804	0	86	954	9	239	(D)	(D)	23	-9	44	(D)	112	(D)	365	183
Panama	1,867	0	81	927	4	190	(D)	(D)	22	-23	31	(D)	104	(D)	255	(D)
Other	938	0	5	28	5	48	31	-59	1	14	13	578	7	2	110	180
Other Western Hemisphere	12,711	272	609	4,333	262	1,659	(D)	(D)	562	1,403	460	0	812	(D)	4,117	595
Bermuda	1,091	(D)	97	303	(D)	(D)	(D)	7	65	292	5	0	6	(D)	83	65
Netherlands Antilles	10,523	15	499	3,883	(D)	1,552	(D)	(D)	463	935	412	-3	548	(D)	3,629	507
U.K. Islands, Caribbean	900	-2	(D)	129	(D)	13	5	23	32	148	28	0	270	0	323	7
Other	197	(D)	(D)	18	0	13	1	3	2	28	15	-3	-13	0	82	16
Middle East	5,159	0	15	94	(D)	(*)	(D)	5	87	148	(D)	448	(D)	0	674	(D)
Israel	497	0	6	89	(D)	0	(D)	1	87	(D)	0	286	(D)	0	0	-6
Other	4,662	0	9	6	(D)	(*)	(D)	4	(*)	(D)	0	162	5	0	674	(D)
Other Africa, Asia, and Pacific	1,146	(D)	25	131	(D)	-8	(D)	-12	66	156	59	300	23	(D)	402	(D)
Memorandum—OPEC [1]	4,725	0	12	-36	7	-4	1	-38	-2	187	(D)	255	5	0	669	(D)

* Less than $500,000 (±).

D Suppressed to avoid disclosure of data of individual companies.

1. OPEC is the Organization of Petroleum Exporting Countries. Its members are Algeria, Ecuador, Gabon, Indonesia, Iran, Iraq, Kuwait, Libya, Nigeria, Qatar, Saudi Arabia, Venezuela, and the United Arab Emirates.

Source: U.S. Department of Commerce, BEA, *Survey of Current Business* (Aug. 1985):52.

Major Industries

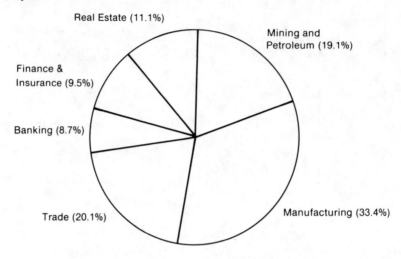

Major Countries

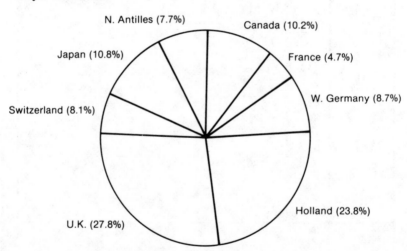

Source: U.S. Department of Commerce, Bureau of Economic Analysis, Foreign Direct Investment in the United States, Country and Industry Detail for Position and Balance of Payments Flows, 1984, August 1984, pp. 47–66.

Figure 3-3. Direct Foreign Investment in the United States, 1984 by Major Industries and Countries

1970s, is likely to remain sluggish unless the global oil situation is radically modified. The finance sector's growth rate, particularly that of banks and other financial services, could expand as new U.S. bank legislation provides attractive opportunities for foreign financial institutions.

DFI Composition by Establishment

In 1982, the last year for which data are available, there were around 22,000 affiliates of foreign companies operating in the United States that were considered by the Department of Commerce to be foreign owned. About 612 of these had sales of at least $1 million. Of these foreign-owned firms, 15.5% were engaged in manufacturing; 18.4% in trade; and 4.7% in insurance and finance, excluding banking (see tables 3-2, 3-3, 3-4 and figure 3-2).

Foreign-owned manufacturing firms are most strongly concentrated in chemicals, machinery, primary and fabricated metals, and electronics. Although they account for only about 16% of foreign-owned businesses, manufacturing firms employ around 50% of the work force of foreign firms.

DFI Location

Direct foreign investment is highly concentrated in a few states. Forty-three percent of all foreign firms are located in seven states. Foreign investors generally prefer states located on the east and west coasts and in the South. California, with 2,015 foreign affiliates, or 9.3% of the total, is the leading state in terms of foreign companies. California was followed by Texas, with 1,790 foreign affiliates, or 8.3% of the total. New York had 1,592, or 7.3%; Florida, 1,229, or 5.7%; Illinois, 940, or 4.3%; Georgia 890, or 4.1%; and New Jersey, 810, or 3.7%. DFI activities are expected to accelerate further in the southern states (see table 3-7 and figure 3-4).

Generally, investors preferred the following locations:

1. Japanese investment is usually located on the west coast because of its geographical proximity to Japan.
2. German investment is concentrated in the Southeast (particularly in South Carolina and Louisiana), the Mideast (particularly in Pennsylvania and New Jersey), the Great Lakes states (especially Illinois and Ohio) and Texas.
3. British investment is generally located on the northeast coast, (particularly in New York and Pennsylvania), the Southeast

Table 3-7
Direct Foreign Investment in the United States, by Region

	Book Value (millions of dollars)	Percentage of Total Book Value	Number of Affiliates	Percentage of Total Affiliates
New England	6,576	2.9	1,280	5.9
Mideast	28,512	12.8	3,644	16.8
Great Lakes	21,825	9.8	2,530	11.6
Plains	10,003	4.5	1,559	7.2
Southeast	54,842	24.6	5,324	24.5
Southwest	36,666	16.4	2,704	12.4
Rocky Mountains	10,530	4.7	1,203	5.5
Far East	29,606	13.3	2,881	13.2
Others	24,705	11.1	627	2.9
Total	223,265		21,752	

Source: U.S. Commerce Department, Bureau of Economic Analysis, *Foreign Direct Investment in the United States*, Annual Survey Results, Preliminary Data for 1982 Estimates, December 1984.
Note: Percentages were rounded off to the nearest decimal point.

(particularly in North Carolina and South Carolina), and the Great Lakes states, especially Ohio.

4. Canadian investment is fairly evenly located throughout the country.

5. Dutch investment is concentrated in the Southeast, Southwest, and far West and to a lesser extent in the Great Lakes area and the Midwest.

Once a corporation decides to invest in the United States, it must make several crucial decisions. Among these decisions are its mode of operation, its means of entering the market, its corporate organization, and its operating site. These decisions will have significant implications on its future success.

More specifically, a company that has decided to enter the U.S. market should prepare a marketing survey and program, select employees and management, and prepare a business and financial plan. Particular attention should be focused on selecting a regional location and a specific site. Generally that selection is based on the following variables:

1. Resources: land, raw materials, natural energy sources, and climate

2. Markets: population, income, industrial buyers of intermediate manufactured goods, and transportation

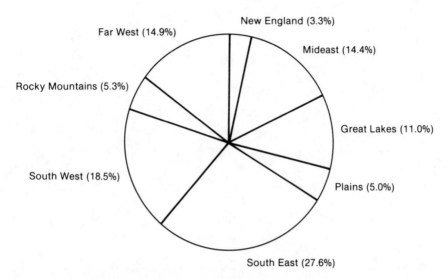

New England (3.3%)

Far West (14.9%)

Mideast (14.4%)

Rocky Mountains (5.3%)

Great Lakes (11.0%)

South West (18.5%)

Plains (5.0%)

South East (27.6%)

Source: U.S. Department of Commerce, Bureau of Economic Analysis, *Foreign Direct Investment in the U.S.*, Preliminary 1982 Estimates, December 1984.

Figure 3-4. U.S. Affiliates of Foreign Companies, by Region and Book Value

3. Labor: wages, unionization, education, and productivity
4. Quality of life: crime, cultural facilities, education, and housing
5. Government: attitudes, regulation, taxation, and stability
6. Financial resources: availability and cost of funds.

Such decision making can be assisted by information on the U.S. business environment and practices, and, of course, through careful planning and implementation. The following chapters discuss some of these areas, and are meant to assist corporations so they can make appropriate decisions.

4

The U.S. Economy and
Its Structure

The United States includes fifty states, the District of Columbia, the Commonwealth of Puerto Rico, and the territories of Guam, the Virgin Islands, American Samoa, Midway Islands, Wake Island, and several other Pacific islands. The gross area (land and water) of the fifty states comprises some 3.6 million square miles or 9.3 million square kilometers. The climate and seasons vary greatly, offering substantial options for an investor.

The United States is richly endowed with raw materials and human resources. Its strength is based on a free-enterprise economy and a huge market of 237 million people, whose standard of living is high. The labor force is extremely mobile. The various regions have different cultural and behavioral patterns and a diversity of economic activity. The U.S. is an urbanized industrial society, heavily engaged in the service industry. The number of agricultural workers has declined to about 3% of the total labor force.

The significance of the service sector has increased substantially, now accounting for two-thirds of GNP. It has grown faster than the goods-producing industries. The strength of the service sector in the past decade was evidenced by the rapid growth in its employment, its contributions to personal income, and its increasing importance in international trade.

The diversity of the population and regions of the United States create a heterogeneous marketplace, which is nevertheless highly integrated, thanks to efficient communications and transportation networks and a common language and legal system. The huge U.S. market with its $3,660 billion GNP is easily accessible and offers tremendous potential. The market is in close proximity to Canada, Latin America, and the Pacific basin.

During the industrialization of the United States, the availability of power and transportation attracted industry primarily to the Northeast and the region around the Great Lakes. In recent years, because of the lower taxes, the lower cost of living, and the milder climate, the population and industry of the United States have shifted to the South and West, substantially modifying regional patterns. This trend, which is likely to continue, will have major business and political implications.

Population and the Labor Force

The U.S. population reached 237 million in 1984, an increase from 205 million in 1970 and 180.7 million in 1960, constituting an average annual growth rate of 1.1% for 1970 to 1984 and 1.3% for 1960 to 1970. The population is expected to grow in the 1980s at an average annual rate of 0.9%, a significant reduction from the 1.3% average in the past 25 years. In 1984 the labor force—the 16- to 64-year-old group—accounted for 115.2 million people, or 49% of the entire population, compared with 84.9 million in 1970 and 71.5 million in 1960—an average annual growth rate of 2.6% throughout the three decades. The civilian labor force participation rate was 65% in 1984; male participation was 78.3%; female; 54.0%.

The labor force is projected to expand by 20 million, or 18%, between 1983 and 1995. This will mean a slowdown in employment's growth rate—from a record 2.3% per annum between 1971 and 1983 to 1.8% between 1983 and 1995.

During the past two decades, the baby-boom generation entered the labor force in large numbers, and women's participation in the labor market increased significantly. The number of young workers under 35 years of age increased from 45% of the civilian labor force in 1972 to 50.3% in 1983. This rise is attributed to the post–World War II baby boom and should level off or decrease as these workers reach age 35. Women's role in the labor market increased from 37.7% in 1970 to 43.8% in 1984. They comprised some 50% of employees in the service industry in 1984.

The Regions: Population and Industries

In the post–World War II period, U.S. population, economic activities, and personal income have generally shifted away from the North and Central toward the South and West.[22] While this trend still continues in the early 1980s, New England and, to a lesser extent, the Mideast have rebounded, due to their industrial diversification and the service sector, which helped to offset weaknesses in their traditional industries. The South and West together contained over half the country's population. (Tables 4-1, 4-2, and 4-3 show population by state, region, and city as well as personal income by state and region. Figures 4-1, and 4-2 show the regional distribution of population and income, and the geographic location of the various regions.)

Over the years, the South and West attracted a great number of large companies, and construction and services followed to provide for the expanding population. The South and West offer competitive wage rates, advantageous energy and land costs, and lower state and local taxes than the North. Further, improved highways and transportation networks gave the South and West competitive access to national markets. Table 4-4 shows regional growth patterns from the late 1950s to the early 1980s.

The outlook to the year 2000 suggests that the southern regions (Rocky Mountains, Southwest, Far West, and Southeast) as well as the New England region, are likely to continue to grow. Other regions are expected to grow below the national average.

There were considerable shifts in economic activities, and income and population growth patterns of metropolitan and nonmetropolitan areas in the past three decades, and there is substantial variability in regional patterns. It seems that in the early 1980s, all the factors that contributed to nonmetropolitan growth were reversed (that is, immigration of population, manufacturing activities, and employment).

The population in a number of cities declined in the 1960s, while their suburbs grew. But in the 1970s, suburban growth was insufficient to offset population decline of many cities, especially in the old industrial areas of New England, the Mideast, and the Great Lakes region. In the 1980s, the growth industries—high technology, defense-oriented manufacturing, and services—provide a strong impetus to the large metropolitan areas, except for the Great Lakes areas. Low-growth industries—agriculture, energy, and those that are natural-resources intensive—are contributing negatively to the Plains and northern regions.

Bureau of the Census data on the long-term growth of metropolitan areas are informative for marketing and other business purposes. For example, in 1984, about 75% of the U.S. population, or around 178 million people, lived in metropolitan areas.

There are 313 metropolitan areas in the United States, of which 42 have a population of at least 1 million. Population projections to the year 2000 suggest that 22 out of the 42 largest metropolitan areas will have an average annual population growth rate in excess of the national average of 0.8% between 1983 and 2000, while the remaining 20 will either expand below the national average or experience a decline. Some 85% of the rapidly growing metropolitan areas are

Table 4-1
Total Personal Income and Population, 1973–2000, United States, Regions, and States

	Total personal income								Population							
	Millions of 1972 dollars				Average annual growth rate (percent)		Index, U.S. average annual growth rate=100		Thousands of persons				Average annual growth rate (percent)		Index, U.S. average annual growth rate=100	
	1973	1983	1990	2000	1973–1983	1983–2000	1973–1983	1983–2000	1973	1983	1990	2000	1973–1983	1983–2000	1973–1983	1983–2000
United States	1,001,799	1,280,180	1,603,313	1,970,899	2.5	2.6	100	100	211,349	234,023	249,203	267,464	1.0	0.8	100	100
Fast-growing regions	494,881	708,852	910,540	1,155,084	3.7	2.9	147	113	110,937	132,588	144,893	159,923	1.8	1.1	176	141
Rocky Mountain	24,802	36,677	48,685	64,686	4.0	3.4	161	132	5,527	7,082	7,962	9,170	2.5	1.5	245	194
Utah	4,502	6,823	9,344	12,771	4.2	3.8	171	146	1,169	1,618	1,859	2,165	3.3	1.7	323	219
Colorado	11,993	18,768	25,030	33,596	4.6	3.5	184	136	2,496	3,146	3,618	4,291	2.3	1.8	229	234
Wyoming	1,685	2,870	3,794	5,061	5.5	3.4	220	132	353	516	562	638	3.9	1.3	377	160
Idaho	3,345	4,414	5,692	7,298	2.8	3.0	113	116	782	987	1,061	1,159	2.4	.9	230	120
Montana	3,277	3,802	4,824	5,970	1.5	2.7	60	105	727	815	862	918	1.1	.7	112	89
Southwest	75,386	124,096	162,816	209,530	5.1	3.1	206	122	17,943	23,458	25,991	29,145	2.7	1.3	265	163
Arizona	9,447	14,779	21,497	30,300	4.6	4.3	184	168	2,125	2,970	3,600	4,397	3.4	2.3	332	296
New Mexico	4,120	6,326	8,219	10,637	4.4	3.1	176	121	1,104	1,399	1,538	1,711	2.4	1.2	234	151
Texas	50,899	86,027	111,916	142,261	5.4	3.0	217	117	12,019	15,779	17,391	19,339	2.8	1.2	269	153
Oklahoma	10,919	16,965	21,188	26,333	4.5	2.6	181	102	2,694	3,310	3,461	3,698	2.1	.7	203	83
Far West	138,564	199,323	254,752	321,970	3.7	2.9	149	111	27,163	33,043	36,631	40,872	2.0	1.3	194	160
Nevada	3,039	5,191	7,179	9,955	5.5	3.9	222	152	569	897	1,058	1,301	4.7	2.2	455	280
Washington	16,779	24,486	31,542	39,782	3.9	2.9	155	113	3,477	4,302	4,762	5,310	2.2	1.2	210	158
Oregon	10,241	13,417	17,103	21,784	2.7	2.9	110	112	2,239	2,658	2,842	3,092	1.7	.9	169	113
California	108,505	156,229	198,928	250,448	3.7	2.8	150	110	20,868	25,186	27,970	31,170	1.9	1.3	185	160
Southeast	189,093	262,939	336,432	424,208	3.4	2.9	135	111	44,992	55,020	59,195	64,117	1.6	.9	155	115
Florida	37,132	57,965	78,319	104,148	4.6	3.5	183	136	7,927	10,742	12,528	14,628	3.1	1.8	301	232
Georgia	20,298	27,880	36,431	46,396	3.2	3.0	130	118	4,907	5,732	6,323	6,905	1.6	1.1	153	140
South Carolina	10,247	14,009	17,853	22,742	3.2	2.9	128	112	2,775	3,256	3,463	3,757	1.6	.8	157	107
Arkansas	7,383	9,739	12,507	15,655	2.8	2.8	113	110	2,058	2,325	2,454	2,617	1.2	.7	120	89
North Carolina	21,596	27,916	35,614	44,380	2.6	2.8	105	108	5,382	6,076	6,487	6,963	1.2	.8	119	102
Mississippi	7,676	9,877	12,587	15,595	2.6	2.7	103	106	2,350	2,581	2,708	2,784	.9	.4	92	57
Tennessee	16,094	20,871	26,512	32,843	2.6	2.6	106	105	4,138	4,676	4,895	5,209	1.2	.6	120	81
Louisiana	13,820	21,320	26,626	33,023	4.4	2.6	179	101	3,789	4,440	4,656	4,915	1.6	.6	156	76
Virginia	22,484	31,494	38,822	47,573	3.4	2.5	138	98	4,907	5,556	5,906	6,331	1.3	.8	122	98
Alabama	12,958	17,105	20,936	25,682	2.8	2.4	113	94	3,581	3,961	4,032	4,163	1.0	.3	103	37
Kentucky	12,751	16,338	20,127	24,274	2.5	2.4	101	92	3,372	3,713	3,774	3,862	1.0	.2	95	29
West Virginia	6,664	8,427	10,100	11,896	2.4	2.0	96	80	1,805	1,962	1,970	1,984	.8	.1	82	8

	1	2	3	4	5	6	7	8	9	10	11	12	13	14	15	16
New England	60,712	76,153	95,545	118,958	2.3	2.7	92	103	12,148	12,486	13,442	14,736	.3	1.0	27	124
New Hampshire	3,557	5,435	6,956	9,151	4.3	3.1	174	121	802	958	1,071	1,235	1.8	1.5	175	191
Vermont	1,902	2,449	3,215	4,090	2.6	3.1	103	119	469	525	566	619	1.1	1.0	112	124
Connecticut	17,403	21,952	27,642	34,456	2.3	2.7	96	105	3,069	3,139	3,393	3,772	1.2	1.1	22	138
Massachusetts	29,351	35,797	44,924	55,643	2.0	2.6	81	102	5,784	5,763	6,209	6,780	0	1.0		122
Rhode Island	4,416	5,231	6,418	7,833	1.7	2.4	69	93	978	956	1,007	1,072	−.2	.7	88	86
Maine	4,083	5,289	6,391	7,785	2.6	2.3	106	89	1,046	1,145	1,196	1,258	−.9	.6		70
Alaska	1,924	3,859	5,099	6,725	7.2	3.3	290	129	333	481	565	675	3.7	2.0	365	256
Hawaii	4,400	5,803	7,212	9,006	2.8	2.6	113	102	842	1,018	1,107	1,207	1.9	1.0	187	128
Slow-growing regions	506,918	571,328	692,773	815,816	1.2	2.1	48	82	100,412	101,435	104,310	107,541	.1	.3	10	44
Plains	81,282	92,341	114,738	138,406	1.3	2.4	52	94	16,628	17,413	18,150	19,059	.5	.5	45	68
Minnesota	19,273	23,090	29,183	36,245	1.8	2.7	73	105	3,885	4,144	4,416	4,827	.6	.9	63	114
Kansas	11,288	13,741	17,204	20,753	2.0	2.5	80	95	2,264	2,426	2,586	2,678	.7	.6	68	74
Nebraska	7,667	8,356	10,333	12,561	.9	2.4	35	94	1,529	1,596	1,651	1,734	.3	.5	42	62
South Dakota	3,229	3,228	3,971	4,821	0	2.4	0	93	679	699	723	749	.7	.4	28	52
North Dakota	3,850	3,716	4,526	5,527	−.4	2.2		92	632	681	712	758	.3	.6	73	80
Missouri	21,340	25,664	31,467	37,342	.5	2.2	75	87	4,775	4,963	5,176	5,347	.7	.4	38	56
Iowa	14,634	14,546	18,063	21,158	−.1	2.2		87	2,864	2,904	2,937	2,966	.1	.1	14	16
Great Lakes	203,701	224,096	272,309	317,474	1.0	2.1	39	81	40,947	41,478	42,137	42,891	.1	.2	13	25
Indiana	25,019	27,114	34,000	40,543	.8	2.4	33	98	5,329	5,472	5,602	5,757	.3	.3	26	38
Wisconsin	20,588	25,140	30,894	37,191	2.0	2.3	81	91	4,518	4,746	4,923	5,143	.5	.5	48	60
Michigan	45,744	48,722	59,966	69,126	.6	2.1	25	82	9,072	9,050	9,221	9,358	0	.2		25
Ohio	51,045	56,432	68,035	78,910	1.0	2.0	41	77	10,767	10,736	10,774	10,859	0	.1		8
Illinois	61,275	66,687	79,413	91,404	.9	1.9	34	73	11,260	11,474	11,617	11,774	.2	.2	18	19
Mideast	221,936	254,891	305,727	359,936	1.4	2.1	56	80	42,837	42,544	44,023	45,590	−.1	.4	52	52
New Jersey	40,592	48,946	60,868	74,163	1.9	2.5	76	96	7,335	7,464	7,943	8,562	.8	.8	17	103
Delaware	3,110	3,578	4,366	5,258	1.4	2.3	57	89	579	606	639	682	.7	.7	44	88
Maryland	21,245	26,292	32,184	38,214	2.2	2.2	87	87	4,109	4,299	4,503	4,711	.5	.5	44	68
New York	97,368	107,641	127,448	148,991	1.0	1.9	41	75	18,195	17,663	18,262	18,971	−.3	.4	0	53
Pennsylvania	55,413	63,862	75,568	87,243	1.4	1.7	58	72	11,885	11,989	12,050	12,024	0	−.1		8
District of Columbia	4,208	4,572	5,293	6,067	.8	1.7	34	65	734	623	626	641	−1.6	−.2	21	21

NOTE.—The regions within the two groupings (fast growing and slow growing) and the States within each region are ranked in descending order by the average annual growth rate in total personal income, 1983–2000 (column 6).

Source: Kenneth P. Johnson and Howard L. Friedenberg, "Regional and State Projections of Income, Employment, and Population to the Year 2000," U.S. Department of Commerce, BEA, *Survey of Current Business* (May 1985):42.

Table 4-2
Per Capita Income, 1973-2000, United States, Regions, and States

	1972 dollars				Percent of U.S. average				Average annual growth rate (percent)		Index, U.S. average annual growth rate=100	
	1973	1983	1990	2000	1973	1983	1990	2000	1973–1983	1983–2000	1973–1983	1983–2000
United States....................	4,740	5,470	6,434	7,369	100	100	100	100	1.4	1.8	100	100
Fast-growing regions	4,461	5,346	6,284	7,223	94	98	98	98	1.8	1.8	127	101
Rocky Mountain....................	4,487	5,179	6,115	7,054	95	95	95	96	1.4	1.8	100	104
Utah	3,852	4,217	5,026	5,899	81	77	78	80	.9	2.0	63	113
Colorado..........................	4,805	5,966	6,918	7,829	101	109	108	106	2.2	1.6	151	91
Wyoming..........................	4,768	5,562	6,752	7,928	101	102	105	108	1.6	2.1	108	119
Idaho..............................	4,277	4,473	5,365	6,290	90	82	83	85	.4	2.0	31	115
Montana..........................	4,505	4,665	5,599	6,506	95	85	87	88	.3	2.0	24	112
Southwest..........................	4,201	5,290	6,264	7,189	89	97	97	98	2.3	1.8	161	103
Arizona............................	4,445	4,976	5,971	6,891	94	91	93	94	1.1	1.9	79	109
New Mexico	3,731	4,522	5,344	6,217	79	83	83	84	1.9	1.9	134	107
Texas..............................	4,235	5,452	6,435	7,356	89	100	100	100	2.6	1.8	177	101
Oklahoma.........................	4,053	5,126	6,120	7,121	86	94	95	97	2.4	2.0	165	110
Far West..........................	5,103	6,032	6,954	7,877	108	110	108	107	1.7	1.6	117	90
Nevada............................	5,342	5,787	6,787	7,652	113	106	105	104	.8	1.7	56	94
Washington	4,826	5,692	6,624	7,492	102	104	103	102	1.7	1.6	115	92
Oregon............................	4,574	5,048	6,019	7,046	96	92	94	96	1.0	2.0	69	112
California..........................	5,200	6,203	7,112	8,035	110	113	111	109	1.8	1.5	123	87
Southeast	4,024	4,779	5,683	6,616	85	87	88	90	1.7	1.9	120	109
Florida............................	4,684	5,396	6,252	7,120	99	99	97	97	1.4	1.6	99	93
Georgia............................	4,135	4,864	5,761	6,719	87	89	90	91	1.6	1.9	113	109
South Carolina	3,692	4,302	5,155	6,054	78	79	80	82	1.5	2.0	107	115
Arkansas..........................	3,587	4,189	5,097	5,982	76	77	79	81	1.6	2.1	108	120
North Carolina	4,012	4,594	5,490	6,373	85	84	85	86	1.4	1.9	94	110
Mississippi........................	3,267	3,827	4,649	5,601	69	70	72	76	1.6	2.3	111	128
Tennessee	3,889	4,463	5,416	6,305	82	82	84	86	1.4	2.1	96	116
Louisiana..........................	3,647	4,802	5,718	6,719	77	88	89	91	2.8	2.0	193	113
Virginia............................	4,582	5,668	6,573	7,515	97	104	102	102	2.1	1.7	149	95
Alabama...........................	3,619	4,318	5,192	6,170	76	79	81	84	1.8	2.1	124	120
Kentucky..........................	3,782	4,400	5,333	6,285	80	80	83	85	1.5	2.1	106	120
West Virginia......................	3,692	4,295	5,127	5,996	78	79	80	81	1.5	2.0	106	112
New England........................	4,998	6,099	7,108	8,072	105	111	110	110	2.0	1.7	139	94
New Hampshire	4,436	5,674	6,498	7,413	94	104	101	101	2.5	1.6	173	90
Vermont...........................	4,059	4,664	5,679	6,606	86	85	88	90	1.4	2.1	97	117
Connecticut	5,670	6,993	8,146	9,134	120	128	127	124	2.1	1.6	147	90
Massachusetts	5,075	6,212	7,236	8,207	107	114	112	111	2.0	1.7	141	93
Rhode Island	4,516	5,472	6,371	7,305	95	100	99	99	1.9	1.7	134	97
Maine..............................	3,902	4,619	5,341	6,187	82	84	83	84	1.7	1.7	118	98
Alaska...............................	5,774	8,023	9,025	9,958	122	147	140	135	3.3	1.3	232	72
Hawaii...............................	5,226	5,701	6,517	7,461	110	104	101	101	.9	1.6	61	90
Slow-growing regions..................	5,048	5,632	6,641	7,586	107	103	103	103	1.1	1.8	76	100
Plains..............................	4,888	5,303	6,322	7,262	103	97	98	99	.8	1.9	57	106
Minnesota..........................	4,961	5,572	6,609	7,509	105	102	103	102	1.2	1.8	81	100
Kansas............................	4,985	5,664	6,785	7,750	105	104	105	105	1.3	1.9	89	105
Nebraska..........................	5,016	5,236	6,257	7,244	106	96	97	98	.4	1.9	30	109
South Dakota	4,756	4,617	5,495	6,435	100	84	85	87	-.3	2.0	....	112
North Dakota	6,088	5,456	6,359	7,288	128	100	99	99	-1.1	1.7	....	97
Missouri...........................	4,469	5,171	6,078	6,984	94	95	94	95	1.5	1.8	102	101
Iowa..............................	5,110	5,009	6,151	7,132	108	92	96	97	-.2	2.1	....	119
Great Lakes........................	4,975	5,403	6,462	7,402	105	99	100	100	.8	1.9	57	106
Indiana............................	4,695	4,955	6,069	7,042	99	91	94	96	.5	2.1	37	118
Wisconsin..........................	4,556	5,297	6,276	7,232	96	97	98	98	1.5	1.8	105	105
Michigan..........................	5,046	5,384	6,503	7,419	106	98	101	101	.7	1.9	45	108
Ohio..............................	4,741	5,256	6,315	7,267	100	96	98	99	1.0	1.9	72	109
Illinois	5,442	5,812	6,836	7,763	115	106	106	105	.7	1.7	46	97

Table 4-2 *(continued)*

Mideast	5,181	5,991	6,945	7,895	109	110	108	107	1.5	1.6	101	93
New Jersey	5,534	6,558	7,663	8,662	117	120	119	118	1.7	1.7	119	93
Delaware	5,370	5,905	6,830	7,709	113	108	106	105	1.0	1.6	66	89
Maryland	5,170	6,116	7,147	8,112	109	112	111	110	1.7	1.7	117	95
New York	5,351	6,094	6,979	7,854	113	111	108	107	1.3	1.5	91	85
Pennsylvania	4,662	5,372	6,271	7,256	98	98	97	98	1.4	1.8	99	101
District of Columbia	5,735	7,339	8,453	9,467	121	134	131	128	2.5	1.5	173	85

Source: Kenneth P. Johnson and Howard L. Friedenberg, "Regional and State Projections of Income, Employment, and Population to the Year 2000," U.S. Department of Commerce, BEA, *Survey of Current Business* (May 1985):43.

Note: For ranking of regions and states, see note to table 4-1.

located in the southern or western United States, while 75% of the slow growth cities are in the northern regions and plains. See table 4-3 for details. For example, among the fastest growing metropolitan areas are:

Phoenix, AZ	2.6%
Tallahassee, FL	1.9%
Houston, TX	1.8%
Denver, CO	1.8%
Anaheim-Santa Ana, CA	1.7%
Forth Myer-Cape Coral, FL	1.7%
Sacramento, CA	1.7%
San Diego, CA	1.6%
Atlanta, GA	1.6%

Among the slowest growing metropolitan areas are:

Detroit, MI	–0.1%
Indianapolis, IN	0.2%
Buffalo, NY	0.3%
Baltimore, MD	0.4%
San Francisco, CA	0.4%
Kansas City, MO-KS	0.5%
Bergen-Passaic, NJ	0.6%

For the direct investor or prospective investor, the following data on population and personal income growth trends may be helpful. These data are delineated by state and region.

New England and Mideast States

The New England population grew 3.8% between 1970 and 1980, falling below the national growth rate of 10.7%. In the early 1980s, population growth is below the national average, at 0.3% per year. In half of the region's states, per capita income is above the national average; the region accounts for 5.7% of total U.S. personal income. Traditionally, capital goods, textile, leather, and apparel constituted the core of the region's manufacturing activities. But in the late 1970s and early 1980s, the region successfully diversified into high technology and R&D-oriented activities.

In the Mideast states the population decreased 0.3% in the past two decades, and its share of U.S. personal income dropped to 20%, down from 23.8% in 1970. In all but one state, personal income is above the national average. This region, like New England, is notable for its educational institutions. It is the nation's financial center.

After declining in the 1960s and 1970s, the Mideast region rebounded. Financial, business, and other services were major factors that simulated growth. Following a decade of high growth of nonmetropolitan areas, the trend reversed in the early 1980s, with metropolitan areas exceeding the growth rate of nonmetropolitan areas. Three-fifths of the region's population is concentrated in four metropolitan areas. Thus, the entire region is more favorably affected by the higher growth of metropolitan areas than is, the South, for example, where metropolitan areas account for only one-fifth of the population.

New York and Rhode Island registered absolute population declines for the 1970–1980 period, while Pennsylvania experienced stagnation. In the New England and Mideast regions as a whole, average growth in personal income from 1970 to 1980 was below that of other regions. New England is expected to exceed the national growth in population and income, while the Mideast region is expected to fall below until the year 2000.

Major manufacturing industries of the Mideast region include electrical equipment, rubber and plastic products, paper, machinery, fabricated metal products, printing and publishing, scientific instruments, apparel, food, and chemicals.

Great Lakes and Plains

To some extent the Great Lakes and plains regions possess many of the characteristics of New England and the Mideast states. The Great Lakes and Plains are older industrialized areas, both experiencing emigration from their central cities and a substantially slower growth in population, income, and employment than the nation as a whole. However, the industrial base of the Great Lakes

Table 4-3
Total Personal Income, Per Capita Personal Income, Population, and Employment by Metropolitan Area, 1983, 1990, and 2000

	Total personal income (Millions of 1972 dollars)				Per capita personal income (1972 dollars)					Population (Thousands of persons)				Employment (Thousands of jobs)			
	1983	1990	2000	Average annual growth rate (percent) 1983–2000	1983	1990	2000	Rank in the United States 2000	Average annual growth rate (percent) 1983–2000	1983	1990	2000	Average annual growth rate (percent) 1983–2000	1983	1990	2000	Average annual growth rate (percent) 1983–2000
United States [1]	1,280,180	1,603,313	1,970,899	2.6	5,471	6,434	7,369		1.8	233,975.0	249,203.0	267,464.0	0.8	106,891.0	123,071.0	138,338.0	1.5
Consolidated Metropolitan Statistical Areas [2]																	
Buffalo, NY	6,504	7,650	8,842	1.8	5,304	6,163	6,942		.9	1,226.3	1,241.3	1,273.6	.2	511.9	558.5	599.8	.9
Chicago, IL	49,720	58,597	67,655	1.8	6,203	7,231	8,191		1.1	8,015.9	8,103.2	8,259.4	.2	3,695.4	4,104.4	4,463.9	1.1
Cincinnati, OH	9,103	11,173	13,276	2.2	5,465	6,594	7,677		1.3	1,665.6	1,694.5	1,729.3	.2	734.2	835.6	908.3	1.3
Cleveland, OH	16,407	18,908	21,238	1.5	5,853	7,045	8,107		.8	2,802.9	2,683.9	2,619.8	-.4	1,255.9	1,365.2	1,427.8	.8
Dallas, TX	21,172	27,412	34,622	2.9	6,482	7,519	8,478		1.3	3,266.1	3,645.8	4,084.0	1.3	1,771.9	2,117.8	2,465.2	2.0
Denver, CO	11,937	15,792	21,188	3.4	6,752	7,783	8,803		1.8	1,767.8	2,029.0	2,406.8	1.8	985.8	1,211.2	1,497.6	2.5
Detroit, MI	27,134	32,442	36,682	1.8	5,892	7,104	8,094		1.9	4,605.0	4,566.8	4,531.8	-.1	1,871.5	2,097.2	2,190.8	.9
Houston, TX	22,475	30,420	39,604	3.4	6,312	7,361	8,344		1.7	3,561.0	4,132.7	4,746.1	1.7	1,735.3	2,154.1	2,570.4	2.3
Los Angeles, CA	76,360	96,030	120,153	2.7	6,264	7,146	8,075		1.2	12,190.6	13,438.0	14,879.1	1.2	5,773.4	6,762.2	7,786.5	1.8
Miami, FL	16,960	20,760	25,828	2.5	6,073	6,911	7,808		1.0	2,792.6	3,003.7	3,308.0	1.0	1,273.6	1,495.7	1,732.6	1.8
Milwaukee, WI	9,482	11,232	13,143	1.9	6,037	7,106	8,175		1.0	1,570.8	1,580.6	1,607.6	.1	763.4	887.5	903.9	1.0
New York, NY	119,233	142,190	168,568	2.1	6,791	7,811	8,796		1.1	17,558.1	18,203.5	19,163.5	.5	8,447.6	9,471.6	10,432.2	1.2
Philadelphia, PA	34,191	41,066	48,360	2.1	5,959	7,011	8,063		1.0	5,737.8	5,857.0	5,997.7	.3	2,652.7	2,928.9	3,155.1	1.0
Pittsburgh, PA	13,280	15,220	17,265	1.6	5,534	6,370	7,305		.8	2,399.8	2,389.3	2,363.3	-.1	983.8	1,074.0	1,130.9	.8
Portland, OR	7,490	9,498	12,044	2.8	5,626	6,613	7,640		1.8	1,331.5	1,436.4	1,576.3	1.0	622.7	737.2	861.2	1.9
San Francisco, CA	40,807	51,337	64,122	2.7	7,256	8,388	9,523		1.6	5,623.5	6,120.1	6,733.6	1.1	2,960.6	3,546.8	4,147.7	2.0
Seattle, WA	13,587	17,656	22,227	2.9	6,212	7,251	8,156		1.3	2,187.2	2,434.9	2,725.3	1.3	1,074.1	1,298.4	1,508.6	2.0
Other Metropolitan Areas [3]																	
Abilene, TX	667	909	1,189	3.5	5,513	6,508	7,407	109	1.7	121.1	139.8	160.5	1.7	65.2	78.1	91.5	2.0
Akron, OH [1]	3,537	4,105	4,641	1.6	5,423	6,531	7,470	99	-.3	652.1	628.5	621.3	-.3	266.7	293.2	310.5	.9
Albany, GA	501	667	867	3.3	4,320	5,297	6,320	248	1.0	116.0	126.0	137.2	1.0	53.4	61.9	70.0	1.6
Albany–Schenectady–Troy, NY	4,656	5,544	6,513	2.0	5,538	6,407	7,244	136	.4	840.7	865.3	899.1	.4	389.9	431.0	467.6	1.1
Albuquerque, NM	2,387	3,093	4,040	3.1	5,393	6,272	7,268	129	1.4	442.5	493.1	555.9	1.4	221.3	266.1	318.4	2.2
Alexandria, LA	552	662	791	2.1	4,030	4,705	5,501	306	.3	137.0	140.7	143.8	.3	54.6	56.9	59.7	.5
Allentown–Bethlehem, PA–NJ	3,659	4,471	5,260	2.2	5,688	6,605	7,575	88	.4	643.3	676.9	694.0	.4	281.3	316.9	340.7	1.1
Altoona, PA	564	660	760	1.8	4,172	4,966	5,822	292	-.2	135.1	132.9	130.6	-.2	52.6	56.7	59.2	.7
Amarillo, TX	1,039	1,322	1,644	2.7	5,582	6,528	7,387	111	1.1	186.1	202.5	222.5	1.1	90.6	105.3	120.0	1.7

Table 4-3 (continued)

	Total personal income (Millions of 1972 dollars)			Avg. annual growth rate (percent)	Per capita personal income (1972 dollars)			Rank in the United States	Population (Thousands of persons)			Avg. annual growth rate (percent)	Employment (Thousands of jobs)			Avg. annual growth rate (percent)
	1983	1990	2000	1983–2000	1983	1990	2000	2000	1983	1990	2000	1983–2000	1983	1990	2000	1983–2000
Anaheim–Santa Ana, CA *	14,700	20,131	26,385	3.5	7,140	8,414	9,677	7	2,059.0	2,392.5	2,726.4	1.7	1,002.0	1,330.7	1,649.1	3.0
Anchorage, AK	1,881	2,490	3,314	3.4	8,904	9,862	10,811	2	211.2	252.4	306.6	2.2	126.0	158.5	201.7	2.8
Anderson, IN	631	764	873	1.9	4,681	5,790	6,682	205	134.7	132.0	130.6	-.2	52.2	56.8	58.3	.7
Anderson, SC	573	736	928	2.9	4,160	5,081	6,041	272	137.7	144.8	153.5	.6	56.0	61.9	67.1	1.1
Ann Arbor, MI	1,618	2,052	2,418	2.4	6,280	7,789	9,076	15	257.7	263.4	266.4	.2	148.1	181.3	204.3	1.9
Anniston, AL	497	587	702	2.1	4,003	4,725	5,572	303	124.1	124.3	126.0	.1	54.8	58.3	62.2	.7
Appleton–Oshkosh–Neenah, WI	1,586	1,966	2,373	2.4	5,339	6,300	7,234	139	297.1	312.1	328.1	.6	147.4	168.0	187.0	1.4
Asheville, NC	774	963	1,189	2.6	4,682	5,499	6,319	249	165.3	175.1	188.1	.8	80.8	91.2	100.3	1.3
Athens, GA	605	762	952	2.7	4,474	5,225	6,005	273	135.2	145.8	158.5	.9	64.3	73.5	82.5	1.5
Atlanta, GA	13,481	18,011	23,590	3.3	5,848	6,779	7,782	64	2,305.0	2,656.9	3,031.5	1.6	1,238.3	1,499.2	1,756.0	2.1
Atlantic City, NJ	1,724	2,237	2,873	3.0	6,072	7,081	8,065	41	284.0	316.0	356.3	1.3	152.0	185.6	220.3	2.2
Augusta, GA–SC	1,702	2,085	2,557	2.4	4,716	5,498	6,340	244	360.8	379.2	403.3	.7	163.1	182.9	201.1	1.2
Aurora–Elgin, IL *	1,881	2,380	2,849	2.5	5,880	6,906	7,815	57	320.0	344.6	364.6	.8	137.4	161.7	183.6	1.7
Austin, TX	3,456	4,971	6,812	4.1	5,588	6,516	7,416	108	618.4	762.8	918.6	2.4	333.3	426.4	523.6	2.7
Bakersfield, CA	2,269	2,940	3,745	3.0	5,079	5,726	6,381	241	446.8	513.5	586.8	1.6	190.5	223.7	259.7	1.8
Baltimore, MD	12,806	15,480	18,108	2.1	5,737	6,698	7,576	87	2,232.2	2,311.3	2,390.0	.4	1,091.6	1,196.2	1,272.5	.9
Bangor, ME (NECMA)	619	736	888	2.1	4,512	5,180	5,969	282	137.3	142.2	148.7	.5	64.7	70.7	77.8	1.1
Baton Rouge, LA	2,798	3,573	4,532	2.9	5,269	6,244	7,286	127	531.1	572.3	622.0	.9	229.5	274.4	322.6	2.0
Battle Creek, MI	715	876	985	1.9	5,188	6,340	7,263	131	137.8	138.1	135.6	-.1	55.6	60.8	61.6	.6
Beaumont–Port Arthur, TX	2,183	2,558	3,012	1.9	5,624	6,494	7,336	118	388.1	393.9	410.6	.3	158.8	173.8	189.8	1.1
Beaver County, PA *	1,015	1,201	1,389	1.9	5,025	5,939	6,940	177	201.9	202.2	200.2	-.1	63.6	75.0	81.2	1.4
Bellingham, WA	525	700	919	3.3	4,753	5,452	6,205	263	110.4	128.4	148.0	1.7	46.8	58.1	69.9	2.4
Benton Harbor, MI	791	937	1,032	1.6	4,829	5,944	6,807	193	163.9	157.6	151.6	-.5	64.3	69.9	70.7	.6
Bergen–Passaic, NJ *	9,734	11,871	14,217	2.3	7,540	8,807	9,931	4	1,291.0	1,347.9	1,431.5	.6	660.2	751.7	836.8	1.4
Billings, MT	636	813	1,038	2.9	5,462	6,301	7,192	149	116.4	129.0	144.4	1.3	58.3	70.3	83.3	2.1
Biloxi–Gulfport, MS	788	1,037	1,352	3.2	4,095	4,895	5,895	286	192.5	211.9	229.4	1.0	86.1	99.4	113.3	1.6
Binghamton, NY	1,382	1,717	2,028	2.3	5,212	6,081	6,886	186	265.1	282.3	294.5	.6	121.6	140.0	153.1	1.4
Birmingham, AL	4,428	5,413	6,716	2.5	4,972	5,891	6,952	175	890.5	919.0	966.0	.5	392.9	430.8	477.2	1.1
Bismarck, ND	492	628	805	2.9	5,538	6,755	7,679	76	84.2	92.9	104.8	1.3	41.7	49.2	57.5	1.9
Bloomington, IN	404	542	690	3.2	4,047	5,112	6,140	269	99.8	106.0	112.4	.7	48.0	56.6	63.3	1.6
Bloomington–Normal, IL	648	835	1,000	2.6	5,356	6,589	7,566	90	121.0	126.8	132.1	.5	58.4	68.4	78.2	1.7
Boise City, ID	1,007	1,313	1,740	3.3	5,465	6,292	7,273	128	184.3	208.6	239.3	1.5	91.3	112.3	137.3	2.4
Boston–Lawrence–Salem–Lowell–Brockton, MA (NECMA)	24,586	30,847	38,359	2.7	6,693	7,835	8,918	18	3,673.4	3,936.8	4,301.3	.9	2,064.9	2,439.1	2,784.7	1.8
Boulder–Longmont, CO *	1,334	1,868	2,694	4.2	6,465	7,688	9,032	17	206.4	243.0	298.3	2.2	112.3	148.4	196.0	3.3
Bradenton, FL	925	1,277	1,749	3.8	5,568	6,472	7,417	107	166.1	197.3	235.8	2.1	60.5	84.0	110.4	3.6
Brazoria, TX *	1,034	1,419	1,848	3.5	5,553	6,537	7,442	104	186.3	217.1	248.3	1.7	65.7	84.1	101.5	2.6
Bremerton, WA	911	1,217	1,566	3.2	5,706	6,383	7,213	145	159.7	190.6	217.1	1.8	68.2	88.2	104.2	2.5
Bridgeport–Stamford–Norwalk–Danbury, CT *	7,032	8,923	11,239	2.8	8,604	9,772	10,809	3	817.2	913.1	1,039.8	1.4	427.7	524.4	617.0	2.2
Brownsville–Harlingen, TX	725	967	1,254	3.3	3,115	3,747	4,330	311	232.7	258.2	289.7	1.3	77.0	91.2	106.2	1.9
Bryan–College Station, TX	473	680	937	4.1	4,253	5,070	5,861	290	111.2	134.2	159.8	2.2	51.9	66.9	82.7	2.8

Buffalo, NY *	5,346	6,292	7,298	1.8	5,336	6,193	6,979	172	1,001.8	1,016.0	1,045.8	.3	428.2	466.3	501.2	.9
Burlington, NC	489	598	728	2.4	4,812	5,545	6,302	252	101.6	107.8	115.5	.8	50.6	56.6	61.7	1.2
Burlington, VT (NECMA)	646	891	1,171	3.6	5,221	6,316	7,333	121	123.8	141.0	159.7	1.5	69.6	88.6	105.7	2.5
Canton, OH	2,019	2,445	2,825	3.0	5,010	6,156	7,170	153	403.0	397.1	393.9	-1.6	157.8	177.1	189.2	1.6
Casper, WY	522	679	915	3.4	6,762	7,845	9,075	16	77.2	86.5	100.9	1.6	39.5	49.1	60.6	1.6
Cedar Rapids, IA	967	1,152	1,345	2.0	5,715	6,724	7,755	70	169.2	171.5	173.4	.4	86.8	98.5	108.1	1.3
Champaign-Urbana-Rantoul, IL	799	989	1,175	2.3	4,723	5,638	6,502	228	169.1	175.4	180.8	.4	83.3	93.5	103.9	1.7
Charleston, SC	2,021	2,604	3,383	3.1	4,354	5,193	6,072	270	464.1	501.5	557.1	1.1	209.6	241.7	276.9	1.7
Charleston, WV	1,452	1,727	2,010	1.9	5,394	6,355	7,310	123	269.1	271.7	274.9	.1	118.3	133.4	145.8	1.2
Charlotte-Gastonia-Rock Hill, NC-SC	5,323	6,760	8,554	2.8	5,221	6,054	6,911	182	1,019.5	1,116.6	1,237.4	1.1	540.3	625.1	705.9	1.6
Charlottesville, VA	599	783	992	3.0	5,103	6,083	7,066	165	117.4	128.7	140.4	1.1	65.3	78.5	90.6	1.9
Chattanooga, TN-GA	1,986	2,507	3,092	2.6	4,657	5,582	6,425	239	426.5	449.0	481.3	.7	186.5	209.7	228.8	1.2
Chicago, IL *	38,549	44,598	50,788	1.6	6,300	7,324	8,284	33	6,119.0	6,089.3	6,130.6	0	2,973.0	3,266.1	3,528.1	1.0
Chico, CA	686	894	1,167	3.2	5,514	5,077	5,747	296	154.7	176.1	203.0	1.6	54.0	68.4	84.3	2.6
Cincinnati, OH-KY-IN *	7,744	9,419	11,146	2.2	5,514	6,651	7,767	67	1,404.5	1,416.1	1,435.0	.6	642.9	729.5	791.6	1.2
Clarksville-Hopkinsville, TN-KY	621	760	919	2.3	4,114	4,985	5,914	285	151.0	152.4	155.3	.2	70.8	77.2	82.9	.9
Cleveland, OH *	11,517	13,128	14,624	1.4	6,134	7,369	8,486	21	1,877.5	1,781.6	1,723.2	-.5	899.4	971.8	1,010.6	.7
Colorado Springs, CO	1,785	2,486	3,430	3.9	5,252	6,215	7,155	157	339.9	399.9	479.4	2.0	172.5	217.2	269.6	2.7
Columbia, MO	501	640	816	2.9	4,818	5,612	6,500	229	103.9	114.0	125.5	1.1	55.3	65.4	75.4	2.1
Columbia, SC	2,127	2,647	3,371	2.7	4,967	5,683	6,495	230	428.2	465.8	519.1	1.1	226.6	261.0	298.6	1.6
Columbus, GA-AL	1,056	1,285	1,560	2.3	4,367	5,146	5,994	277	241.9	249.7	260.3	.4	118.2	128.5	138.0	.9
Columbus, OH	6,765	8,505	10,354	2.5	6,379	6,377	7,336	119	1,262.6	1,333.2	1,411.4	.7	613.8	716.1	798.8	1.6
Corpus Christi, TX	1,750	2,187	2,707	2.6	4,917	5,821	6,657	207	356.0	375.8	406.6	.8	152.8	173.5	195.6	1.5
Cumberland, MD-WV	434	509	576	1.7	4,100	4,810	5,447	307	105.8	105.8	37.4	0	37.4	40.0	41.5	1.6
Dallas, TX *	14,450	18,667	23,599	2.9	6,658	7,716	8,701	20	2,170.2	2,419.3	2,712.3	1.3	1,269.6	1,511.3	1,757.4	1.9
Danville, VA	458	551	653	2.1	4,134	4,948	5,775	295	110.7	111.3	113.0	.3	48.1	52.5	52.5	.5
Davenport-Rock Island-Moline, IA-IL	2,090	2,592	3,056	2.3	5,436	6,551	7,574	89	384.4	395.7	403.4	-.1	170.0	189.5	205.2	1.1
Dayton-Springfield, OH	4,992	5,881	6,720	1.8	5,335	6,394	7,335	120	935.7	919.8	916.1	-.3	420.5	467.2	497.4	1.0
Daytona Beach, FL	1,412	2,008	2,765	4.0	4,875	5,662	6,478	232	289.6	354.7	426.8	2.3	104.0	131.7	161.4	2.6
Decatur, IL	690	812	906	1.6	5,331	6,370	7,232	140	129.5	127.5	125.3	-.2	55.3	60.4	64.2	.9
Denver, CO *	10,602	13,924	18,494	3.3	6,790	7,796	8,771	19	1,561.5	1,786.1	2,108.5	1.8	873.4	1,062.8	1,301.6	2.4
Des Moines, IA	2,260	2,745	3,333	2.3	6,030	7,044	8,268	34	374.9	389.8	403.1	-.4	209.3	235.5	259.8	2.3
Detroit, MI *	25,515	30,391	34,264	1.7	5,869	7,062	8,033	44	4,347.4	4,303.4	4,265.4	-.5	1,723.4	1,915.9	1,986.5	1.8
Dothan, AL	517	652	819	2.7	4,125	5,029	6,056	271	125.2	129.6	135.2	.4	63.0	70.1	77.7	1.2
Dubuque, IA	442	540	638	2.2	4,802	5,838	6,798	194	92.5	92.5	93.9	-.7	44.1	48.8	52.4	1.0
Duluth, MN-WI	1,202	1,378	1,600	1.7	4,649	5,475	6,288	253	238.5	251.8	254.4	.7	98.2	104.6	110.7	.7
Eau Claire, WI	609	770	945	2.8	4,545	5,471	6,320	247	133.9	140.7	149.6	.9	60.8	69.6	78.2	1.5
El Paso, TX	1,981	2,507	3,163	2.8	3,881	4,621	5,358	309	510.5	542.5	590.4	-.1	201.9	229.1	228.6	1.5
Elkhart-Goshen, IN	765	1,013	1,285	3.1	5,512	5,512	8,016	45	138.8	148.7	160.3	.9	87.1	106.3	118.4	1.8
Elmira, NY	459	539	621	1.8	4,774	5,706	6,577	223	96.2	94.4	94.4	-.1	37.3	40.2	42.6	.8
Enid, OK	392	492	614	2.7	5,795	7,221	8,521	26	67.7	68.2	72.0	.2	33.1	37.3	42.0	1.4
Erie, PA	1,368	1,646	1,898	1.9	4,880	5,717	6,590	218	290.4	287.9	288.0	.4	118.7	132.1	139.9	1.0
Eugene-Springfield, OR	1,223	1,577	2,028	3.0	4,553	5,461	6,371	243	268.5	288.8	318.3	-.5	108.7	129.0	152.3	2.0
Evansville, IN-KY	1,473	1,914	2,333	2.7	5,298	6,581	7,701	75	278.6	290.8	302.9	.8	132.4	154.6	132.4	1.5
Fargo-Moorhead, ND-MN	786	962	1,188	2.5	5,598	6,487	7,361	115	140.4	148.3	161.3	.4	73.3	83.3	93.9	1.5
Fayetteville, NC	1,023	1,229	1,474	2.2	4,107	4,840	5,566	304	249.0	254.0	264.8	-.4	122.6	132.7	141.3	.8

Table 4-3 (continued)

Column groups: Total personal income (Millions of 1972 dollars) — 1983, 1990, 2000, Average annual growth rate (percent) 1983–2000; Per capita personal income (1972 dollars) — 1983, 1990, 2000, Average annual growth rate (percent) 1983–2000, Rank in the United States 2000; Population (Thousands of persons) — 1983, 1990, 2000, Average annual growth rate (percent) 1983–2000; Employment (Thousands of jobs) — 1983, 1990, 2000, Average annual growth rate (percent) 1983–2000.

Metropolitan area	TPI 1983	TPI 1990	TPI 2000	TPI gr.	PCI 1983	PCI 1990	PCI 2000	PCI gr.	Rank 2000	Pop 1983	Pop 1990	Pop 2000	Pop gr.	Emp 1983	Emp 1990	Emp 2000	Emp gr.
Fayetteville-Springdale, AR	433	568	733	3.2	4,215	5,118	5,987	2.1	278	102.6	110.9	122.5	1.0	48.6	58.5	68.4	2.0
Flint, MI	2,435	2,933	3,333	1.9	5,560	6,649	7,521	1.8	93	438.0	441.1	443.2	.1	172.2	197.7	208.7	1.1
Florence, AL	613	736	882	2.2	4,511	5,336	6,232	1.9	260	135.9	138.0	141.5	.2	53.5	58.5	63.6	1.0
Florence, SC	458	633	832	3.6	4,044	4,992	5,929	2.3	284	113.2	126.8	140.3	1.3	52.9	62.0	69.9	1.6
Fort Collins-Loveland, CO	811	1,177	1,659	4.3	5,006	5,825	6,577	1.6	222	162.1	202.1	252.2	2.6	68.8	91.8	118.7	3.3
Fort Lauderdale-Hollywood-Pompano Beach, FL	7,195	9,432	12,281	3.2	6,704	7,617	8,581	1.5	24	1,073.2	1,238.2	1,431.1	1.7	431.4	551.0	675.7	2.7
Fort Myers-Cape Coral, FL	1,311	2,066	3,054	5.1	5,437	6,301	7,158	1.6	156	241.2	327.9	426.7	3.4	95.0	137.0	184.2	4.0
Fort Pierce, FL	914	1,441	2,123	5.1	5,076	5,795	6,566	1.5	225	180.1	248.7	323.4	3.5	67.8	94.6	123.6	3.6
Fort Smith, AR-OK	716	953	1,237	3.3	4,280	5,014	5,797	1.8	294	167.3	190.0	213.4	1.4	74.5	91.0	105.9	2.1
Fort Walton Beach, FL	557	806	1,118	4.2	4,630	5,444	6,271	1.8	254	120.3	148.1	178.2	2.3	58.0	71.1	85.3	2.3
Fort Wayne, IN	1,796	2,234	2,668	2.4	5,147	6,236	7,208	2.0	146	349.0	358.2	370.1	.3	170.2	194.9	210.7	1.3
Fort Worth-Arlington, TX *	6,722	8,744	11,024	3.0	6,135	7,130	8,037	1.6	43	1,095.8	1,226.4	1,371.6	1.3	502.3	606.4	707.8	2.0
Fresno, CA	2,789	3,579	4,515	2.9	5,113	5,876	6,586	1.5	220	545.5	609.2	685.5	1.4	241.5	288.9	339.5	2.0
Gadsden, AL	431	515	615	2.1	4,163	4,952	5,815	2.0	293	103.6	104.0	105.7	.1	37.0	40.0	43.1	.9
Gainesville, FL	759	1,065	1,459	3.9	4,125	4,858	5,629	1.8	301	184.0	219.2	259.1	2.0	87.2	107.7	129.9	2.4
Galveston-Texas City, TX *	1,231	1,486	1,769	2.2	5,769	6,652	7,505	1.6	94	213.3	223.5	235.7	.6	76.8	83.8	90.8	1.0
Gary-Hammond, IN *	3,346	4,043	4,731	2.1	5,229	6,261	7,199	1.9	147	639.9	645.7	657.2	.2	242.0	272.3	290.0	1.1
Glens Falls, NY	497	633	765	2.6	4,184	5,251	5,986	2.1	279	118.8	120.6	127.8	.4	46.5	54.1	59.9	1.5
Grand Forks, ND	336	403	497	2.3	5,017	5,814	6,727	1.7	202	67.0	69.3	73.9	.6	35.7	39.5	43.7	1.2
Grand Rapids, MI	3,242	4,307	5,250	2.9	5,306	6,465	7,371	1.9	113	611.0	666.2	712.3	.9	300.7	375.9	425.1	2.1
Great Falls, MT	398	469	558	2.0	4,912	5,742	6,626	1.8	211	80.9	81.7	84.2	.2	37.7	41.4	45.0	1.0
Greeley, CO	647	861	1,139	3.4	4,969	5,773	6,524	1.6	227	130.4	149.2	174.5	1.7	52.3	62.3	74.3	2.1
Green Bay, WI	984	1,249	1,550	2.7	5,479	6,514	7,550	1.9	91	179.6	191.8	205.3	.8	90.4	108.3	124.6	1.9
Greensboro-Winston-Salem-High Point, NC	4,629	5,861	7,274	2.7	5,284	6,247	7,216	1.8	144	876.0	938.2	1,008.1	.8	465.7	531.4	584.6	1.3
Greenville-Spartanburg, SC	2,795	3,502	4,416	2.7	4,738	5,564	6,451	1.8	235	590.0	629.5	684.6	.9	295.9	338.1	380.0	1.5
Hagerstown, MD	518	633	763	2.3	4,603	5,550	6,494	2.0	231	112.5	114.0	117.5	.3	45.7	52.9	57.5	1.4
Hamilton-Middletown, OH *	1,359	1,754	2,130	2.7	5,206	6,301	7,238	2.0	137	261.1	278.4	294.2	.7	91.3	106.1	116.8	1.5
Harrisburg-Lebanon-Carlisle, PA	3,133	3,780	4,432	2.1	5,550	6,374	7,337	1.6	117	564.4	593.0	604.1	.4	292.1	327.2	349.4	1.1
Hartford-New Britain-Middletown-Bristol, CT (NECMA)	7,190	9,059	11,296	2.7	6,799	8,062	9,112	1.7	13	1,057.5	1,123.7	1,239.7	.9	599.1	713.8	824.3	1.9
Hickory, NC	978	1,306	1,669	3.2	4,681	5,546	6,436	1.9	238	209.0	235.6	259.4	1.3	117.7	138.5	154.2	1.6
Honolulu, HI	4,749	5,814	7,149	2.4	5,944	6,829	7,802	1.6	60	798.9	851.4	916.3	.8	429.1	484.5	547.1	1.4
Houma-Thibodaux, LA	960	1,116	1,389	2.2	4,727	5,515	6,439	1.8	237	190.3	202.4	217.2	.8	73.3	85.6	98.7	1.8
Houston, TX	20,211	27,514	35,987	3.5	6,393	7,452	8,443	1.6	29	3,161.4	3,692.1	4,262.1	1.8	1,592.7	1,986.2	2,378.1	2.4
Huntington-Ashland, WV-KY-OH	1,406	1,716	2,046	2.2	4,186	5,009	5,875	2.0	287	335.9	342.5	348.3	.2	113.4	127.1	136.7	1.1
Huntsville, AL	1,102	1,397	1,756	2.8	5,317	6,402	7,628	2.1	79	207.2	218.2	230.2	.6	113.4	129.2	145.2	1.5
Indianapolis, IN	6,562	8,064	9,536	2.2	5,551	6,712	7,763	2.0	69	1,182.0	1,201.5	1,228.4	.2	583.2	665.4	718.5	1.2
Iowa City, IA	435	544	664	2.5	5,216	6,122	7,252	2.0	133	83.4	88.8	91.6	.6	49.1	55.4	61.2	1.3
Jackson, MI	709	873	1,004	2.1	4,836	5,995	6,926	2.1	180	146.6	145.1	145.0	-.1	54.4	60.2	65.2	1.1
Jackson, MS	1,828	2,320	2,923	2.8	4,892	5,639	6,628	1.8	210	373.8	411.5	440.9	1.0	181.7	212.3	241.2	1.7
Jacksonville, FL	4,034	5,164	6,575	2.9	5,219	6,086	6,977	1.7	173	772.8	848.5	942.4	1.2	380.3	437.2	498.1	1.6

Area																
Jacksonville, NC	482	574	686	2.1	4,063	4,743	5,414	308	118.8	121.1	126.6	.4	64.3	69.6	74.3	.9
Janesville-Beloit, WI	712	867	1,035	2.2	5,123	6,047	6,966	174	139.0	143.3	148.6	.4	59.2	66.1	72.6	1.2
Jersey City, NJ *	2,943	3,344	3,760	1.5	5,241	6,124	6,909	183	561.6	546.0	544.3	−.2	234.3	241.3	247.8	1.3
Johnson City-Kingsport-Bristol, TN-VA	1,818	2,300	2,834	2.6	4,131	5,088	5,996	276	440.0	452.1	472.6	−.4	178.9	202.5	222.9	1.3
Johnstown, PA	1,126	1,246	1,380	1.2	4,326	4,943	5,611	302	260.3	252.1	246.0	−.3	85.1	88.5	90.8	.4
Joliet, IL *	1,996	2,652	3,315	3.0	5,541	6,556	7,428	106	360.3	404.5	446.2	1.3	101.3	117.2	133.2	1.6
Joplin, MO	558	740	934	3.1	4,295	5,263	6,240	258	129.9	140.6	149.7	.8	57.8	67.4	75.1	1.6
Kalamazoo, MI	1,184	1,464	1,719	2.2	5,602	5,602	7,599	83	211.4	218.3	226.3	.4	103.9	123.9	136.6	1.6
Kankakee, IL	501	604	698	2.0	4,934	5,873	7,635	209	101.5	102.9	105.2	2.2	41.0	44.9	49.2	1.1
Kansas City, MO-KS	8,675	10,302	12,121	2.0	5,924	6,726	7,577	86	1,464.4	1,531.7	1,599.7	2.5	734.0	823.1	895.6	1.2
Kenosha, WI *	681	800	931	1.9	5,576	6,474	7,381	112	122.1	123.6	126.2	.2	45.4	50.5	54.7	1.1
Killeen-Temple, TX	1,004	1,255	1,562	2.6	4,649	5,557	6,446	236	216.0	225.8	242.3	.7	112.1	125.1	139.3	1.3
Knoxville, TN	2,664	3,410	4,330	2.9	4,603	5,502	6,332	245	578.6	619.8	643.8	1.0	259.4	307.0	354.0	1.8
Kokomo, IN	544	679	800	2.3	5,330	6,469	7,456	102	102.1	105.0	107.3	.3	47.4	54.5	58.6	1.3
La Crosse, WI	481	594	729	2.5	5,234	6,174	7,152	159	92.0	96.3	102.0	.6	50.9	60.7	70.7	1.9
Lafayette, LA	1,245	1,799	2,475	4.1	5,759	6,742	7,785	63	216.1	266.9	317.9	2.3	111.0	148.4	188.2	3.2
Lafayette, IN	572	733	887	2.6	4,668	5,837	6,856	188	122.6	125.6	129.4	.3	60.5	70.0	77.0	2.4
Lake Charles, LA	884	1,121	1,395	2.7	4,999	6,120	7,249	135	176.9	183.1	192.5	.5	69.7	80.0	90.9	1.6
Lake County, IL *	3,266	4,124	5,042	2.6	7,185	8,323	9,430	10	454.6	495.5	534.6	1.0	196.2	236.5	274.4	2.0
Lakeland-Winter Haven, FL	1,580	2,159	2,865	3.6	4,567	5,384	6,217	261	345.9	401.1	460.9	1.7	146.3	178.4	210.7	2.2
Lancaster, PA	1,998	2,512	2,958	2.3	5,369	6,242	7,175	152	372.2	402.4	412.2	.6	180.5	207.3	222.1	1.2
Lansing-East Lansing, MI	2,233	2,817	3,340	2.4	5,435	6,583	7,489	96	410.8	427.9	446.0	.5	194.1	228.5	250.5	1.5
Laredo, TX	313	420	544	3.3	2,817	3,321	3,798	313	111.1	126.4	143.2	1.5	34.8	43.5	51.9	2.4
Las Cruces, NM	406	540	695	3.2	3,972	4,778	5,532	305	102.3	112.9	125.6	1.2	41.4	57.1	57.1	1.9
Las Vegas, NV	2,937	4,076	5,686	4.0	5,642	6,554	7,404	110	520.6	621.8	768.0	2.3	252.1	320.7	412.8	2.9
Lawrence, KS	304	388	491	2.9	4,353	5,216	6,185	265	69.8	73.4	79.4	.8	31.9	37.0	42.2	1.6
Lawton, OK	509	619	753	2.3	4,558	5,283	6,181	266	122.5	118.6	121.8	0	57.4	62.0	67.1	.9
Lewiston-Auburn, ME (NECMA)	453	531	629	1.9		5,289	6,148	268	99.5	100.4	102.3	.2	44.4	46.8	49.9	.7
Lexington-Fayette, KY	1,900	2,243	2,718	2.1	5,891	6,779	7,911	53	322.6	330.9	343.6	.4	173.0	199.8	222.6	1.5
Lima, OH	763	943	1,096	2.2	4,993	6,067	6,995	170	152.7	155.4	156.7	.1	69.6	77.4	81.9	1.0
Lincoln, NE	1,093	1,342	1,631	2.4	5,477	6,411	7,301	124	199.5	209.3	223.9	.7	107.6	122.8	139.5	1.5
Little Rock-North Little Rock, AR	2,518	3,159	3,972	2.7	5,168	6,029	6,947	176	487.3	523.9	571.9	.9	242.0	285.9	327.5	1.8
Longview-Marshall, TX	869	1,137	1,445	3.0	5,154	6,109	7,003	169	168.6	186.1	206.3	1.2	78.0	92.4	106.6	1.9
Lorain-Elyria, OH *	1,353	1,676	1,972	2.2	4,951	6,121	7,165	154	273.3	273.8	275.2	0	89.7	100.2	106.7	1.0
Los Angeles-Long Beach, CA *	49,109	58,631	70,957	2.2	6,281	7,106	8,000	47	7,818.3	8,251.3	8,870.2	.7	3,998.2	4,481.4	5,004.3	1.3
Louisville, KY-IN	5,149	6,200	7,422	2.6	5,207	6,484	7,593	84	955.8	956.2	977.5	.1	436.5	486.0	527.6	1.1
Lubbock, TX	1,142	1,423	1,756	2.5	4,889	6,004	6,787	195	219.3	237.0	258.7	1.0	108.5	123.8	139.2	1.5
Lynchburg, VA	695	874	1,064	2.4	4,775	5,809	6,734	201	142.1	150.4	158.1	.6	74.0	83.1	90.5	1.2
Macon-Warner Robins, GA	1,307	1,616	1,968	2.5	6,096	5,768	6,785	196	273.8	280.2	290.1	.3	126.6	139.6	150.7	1.0
Madison, WI	2,014	2,498	3,080			7,057	8,058	42	330.4	354.0	382.3	.9	204.3	237.4	271.4	1.7
Manchester-Nashua, NH (NECMA)	1,764	2,266	2,977	3.1	6,079	6,903	7,791	61	290.1	328.3	382.1	1.6	164.1	202.8	246.6	2.4
Mansfield, OH	652	794	915	2.0	5,048	6,101	7,051	166	129.1	130.1	129.8	0	59.2	66.1	69.9	1.0
McAllen-Edinburg-Mission, TX	908	1,211	1,572	3.3	2,814	3,311	3,820	312	322.8	365.6	411.6	.4	102.3	123.8	146.3	2.1
Medford, OR	597	801	1,069	3.5	4,448	5,391	6,415	240	134.1	148.5	166.7	1.3	50.5	61.7	74.2	2.3
Melbourne-Titusville-Palm Bay, FL	1,649	2,387	3,315	4.2	5,375	6,225	7,121	161	306.8	383.5	465.6	2.5	133.6	173.6	215.2	2.8
Memphis, TN-AR-MS	4,612	5,599	6,821	2.3	4,958	5,851	6,771	198	930.3	957.0	1,007.3	.5	437.3	487.9	537.2	1.2

Table 4-3 *(continued)*

	Total personal income (Millions of 1972 dollars)				Per capita personal income (1972 dollars)					Population (Thousands of persons)				Employment (Thousands of jobs)			
	1983	1990	2000	Avg. annual growth rate (percent) 1983–2000	1983	1990	2000	Avg. annual growth rate (percent) 1983–2000	Rank in the United States 2000	1983	1990	2000	Avg. annual growth rate (percent) 1983–2000	1983	1990	2000	Avg. annual growth rate (percent) 1983–2000
Miami–Hialeah, FL *	9,765	11,328	13,547	1.9	5,679	6,416	7,218	1.3	143	1,719.4	1,765.5	1,876.8	0.5	842.1	944.7	1,056.9	1.3
Middlesex–Somerset–Hunterdon, NJ *	6,553	8,628	10,869	3.0	7,221	8,360	9,372	1.5	11	907.6	1,032.0	1,159.7	1.5	465.7	580.1	685.2	2.3
Midland, TX *	776	1,087	1,476	3.9	7,260	8,373	9,497	1.5	9	107.0	129.9	155.4	2.2	57.9	75.0	93.1	2.8
Milwaukee, WI *	8,504	10,063	11,777	1.9	6,086	7,172	8,266	1.8	35	1,397.3	1,403.1	1,424.7	.1	690.0	755.6	815.1	1.0
Minneapolis–St. Paul, MN–WI	14,245	17,762	22,088	2.6	6,452	7,339	8,216	1.4	37	2,207.9	2,420.2	2,688.6	1.2	1,211.8	1,444.7	1,668.5	1.9
Mobile, AL	1,971	2,355	2,868	2.2	4,294	5,026	5,864	1.8	289	459.0	468.5	489.1	.4	175.5	192.8	213.7	1.2
Modesto, CA *	1,436	1,918	2,463	3.2	5,003	5,754	6,473	1.5	234	287.0	333.4	380.5	1.7	111.0	134.6	158.0	2.1
Monmouth–Ocean, NJ *	5,459	7,339	9,463	3.3	6,176	7,232	8,224	1.7	36	884.0	1,014.8	1,150.6	1.6	301.6	374.3	442.4	2.3
Monroe, LA *	620	786	990	2.8	4,354	5,236	6,215	2.1	262	142.5	150.1	159.3	.7	59.7	66.5	74.2	1.3
Montgomery, AL	1,371	1,687	2,101	2.5	4,884	5,803	6,862	2.0	187	280.8	290.8	306.1	.5	133.6	147.0	163.1	1.2
Muncie, IN	562	678	781	2.0	4,482	5,612	6,570	2.3	224	125.5	120.9	118.9	-.3	50.9	55.6	57.9	.8
Muskegon, MI	699	848	959	1.9	4,528	5,525	6,314	2.0	250	154.5	153.4	151.8	-.1	55.9	63.6	66.7	1.0
Naples, FL	654	972	1,384	4.5	6,286	6,859	7,603	1.1	82	104.0	141.7	182.1	3.4	43.3	60.5	78.9	3.6
Nashville, TN *	4,546	5,889	7,486	3.0	5,177	6,245	7,235	2.0	138	878.0	942.9	1,034.7	1.0	447.7	531.9	610.2	1.8
Nassau–Suffolk, NY *	19,439	24,567	29,842	2.6	7,321	8,498	9,651	1.6	8	2,655.3	2,891.0	3,092.3	.9	1,101.0	1,335.1	1,524.9	1.9
New Bedford–Fall River–Attleboro, MA (NECMA)	2,438	3,081	3,783	2.6	5,067	5,858	6,605	1.6	215	481.2	525.9	572.8	1.0	205.6	239.3	266.9	1.5
New Haven–Waterbury–Meriden, CT (NECMA)	4,721	5,783	7,066	2.4	6,174	7,142	7,990	1.5	48	764.8	809.7	884.4	.9	357.8	409.1	457.2	1.5
New London–Norwich, CT (NECMA) *	1,499	1,959	2,469	3.0	6,158	7,384	8,400	1.8	30	243.5	265.3	294.0	1.1	130.8	159.2	184.2	2.0
New Orleans, LA *	7,211	8,713	10,613	2.3	5,481	6,457	7,536	1.9	92	1,315.7	1,349.4	1,408.3	.4	600.2	654.0	718.8	1.1
New York, NY *	53,595	60,181	68,602	1.5	6,465	7,291	8,135	1.3	42	8,290.6	8,253.8	8,433.2	.1	4,207.9	4,506.6	4,813.9	.8
Newark, NJ *	13,084	15,567	18,414	2.0	6,951	8,134	9,208	1.7	12	1,882.4	1,913.9	1,999.4	.4	947.8	1,040.5	1,132.9	1.1
Niagara Falls, NY *	1,158	1,358	1,543	1.7	5,158	6,027	6,777	1.6	197	224.5	225.3	227.7	.1	83.7	92.2	98.6	1.0
Norfolk–Virginia Beach–Newport News, VA.	6,501	7,874	9,547	2.3	5,297	6,101	6,939	1.6	178	1,227.4	1,290.6	1,376.0	.7	633.3	705.7	779.4	1.2
Oakland, CA *	12,782	15,492	18,993	2.4	6,860	7,724	8,636	1.4	22	1,863.3	2,005.7	2,199.3	1.0	809.3	927.8	1,058.5	1.6
Ocala, FL	608	941	1,356	4.8	4,103	4,874	5,675	1.9	300	148.3	193.1	239.0	2.8	51.3	67.8	84.5	3.0
Odessa, TX	739	997	1,299	3.4	5,390	6,448	7,433	1.9	105	137.1	154.7	174.7	1.4	60.4	75.2	84.9	2.4
Oklahoma City, OK	5,568	7,152	9,120	2.9	5,818	6,884	8,012	1.9	46	957.1	1,038.9	1,138.4	1.0	493.5	580.0	669.8	1.8
Olympia, WA *	728	956	1,300	3.5	5,322	6,102	7,080	1.7	168	136.8	156.7	184.9	1.8	52.0	64.5	79.0	2.5
Omaha, NE–IA	3,421	4,152	5,028	2.3	5,667	6,685	7,773	1.9	65	603.6	621.1	646.9	.4	314.8	358.6	405.3	1.5
Orange County, NY *	1,393	1,771	2,161	2.6	5,192	6,085	6,922	1.7	181	268.4	291.0	312.2	.9	101.3	117.4	131.3	1.5
Orlando, FL	4,241	6,131	8,504	4.2	5,346	6,219	7,122	1.7	160	793.3	985.9	1,194.0	2.4	403.1	536.0	674.3	3.1
Owensboro, KY	438	549	661	2.4	5,011	6,140	7,183	2.1	151	87.5	89.4	92.0	.3	37.7	42.6	46.5	1.3
Oxnard–Ventura, CA *	3,448	4,815	6,490	3.8	5,991	6,972	7,941	1.7	50	575.5	690.7	817.3	2.1	209.4	269.2	332.5	2.8
Panama City, FL	475	644	858	3.5	4,630	5,231	5,875	1.4	288	102.5	123.1	146.0	2.1	47.5	57.8	69.0	2.2
Parkersburg–Marietta, WV–OH	752	929	1,113	2.3	4,737	5,687	6,607	2.0	214	158.7	163.4	168.5	.4	64.6	74.1	81.4	1.4
Pascagoula, MS	522	753	951	3.6	4,140	5,207	5,999	2.2	274	126.1	144.5	158.6	1.4	45.2	56.9	63.6	2.0
Pensacola, FL	1,394	1,774	2,227	2.8	4,455	5,082	5,726	1.5	297	313.0	349.1	389.0	1.3	131.5	150.6	170.2	1.5
Peoria, IL	1,934	2,381	2,769	2.1	5,351	6,589	7,663	2.1	77	361.5	361.3	361.3	0	149.2	166.9	182.8	1.2
Philadelphia, PA–NJ *	28,302	33,854	39,701	2.0	5,946	7,002	8,079	1.8	40	4,760.0	4,835.0	4,914.2	.2	2,147.1	2,369.8	2,540.9	1.0
Phoenix, AZ	9,175	13,695	19,645	4.6	5,515	6,613	7,635	1.9	78	1,663.8	2,070.9	2,573.0	2.6	781.9	1,058.3	1,380.8	3.4

Area																
Pine Bluff, AR	380	456	548	2.2	4,198	5,078	5,954	283	90.4	89.8	92.1	.1	36.0	40.1	43.7	1.1
Pittsburgh, PA *	12,265	14,019	15,876	1.5	5,581	6,410	7,339	116	2,197.9	2,187.1	2,163.2	—1	920.2	999.0	1,049.7	.8
Pittsfield, MA (NECMA)	786	935	1,101	2.0	5,559	6,433	7,187	150	141.4	145.0	152.2	—	66.8	75.8	83.6	1.3
Portland, ME (NECMA)	1,236	1,489	1,824	2.3	5,566	6,336	7,254	132	222.0	235.0	251.4	.5	125.4	140.9	159.1	1.4
Portland, OR *	6,486	8,160	10,296	2.8	5,743	6,763	7,846	54	1,129.4	1,206.7	1,312.3	.7	558.4	658.0	766.8	1.9
Portsmouth-Dover-Rochester, NH (NECMA)	1,685	2,199	2,947	3.3	5,782	6,570	7,495	95	291.4	334.7	393.3	1.8	132.6	167.9	207.3	2.7
Poughkeepsie, NY	1,496	1,967	2,402	2.8	5,974	6,928	7,807	59	250.3	284.0	307.7	1.2	116.3	142.4	161.5	1.9
Providence-Pawtucket-Woonsocket, RI (NECMA)	4,761	5,783	7,010	2.3	5,465	6,363	7,300	125	871.2	908.9	960.3	.6	408.5	460.6	507.9	1.3
Provo-Orem, UT	743	1,034	1,434	3.9	3,156	3,838	4,647	310	235.6	269.4	308.7	1.6	69.7	86.4	107.5	2.6
Pueblo, CO	559	684	799	2.1	4,501	5,601	6,323	246	124.2	122.1	126.3	.1	43.8	47.6	51.2	2.9
Racine, WI *	978	1,169	1,366	2.0	5,636	6,584	7,470	100	173.5	177.5	182.9	.3	73.4	81.8	88.8	1.1
Raleigh-Durham, NC	3,303	4,528	6,081	3.7	5,595	6,775	7,931	51	590.4	668.3	766.7	1.5	348.6	429.0	509.9	2.3
Reading, PA	1,808	2,223	2,603	2.2	5,744	6,752	7,835	56	314.8	329.3	332.2	.3	155.7	173.5	183.3	1.0
Redding, CA	568	767	999	3.4	4,562	5,280	5,982	280	124.6	145.2	166.9	1.7	44.0	54.9	65.9	2.4
Reno, NV	1,385	1,916	2,677	4.0	6,613	7,578	8,367	31	209.4	252.8	319.9	2.5	122.5	154.2	196.4	2.8
Richland-Kennewick-Pasco, WA	873	1,190	1,600	3.6	5,786	6,501	7,250	134	150.8	183.1	220.7	2.3	69.2	91.2	114.3	3.0
Richmond-Petersburg, VA	4,795	5,737	6,883	2.1	6,105	6,909	7,767	68	785.5	830.4	886.3	.7	430.3	474.4	519.5	1.1
Riverside-San Bernardino, CA *	9,103	12,453	16,321	3.5	5,238	5,920	7,620	212	1,737.8	2,103.4	2,465.2	2.1	563.8	681.0	800.6	2.1
Roanoke, VA	1,204	1,419	1,667	1.9	5,448	6,271	7,099	163	220.9	226.3	234.8	.4	116.5	126.0	135.1	.9
Rochester, MN	610	805	1,044	3.2	6,528	7,626	8,596	23	93.4	105.6	121.4	1.6	60.2	74.0	88.5	2.3
Rochester, NY	5,861	7,438	8,881	2.5	5,922	6,924	7,843	55	989.8	1,074.3	1,132.3	.8	465.4	540.2	593.3	1.4
Rockford, IL	1,504	1,856	2,182	3.2	5,366	6,325	7,232	141	280.3	293.4	301.8	.4	126.4	145.4	160.4	1.4
Sacramento, CA	6,544	8,863	11,682	3.5	5,466	6,364	7,267	130	1,197.2	1,392.7	1,607.6	1.7	524.9	646.4	773.6	2.3
Saginaw-Bay City-Midland, MI	2,096	2,589	2,985	2.1	5,067	6,181	7,047	167	413.6	418.8	423.5	.1	154.2	177.1	188.1	1.2
St. Cloud, MN	722	993	1,318	3.6	4,273	5,327	6,241	257	168.9	186.4	211.2	1.3	72.9	89.7	107.6	2.3
St. Joseph, MO	427	508	592	1.9	4,941	5,834	6,769	199	86.4	87.1	87.5	.1	40.8	44.3	46.6	.8
St. Louis, MO-IL	14,260	16,938	19,757	3.0	5,960	6,847	7,786	62	2,396.5	2,473.7	2,537.5	.3	1,151.4	1,291.9	1,397.7	1.1
Salem, OR	1,186	1,515	1,966	2.4	4,658	5,575	6,598	216	254.7	271.7	298.0	.9	103.8	122.1	143.5	1.9
Salinas-Seaside-Monterey, CA	1,869	2,325	2,820	3.7	6,014	6,878	7,604	81	310.8	338.1	370.9	1.0	151.1	176.1	201.7	1.7
Salt Lake City-Ogden, UT	4,659	6,315	8,594	3.1	4,631	5,442	6,304	251	1,006.1	1,160.3	1,363.3	1.8	438.4	534.9	656.2	2.4
San Angelo, TX	510	668	860	2.7	5,422	6,377	7,324	122	94.0	104.8	117.4	1.3	46.1	54.5	63.0	1.9
San Antonio, TX	5,784	7,301	9,163	3.4	4,948	5,737	6,593	217	1,168.8	1,272.6	1,389.7	1.0	529.7	607.9	692.9	1.6
San Diego, CA	11,578	15,647	20,431	2.4	5,745	6,729	7,703	74	2,015.2	2,325.5	2,652.3	1.6	932.9	1,166.3	1,398.4	2.4
San Francisco, CA *	12,703	15,536	19,046	3.1	8,368	9,982	11,660	5	1,517.9	1,556.4	1,633.5	.4	1,007.4	1,145.4	1,297.3	1.5
San Jose, CA *	10,091	13,322	16,975	3.0	7,422	8,698	8,315	32	1,359.7	1,531.6	1,716.7	1.4	806.8	1,043.9	1,266.5	2.7
Santa Barbara-Santa Maria-Lompoc, CA	2,054	2,678	3,410	3.8	6,481	7,393	7,617	80	317.0	362.3	410.1	1.5	156.7	191.8	226.7	2.2
Santa Cruz, CA *	1,140	1,593	2,165	3.3	5,699	6,642	7,370	114	200.1	239.9	284.2	2.1	100.8	124.7	2.8
Santa Fe, NM	571	752	998	3.3	5,617	6,431	7,973	49	101.6	117.0	135.4	1.7	51.9	61.8	74.1	2.1
Santa Rosa-Petaluma, CA *	1,988	2,676	3,468	4.5	6,194	7,086	9,083	14	321.0	377.6	434.9	1.8	124.6	166.7	208.2	3.1
Sarasota, FL	1,551	2,289	3,253		6,841	7,957			226.8	287.7	358.2	2.7	131.6		170.0	3.3
Savannah, GA	1,134	1,402	1,721	2.5	4,900	5,770	6,696	204	231.4	243.1	257.0	.6	107.2	120.5	132.3	1.2
Scranton-Wilkes-Barre, PA	3,461	4,098	4,777	1.9	4,761	5,597	6,540	226	727.0	732.2	730.4	0	296.6	320.0	335.4	.7

Table 4-3 (continued)

	Total personal income (Millions of 1972 dollars)				Per capita personal income (1972 dollars)				Population (Thousands of persons)				Employment (Thousands of jobs)			
	1983	1990	2000	Average annual growth rate (percent) 1983–2000	1983	1990	2000	Rank in the United States 2000	1983	1990	2000	Average annual growth rate (percent) 1983–2000	1983	1990	2000	Average annual growth rate (percent) 1983–2000
Seattle, WA *	10,959	14,443	18,332	3.1	6,533	7,576	8,472	28	1,677.4	1,906.4	2,163.8	1.5	875.4	1,074.8	1,261.7	2.2
Sharon, PA	573	683	771	1.8	4,520	5,414	6,248	256	126.7	126.2	123.4	-.2	46.4	50.8	53.0	.8
Sheboygan, WI	552	689	829	2.4	5,443	6,465	7,482	97	101.5	106.6	110.8	.5	49.8	56.3	61.6	1.3
Sherman-Denison, TX	488	614	743	2.5	5,219	6,291	7,288	126	93.5	97.5	102.0	.5	41.0	45.7	49.6	1.1
Shreveport, LA	1,807	2,258	2,816	2.6	5,123	5,844	6,736	200	352.7	386.4	418.1	1.0	161.4	181.8	203.3	1.4
Sioux City, IA-NE	597	707	824	1.9	5,076	6,111	7,153	158	117.7	115.7	115.2	-.1	57.2	61.4	65.4	.8
Sioux Falls, SD	628	773	967	2.6	5,497	6,214	7,117	162	114.3	124.5	135.9	1.0	64.4	75.6	88.1	1.9
South Bend-Mishawaka, IN	1,252	1,528	1,809	2.2	5,242	6,566	7,743	72	238.8	232.8	233.6	-.1	107.5	121.4	129.9	1.1
Spokane, WA	1,742	2,218	2,764	2.8	5,006	5,953	6,831	192	348.0	372.6	404.6	.9	150.4	174.4	196.5	1.6
Springfield, IL	1,058	1,265	1,467	1.9	5,634	6,752	7,772	66	187.8	187.3	188.8	0	98.1	107.9	118.7	1.1
Springfield, MO	1,030	1,331	1,686	2.9	4,829	5,614	6,473	233	213.3	237.1	260.5	1.2	106.1	127.1	146.1	1.9
Springfield, MA (NECMA)	3,102	3,826	4,655	2.4	5,333	6,233	7,074	164	581.7	613.8	658.0	.7	261.5	299.3	332.0	1.4
State College, PA	478	611	749	2.7	4,222	4,981	5,833	291	113.3	122.7	128.4	.7	53.6	62.1	68.2	1.4
Steubenville-Weirton, OH-WV	757	920	1,073	2.1	4,780	5,882	6,900	184	158.4	156.4	155.5	-.1	55.3	61.2	64.8	.9
Stockton, CA	1,934	2,534	3,212	3.0	5,106	5,937	6,723	203	378.7	426.8	477.7	1.4	148.9	173.2	198.0	1.7
Syracuse, NY	3,407	4,270	5,114	2.4	5,239	6,148	6,979	171	650.4	694.5	732.7	.7	294.7	340.4	376.6	1.5
Tacoma, WA *	2,628	3,213	3,895	2.3	5,155	6,080	6,937	179	509.8	528.4	561.5	.6	199.1	223.6	246.9	1.3
Tallahassee, FL	881	1,186	1,589	3.5	4,341	4,976	5,689	298	202.9	238.3	279.4	1.9	100.0	120.2	142.6	2.1
Tampa-St. Petersburg-Clearwater, FL	9,413	12,813	17,096	3.6	5,319	6,231	7,161	155	1,769.6	2,056.5	2,387.5	1.8	732.2	926.6	1,129.8	2.6
Terre Haute, IN	614	750	880	2.1	4,514	5,606	6,587	219	136.0	133.9	133.5	-.1	57.8	63.6	66.8	.9
Texarkana, TX-Texarkana, AR	524	636	774	2.3	4,474	5,188	5,971	281	117.0	122.6	129.7	.6	50.3	56.2	62.1	1.2
Toledo, OH	3,306	3,919	4,495	1.8	5,437	6,518	7,465	101	608.1	601.2	602.1	-.1	272.4	300.3	318.5	.9
Topeka, KS	944	1,095	1,290	1.9	5,988	6,860	7,813	58	157.8	159.8	165.1	.3	89.2	96.4	103.7	.9
Trenton, NJ *	2,027	2,447	2,947	2.2	6,522	7,681	8,652	21	310.7	320.7	340.6	.5	187.3	208.2	230.1	1.2
Tucson, AZ	2,866	4,049	5,651	4.1	5,007	5,928	6,834	191	572.3	683.0	826.9	2.2	224.4	293.2	374.4	3.1
Tulsa, OK	4,180	5,173	6,470	2.6	5,796	6,653	7,591	85	721.0	777.5	852.4	1.0	343.2	399.0	460.0	1.7
Tuscaloosa, AL	579	679	814	2.0	4,199	5,058	5,998	275	138.0	134.2	135.7	-.1	54.8	57.8	62.3	.8
Tyler, TX	806	1,055	1,346	3.1	5,706	6,592	7,454	103	141.2	160.0	180.6	1.5	69.8	84.4	98.8	2.1
Utica-Rome, NY	1,534	1,787	2,035	1.7	4,781	5,489	6,149	267	320.9	325.6	331.0	.2	132.0	140.7	147.5	.7
Vallejo-Fairfield-Napa, CA *	2,103	2,719	3,476	3.0	5,816	6,648	7,475	98	361.6	409.0	465.0	1.5	133.9	162.3	192.6	2.2
Vancouver, WA *	1,004	1,338	1,748	3.3	4,967	5,824	6,619	213	202.1	229.7	264.1	1.6	64.3	79.2	94.5	2.3
Victoria, TX	422	570	731	3.3	5,584	6,740	7,722	73	75.6	84.6	94.6	1.3	33.8	41.1	48.3	2.1
Vineland-Millville-Bridgeton, NJ *	648	791	937	2.2	4,869	5,817	6,661	206	133.2	135.9	140.6	.3	58.5	63.6	68.1	.9
Visalia-Tulare-Porterville, CA	1,170	1,520	1,896	2.9	4,425	5,107	5,680	299	264.5	297.6	333.7	1.4	105.0	125.9	147.0	2.0
Waco, TX	913	1,146	1,412	2.6	5,130	5,978	6,852	189	177.9	191.6	206.0	.9	83.8	95.0	106.4	1.4
Washington, DC-MD-VA	25,514	31,501	38,418	2.4	7,572	8,651	9,731	6	3,369.6	3,641.3	3,948.0	.9	1,964.9	2,271.7	2,562.5	1.6
Waterloo-Cedar Falls, IA	830	1,019	1,222	2.3	5,107	6,175	7,194	148	162.5	165.0	169.9	.3	75.1	84.5	92.0	1.2
Wausau, WI	526	677	840	2.8	4,681	5,678	6,585	221	112.3	119.3	127.6	.8	51.5	58.7	66.1	1.5
West Palm Beach-Boca Raton-Delray Beach, FL	4,669	6,625	9,073	4.0	7,089	7,738	8,540	25	658.7	856.2	1,062.5	2.9	296.1	400.7	508.3	3.2
Wheeling, WV-OH	858	1,015	1,174	1.9	4,717	5,704	6,636	208	182.0	178.0	176.9	-.2	67.6	74.7	79.6	1.0

Wichita, KS	2,606	3,315	4,066	2.7	6,077	7,195	8,191	38	428.8	460.8	496.4	.9	222.3	254.6	284.8	1.5
Wichita Falls, TX	718	913	1,145	2.8	5,604	6,673	7,746	71	128.1	136.8	147.9	.8	66.6	75.1	83.6	1.4
Williamsport, PA	538	624	716	1.7	4,555	5,312	6,187	264	118.1	117.5	115.7	-.1	49.8	53.8	56.2	.7
Wilmington, DE-NJ-MD*	3,214	3,974	4,775	2.4	6,020	7,030	7,929	52	533.8	565.3	602.2	.7	259.3	287.3	315.9	1.2
Wilmington, NC	508	660	837	3.0	4,659	5,527	6,371	242	109.1	119.4	131.4	1.1	51.5	61.3	69.9	1.8
Worcester-Fitchburg-Leominster, MA (NECMA)	3,453	4,329	5,298	2.5	5,306	6,114	6,845	190	650.8	708.2	774.0	1.0	281.3	326.8	366.3	1.6
Yakima, WA	831	1,028	1,275	2.5	4,692	5,446	6,237	259	177.2	188.7	204.4	.8	76.2	87.9	98.9	1.5
York, PA	1,968	2,444	2,877	2.3	5,079	5,953	6,896	185	387.6	410.5	417.2	.4	173.1	196.1	209.2	1.1
Youngstown-Warren, OH	2,617	3,101	3,511	1.7	5,012	6,212	7,229	142	522.1	499.3	485.6	-.4	196.9	212.0	219.2	1.1
Yuba City, CA	500	654	815	2.9	4,634	5,491	6,256	255	107.8	119.1	130.3	1.1	41.2	47.2	53.0	1.5

1. The U.S. total includes metropolitan and nonmetropolitan counties.
2. Only the name of the largest city in each Consolidated Metropolitan Statistical Area (CMSA) is shown. Complete titles designated by the Office of Management and Budget include additional city names.

3. Includes Metropolitan Statistical Areas, Primary Metropolitan Statistical Areas (PMSA's, indicated by *), and New England County Metropolitan Areas (NECMA's). The Bridgeport-Stamford-Norwalk-Danbury, CT NECMA is presented as a PMSA (part of the New York CMSA).

Source: Regional Economic Analysis Division, U.S. Department of Commerce, BEA, *Survey of Current Business* (Oct. 1985):32-36.

Distribution of Population

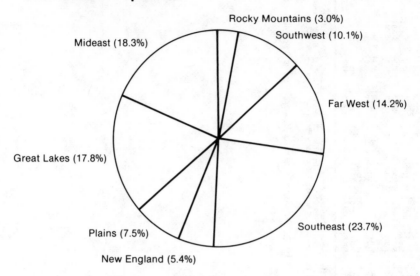

Distribution of Personal Income

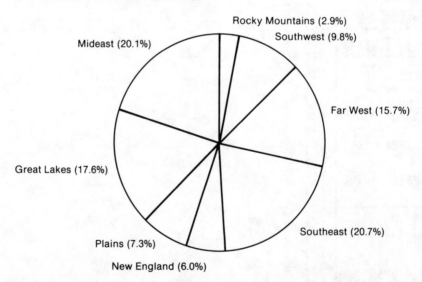

Source: Kenneth P. Johnson and Howard L. Friedenberg, "Regional and State Projections of Income, Employment, and Population to the Year 2000," *Survey of Current Business*, BEA, May 1985.

Figure 4-1. Distribution of Population and Personal Income, by Region, 1983

Figure 4-2. United States of America Regional Markets

Table 4-4
Total Personal Income, Per Capita Income, Population, and Earnings: Average Annual Growth Rates, 1959-69, 1969-79, and 1979-83

Line	United States and Regions: Metro and nonmetro portions [1] Metro size classes [2]	1959-69 Total Personal income	Population	Earnings	Earnings excluding Farm	Manufacturing	Manufacturing and farm	1969-79 Total Personal income	Population	Earnings
1	United States [3]	6.93	1.29	6.72	6.86	6.93	7.14	10.02	1.10	9.35
2	Sum of nonmetro counties [3]	6.70	.35	6.15	6.56	5.77	6.25	10.98	1.29	10.01
3	Sum of metro counties	6.98	1.60	6.84	6.91	7.18	7.30	9.80	1.04	9.21
	Metro size classes:									
4	Less than .5 million [4]	6.97	1.49	6.79	6.92	6.93	7.14	10.83	1.59	10.08
5	.5 to 1 million [5]	7.11	1.58	6.87	6.97	7.17	7.33	10.08	1.22	9.47
6	1 to 2 million	7.47	2.19	7.30	7.38	7.55	7.66	10.37	1.43	9.82
7	Over 2 million	6.64	1.31	6.59	6.61	7.12	7.17	8.66	.25	8.19
8	New England	6.77	1.18	6.49	6.54	7.15	7.26	8.82	.51	8.22
9	Sum of nonmetro counties	6.92	.97	6.20	6.42	6.44	6.79	10.07	1.53	8.72
10	Sum of metro counties	6.75	1.21	6.52	6.56	7.25	7.32	8.64	.33	8.15
	Metro size classes:									
11	Less than .5 million	7.01	1.41	6.74	6.79	7.06	7.15	9.83	1.24	9.14
12	.5 to 1 million	6.65	1.16	6.12	6.15	6.98	7.03	8.46	.24	7.83
13	1 to 2 million	7.34	1.93	7.46	7.56	7.78	7.95	8.49	.26	8.17
14	Over 2 million	6.58	.99	6.53	6.55	7.39	7.42	8.36	-.03	8.04
15	Mideast	6.41	.98	6.16	6.20	6.74	6.80	8.21	.06	7.46
16	Sum of nonmetro counties	6.28	.42	5.65	5.78	5.66	5.86	9.37	.82	8.11
17	Sum of metro counties	6.41	1.03	6.19	6.23	6.80	6.86	8.12	-.02	7.42
	Metro size classes:									
18	Less than .5 million	6.26	.79	6.03	6.10	6.34	6.48	9.18	.59	8.33
19	.5 to 1 million	6.79	1.44	6.25	6.32	6.55	6.69	9.03	.61	8.42
20	1 to 2 million	6.53	1.01	6.33	6.36	6.94	6.98	7.73	-.36	7.52
21	Over 2 million	6.32	.97	6.18	6.20	6.89	6.92	7.77	-.27	6.99
22	Great Lakes	6.53	1.06	6.38	6.44	6.64	6.76	9.16	.42	8.52
23	Sum of nonmetro counties	6.82	.55	6.16	6.34	5.87	6.10	10.13	.96	9.11
24	Sum of metro counties	6.47	1.20	6.42	6.46	6.80	6.88	8.94	.27	8.41
	Metro size classes:									
25	Less than .5 million	6.82	1.42	6.65	6.75	6.94	7.13	9.85	.76	9.18
26	.5 to 1 million	6.52	1.14	6.54	6.58	6.86	6.94	8.93	.19	8.19
27	1 to 2 million	6.10	1.11	6.14	6.17	6.77	6.82	8.66	.09	8.28
28	Over 2 million	6.42	1.09	6.37	6.39	6.71	6.74	8.45	-.02	8.01
29	Plains	6.53	.64	6.38	6.48	6.27	6.38	9.95	.54	9.52
30	Sum of nonmetro counties	6.52	-.11	6.03	6.13	5.73	5.75	10.17	.44	9.47
31	Sum of metro counties	6.53	1.36	6.59	6.64	6.65	6.72	9.79	.63	9.55
	Metro size classes:									
32	Less than .5 million	5.93	1.03	5.92	5.95	6.08	6.13	10.51	.94	10.41
33	.5 to 1 million	6.77	1.64	6.52	6.48	6.92	6.88	9.47	.74	9.32
34	1 to 2 million	6.66	1.32	6.60	6.69	6.65	6.78	9.76	.53	9.36
35	Over 2 million	6.89	1.61	7.06	7.10	7.03	7.10	9.33	.39	9.04
36	Southeast	7.85	1.32	7.61	7.96	7.36	7.80	11.44	1.81	10.61
37	Sum of nonmetro counties	7.42	.32	6.89	7.66	6.03	6.97	11.56	1.42	10.52
38	Sum of metro counties	8.04	1.99	7.92	8.07	7.89	8.08	11.39	2.05	10.64
	Metro size classes:									
39	Less than .5 million	7.85	1.62	7.58	7.74	7.44	7.65	11.33	1.98	10.46
40	.5 to 1 million	7.54	1.63	7.59	7.76	7.63	7.86	11.15	1.77	10.54
41	1 to 2 million	8.49	2.72	8.37	8.49	8.23	8.37	11.75	2.51	10.86
42	Over 2 million	9.23	3.40	9.35	9.44	9.40	9.52	11.52	2.22	11.15
43	Southwest	7.31	1.64	7.05	7.41	6.71	7.13	12.51	2.44	12.06
44	Sum of nonmetro counties	5.84	.21	5.00	5.75	4.69	5.50	12.34	1.75	11.43
45	Sum of metro counties	7.79	2.27	7.66	7.82	7.37	7.57	12.56	2.70	12.22
	Metro size classes:									
46	Less than .5 million	6.36	1.17	6.16	6.35	6.00	6.23	11.95	2.12	11.34
47	.5 to 1 million	7.92	2.27	7.79	7.94	7.39	7.58	12.28	2.68	11.70
48	1 to 2 million	8.87	3.06	8.84	8.99	8.30	8.48	12.12	2.86	11.73
49	Over 2 million	8.30	3.42	8.12	8.21	8.24	8.37	14.50	3.57	14.73
50	Rocky Mountain	6.55	1.58	6.43	6.56	6.42	6.58	12.54	2.68	12.17
51	Sum of nonmetro counties	5.55	.36	5.25	5.37	5.16	5.28	12.41	2.37	11.75
52	Sum of metro counties	7.20	2.57	7.18	7.20	7.27	7.30	12.62	2.90	12.41
	Metro size classes:									
53	Less than .5 million	7.42	2.72	7.33	7.35	7.37	7.39	13.06	3.27	12.57
54	.5 to 1 million	6.46	2.19	6.48	6.51	6.66	6.70	12.08	2.69	11.81
55	1 to 2 million	7.41	2.65	7.42	7.44	7.53	7.55	12.51	2.63	12.56
56	Far West	7.44	2.34	7.26	7.43	7.48	7.73	10.83	1.81	10.10
57	Sum of nonmetro counties	5.99	.91	5.86	6.15	6.23	6.72	12.27	2.58	10.91
58	Sum of metro counties	7.56	2.49	7.37	7.52	7.58	7.79	10.72	1.73	10.04
	Metro size classes:									
59	Less than .5 million	7.25	2.40	7.15	7.56	7.39	7.91	12.24	2.74	11.17
60	.5 to 1 million	8.15	3.42	7.07	7.91	6.95	7.91	13.02	2.73	11.83
61	1 to 2 million	8.14	3.03	7.79	7.91	7.80	7.95	11.21	1.92	10.49
62	Over 2 million	6.84	1.64	6.93	6.98	7.41	7.49	8.76	.57	8.66

1. Metropolitan counties are those defined by the Office of Management and Budget as of October, 1984 as part of Metropolitan Statistical Areas (MSA's).
2. Metropolitan size classes are based on 1980 population.
3. Alaska and Hawaii are included in U.S. totals but are not included in regions.
4. Includes Anchorage, AK.
5. Includes Honolulu, HI.

1969-79 Earnings excluding			1979-83 Total			1979-83 Earnings excluding			Line
Farm	Manufacturing	Manufacturing and farm	Personal income	Population	Earnings	Farm	Manufacturing	Manufacturing and farm	
9.39	9.73	9.81	8.92	1.03	7.13	7.49	7.99	8.50	1
10.31	10.05	10.48	7.93	.88	4.72	6.21	4.78	6.87	2
9.22	9.66	9.69	9.16	1.08	7.62	7.73	8.64	8.79	3
10.12	10.38	10.45	8.80	1.19	6.52	6.77	7.57	7.94	4
9.50	10.07	10.12	9.52	1.16	7.75	7.87	8.82	9.01	5
9.83	10.27	10.29	9.74	1.50	8.49	8.55	9.22	9.31	6
8.19	8.69	8.70	8.81	.63	7.68	7.71	8.82	8.85	7
8.25	8.55	8.59	10.13	.29	9.13	9.18	9.85	9.93	8
8.85	8.83	9.02	9.93	.76	8.13	8.44	8.60	9.06	9
8.17	8.50	8.53	10.16	.20	9.26	9.28	10.02	10.05	10
9.19	9.58	9.68	10.67	.67	9.86	9.93	10.55	10.67	11
7.84	8.32	8.34	9.45	.11	7.90	7.91	9.01	9.03	12
8.21	9.10	9.17	10.23	.22	8.94	8.97	10.80	10.86	13
8.04	8.13	8.13	10.59	.02	10.25	10.25	10.33	10.34	14
7.48	7.92	7.95	8.95	.12	7.55	7.62	8.80	8.90	15
8.25	8.26	8.49	7.87	.18	4.96	5.36	6.00	6.67	16
7.43	7.90	7.92	9.04	.11	7.72	7.76	8.96	9.02	17
8.40	8.86	8.99	8.22	.12	5.59	5.71	7.70	7.93	18
8.47	9.06	9.14	9.34	.39	7.47	7.54	8.73	8.85	19
7.53	8.06	8.07	9.11	-.28	7.61	7.61	9.14	9.15	20
6.99	7.52	7.52	9.08	.10	8.17	8.19	9.16	9.18	21
8.53	8.90	8.92	6.17	.05	3.60	4.05	5.19	5.93	22
9.18	9.22	9.36	5.90	.05	2.28	4.24	2.31	5.40	23
8.42	8.83	8.85	6.24	.08	3.84	4.01	5.74	6.02	24
9.21	9.49	9.54	6.22	.02	3.53	3.92	5.18	5.89	25
8.20	8.80	8.83	6.10	-.09	3.19	3.32	5.09	5.33	26
8.28	8.69	8.70	7.06	.00	4.94	5.07	6.69	6.90	27
8.01	8.50	8.50	5.83	-.22	3.64	3.68	5.74	5.79	28
9.72	9.59	9.86	7.69	.47	5.09	6.44	5.32	7.11	29
9.99	9.18	9.75	6.59	.19	2.26	5.56	1.92	6.04	30
9.59	9.85	9.92	8.44	.71	6.61	6.84	7.32	7.63	31
10.54	10.44	10.61	7.93	.66	5.37	5.74	6.38	6.89	32
9.50	9.83	10.07	8.50	.63	6.93	7.22	7.36	7.70	33
9.33	9.81	9.78	7.96	.64	5.97	6.27	6.54	6.93	34
9.05	9.44	9.45	8.99	.79	7.69	7.77	8.32	8.44	35
10.73	10.85	11.02	9.93	1.42	8.16	8.55	8.56	9.19	36
10.85	10.61	11.11	8.63	.89	5.79	6.83	5.50	7.02	37
10.68	10.94	10.99	10.49	1.72	9.07	9.17	9.72	9.85	38
10.50	10.64	10.70	10.07	1.57	8.00	8.12	8.66	8.83	39
10.59	10.94	11.02	10.08	1.47	8.61	8.73	9.42	9.59	40
10.88	10.99	11.02	11.04	2.03	10.10	10.13	10.46	10.50	41
11.17	11.67	11.69	11.69	2.34	11.79	11.82	11.96	12.00	42
12.13	12.18	12.27	11.43	3.00	10.00	10.48	10.49	11.10	43
11.60	11.19	11.36	9.82	2.34	6.08	8.00	6.15	8.47	44
12.24	12.45	12.48	11.88	3.23	10.88	10.98	11.52	11.65	45
11.40	11.19	11.26	11.05	2.40	9.06	9.21	9.50	9.69	46
11.69	11.99	11.99	12.51	3.40	11.21	11.33	11.61	11.77	47
11.74	12.20	12.22	12.24	3.17	11.98	12.07	12.30	12.42	48
14.72	15.06	15.05	11.72	4.59	11.16	11.17	12.63	12.65	49
12.62	12.10	12.63	10.15	2.39	8.49	8.73	8.71	9.01	50
12.87	11.72	13.01	9.01	2.20	6.29	6.63	6.57	6.99	51
12.50	12.32	12.43	10.80	2.53	9.61	9.74	9.88	10.03	52
12.77	12.04	12.26	9.78	2.06	7.82	8.11	7.75	8.11	53
11.86	11.69	11.75	9.98	3.30	8.61	8.65	8.38	8.43	54
12.60	12.85	12.90	12.04	2.55	11.39	11.40	12.02	12.03	55
10.10	10.42	10.43	9.21	1.92	7.67	7.85	7.72	7.96	56
11.14	10.83	11.13	7.50	1.80	4.15	4.70	4.67	5.48	57
10.03	10.39	10.38	9.36	1.93	7.93	8.07	7.95	8.12	58
11.19	11.13	11.15	8.78	2.28	6.44	6.85	6.44	6.92	59
11.80	11.91	11.89	9.45	2.43	7.18	8.18	6.96	8.10	60
10.51	10.67	10.69	9.72	2.04	8.59	8.65	8.51	8.57	61
8.65	9.33	9.32	9.05	1.38	7.75	7.76	8.07	8.09	62

Source: Daniel H. Garnick, "Patterns of Growth of Metropolitan and Nonmetropolitan Areas: An Update," U.S. Department of Commerce, BEA, *Survey of Current Business* (May 1985):34–35.

region—automobiles, machine tools, electrical equipment, and industrial machinery—is both capital- and energy-intensive. Agriculture and related manufacturing industries, such as food processing, chemicals, and leather are the major factors in the Plains' region economy. Demand for industrial goods and housing diminished, as manufacturing firms and people relocated to the South and West.

The Great Lakes and Plains' populations expanded by 3% and 4.9%, respectively, between 1970 and 1980. Personal income expanded by 14.9% and 16.3% per year in nominal terms. In the early 1980s, the Great Lakes population declined at an average annual rate of 0.5%, and personal income expanded by under 6.1%, while the plains experienced a growth of 0.5% in population and 7.7% in personal income. The average growth of both regions was below the national average, and both regions are expected to experience below-average national growth rates in population and income to the year 2000.

This region is a major supplier of rubber and plastics, primary metals, wood, paper, food and food products, printing, and transportation equipment.

Southeast and Southwest

The most spectacular change in the U.S. interregional population flow from 1970 to 1980 occurred in the Southeast and Southwest. In the 1970s, net migration into the area was more than 3 million, and the population increased by 18%, reaching 24 million.

In the early 1980s, the Southeast's growth in personal income and population exceeds the national average. The Southeast average annual population growth was 1.4% from 1979 to 1983, and personal income grew at 9.9% (with the national average 11.03% and 8.9%, respectively). The Southwest figures were 3.0% and 11.4% for the same indicators and time periods.

With business and commerce relocating to the Southeast, personal income grew at a substantially higher rate than in New England and the Mideast, although the South still lagged in this area. The South led all regions in privately owned housing starts from 1981 to 1983, accounting for more than 55% of the total.

These shifts in population, employment, and housing were caused by various factors. Aggressive solicitation of business and industry by the southern states, supported by state and local lenders, complemented the region's advantages of open land, good transportation, and relatively inexpensive and abundant labor. With racial tensions substantially decreased, more whites moved into the region and fewer blacks moved out of it. The Southeast and Southwest regions are expected to grow above the national average in terms of population and personal income to the year 2000. In the Southeast, manufacturing industries are the major factors that stimulate economic activities. Services—including trucking, warehousing, and transportation—have also gained significantly as the population expanded. In the Southwest, manufacturing activities, including machinery and construction, that supply the energy and the petrochemical industries constitute the backbone of the region. The energy industry has, however, weakened in recent years. Major industries of the region include chemicals, apparel, food, primary metals, textiles, paper and allied products, and petroleum.

Rocky Mountains and Far West

During the past decade, population and income growth in the Rocky Mountain and Far West regions was high but uneven. Since 1970, the population has grown 29.8% in the Rocky Mountain region and 19.4% in the Far West. Personal income has expanded by 23.1% and 19.5%, respectively. By the end of the 1970s, California's growth no longer dominated the Far West as it had in earlier decades. However, California still accounts for 64% of the population in these regions and 68% of the personal income.

Unlike any other section of the country, every state in the West experienced a net population gain. The largest growth rates were not seen on the coast but in several of the sparsely populated mountain and desert states east of the Sierra Nevada—Idaho, Wyoming, Colorado, Nevada, and Arizona. The leaders were Nevada, with a population growth of 62.5% between 1970 and 1980, and Arizona, with 51.5% growth. Wyoming's increase in personal income was the highest in the nation from 1973 to 1980, while Alaska ranked second and Texas ranked third. However, due to its isolated location, cost of living is also significantly higher in Alaska than in the other states. The Rocky Mountain and Far West regions are expected to expand above the national average in terms of population and personal income growth.

The Far West region is heavily endowed with industries that manufacture advanced technological equipment such as scientific instruments, computing and electronic equipment, and plastic industries. These industries supply the aircraft and aerospace manufacturers. The service sector—that is, higher education—played an important role as the population expanded sharply. Military spending also became an important factor.

Oil, gas, and coal mining were major factors in the Rocky Mountain region's economy, particularly after 1973. Machinery manufacturing to service the energy business became important. Construction and services grew fast in response to population and income growth. The region also benefits from the national defense build-up.

The States

Under the U.S. Constitution, powers not given to the federal government are reserved for state governments. Similarly, in state constitutions, powers, particularly those related to local development, are often delegated to local governments. Among the powers exclusively reserved for the federal government are those to grant patents and copyrights and those to regulate interstate and foreign commerce.

Each of the fifty states has its own constitution, and their governments are modeled after the federal government, with executive, legislative, and judiciary branches. The U.S. Constitution gave the states great power to enact laws over matters, such as commercial law, which are not specifically subject to the federal government's jurisdiction. With the exception of a few industries, the federal government has not enacted national statutes governing the incorporation of business enterprises.

Each of the states as well as the District of Columbia, Puerto Rico, and U.S. possessions has its own laws and substantial jurisdiction over business activities and commerce. Each state has its own corporate laws, its own labor laws, and its own system of taxation. No agreements or compacts may be entered into between one state and another state or between a state and a foreign nation without the consent of the U.S. Congress.

The states are composed of small political units, including cities, towns, and villages. State and local governments play important roles in developing and running day-to-day affairs. The foreign entrepreneur will deal primarily with the city or county level. The complexities of federal and state laws require that local legal and professional people who are familiar with and able to deal effectively with local officials, be employed to help you with legal aspects of a business.

Each state has its own tax system, which is independent from that of any other state and the federal government. Many states levy a sales tax, a personal income tax, and a corporate tax with rates and minimum amounts subject to tax varying widely from state to state. Property tax laws are legislated at the state level but assessed and collected at the county level. State and local taxes range from 3 to 12% and thus can add several percentage points to a business's tax rate. Cities may levy some form of tax, such as a city sales tax or franchise tax. When a U.S. corporation operates in more than one state, the amount of income attributable to state operations is determined by various formulas.

In summary, state and local governments have most of the jurisdiction over doing business in the United States. Corporations in the United States are created under state law, and it is therefore necessary to review those laws to determine whether any local restrictions apply to a particular industry. Tax differentials, corporate laws, and the business environment are some of the variables corporations should consider in selecting a location. Although state laws are to some extent similar, there are great variations in the requirements for incorporation and operation of a corporation. For instance, Delaware's corporation laws are the most liberal, so the greatest number of U.S. corporations are organized there.

U.S. Aggregate Income and Production

GNP in current dollars reached $3,661 billion in 1984, and real GNP expanded by an average of about 3.5% per annum between 1970 and 1984. Gross national product per capita, in 1972 dollars, has increased by 1.7% per annum since 1970, while disposable personal income has expanded by 3.4% per annum.

Personal consumption expenditures in current dollars reached $2,342 billion in 1984, constituting almost 64% of GNP, up from about 63% in 1970. In 1984 personal consumption expenditures for durable goods accounted for 13.6% of consumer expenditures, nondurables for 36.7%, and services for 49.8%.

Gross private domestic investment reached $637 billion in 1984. This was 17.4% of GNP, an increase of 2 percentage points from 1970. Business investment expenditures for new plant and equipment reached $426 billion in 1984; residential investment, about $154 billion. New private housing unit starts averaged $1.7 million in 1984.

Federal, state, and local government purchases of goods and services (measured in 1972 dollars) were $748 billion in 1984, or almost 20.4% of GNP. In real terms such purchases expanded by an annual average of 1.4% per annum from 1970 to 1984.

Productivity Trends and Growth Potential

Productivity rises because of long-term improvement in labor skills, increases in the capital available to each worker, and reallocation of resources from lower-valued to higher-valued uses. U.S. productivity growth, measured in terms of output produced per unit of labor used in production, averaged 0.7% per year from 1973 to 1981. But this growth went up to 1.9% between 1981 and 1984, and it is expected to expand at an average rate of 2% per annum between 1985 and 1990. This outlook is attributed to: (1) the skills acquired by the baby-boom generation, which entered the labor force in the 1970s; (2) the high rate of business investment and an increase in capital stock; (3) low inflation; (4) a somewhat reduced government regulation; and (5) improvements in labor–management cooperation.

Substantial productivity variation occurred among the various sectors, and productivity growth has been unusually erratic (see figure 4–3 and tables 4–5 and 4–6).

The declining productivity growth in the 1970s and early 1980s has not been fully explained. However, several factors that generated the strong productivity growth between World War II and the mid-1960s have since been reversed. For example, between 1948 and 1973, high rates of private investment and growth of net capital stock led to an annual increase of nearly 3% in the capital—labor ratio. Because of low rates of investment and a sharp increase in employment, the average annual investment growth rate from 1974 to 1979 was –0.1%. This factor alone could have reduced productivity growth by up to 0.5 percentage points per year from earlier trends.

Since 1965 productivity growth has also been reduced by a demographic shift in the age and sex composition of the labor force. The addition of many young workers to the growing pool of labor has increased the number of less experienced workers. Such demographic shifts in employment reduced the annual growth rate of productivity between 1965 and 1973 by 0.4 percentage points and by one-third of a percentage point after 1974.

Increased economic and social regulations have aggravated the productivity slowdown in a number of ways. Investments for pollution abatement and other social objectives displaced investment that would have expanded capacity. During the late 1960s and 1970s, the direct cost of compliance with environmental, health, and safety regulations may have reduced the annual growth of productivity in the private nonfarm sector by 0.3 percentage points.

A decline in research and development (R&D) in the United States may also be a significant cause of the productivity slowdown.

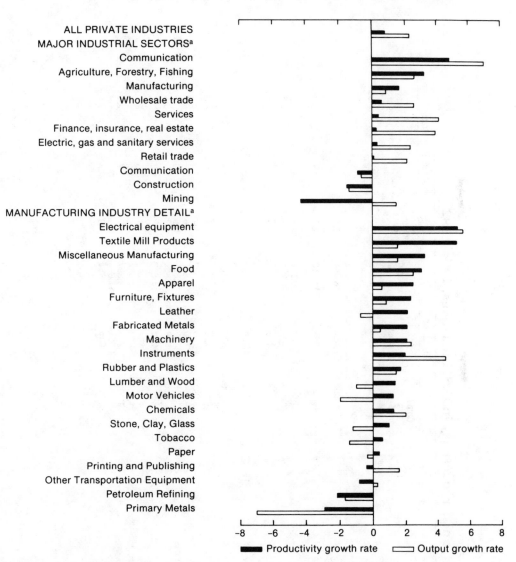

ALL PRIVATE INDUSTRIES
MAJOR INDUSTRIAL SECTORS[a]
Communication
Agriculture, Forestry, Fishing
Manufacturing
Wholesale trade
Services
Finance, insurance, real estate
Electric, gas and sanitary services
Retail trade
Communication
Construction
Mining
MANUFACTURING INDUSTRY DETAIL[a]
Electrical equipment
Textile Mill Products
Miscellaneous Manufacturing
Food
Apparel
Furniture, Fixtures
Leather
Fabricated Metals
Machinery
Instruments
Rubber and Plastics
Lumber and Wood
Motor Vehicles
Chemicals
Stone, Clay, Glass
Tobacco
Paper
Printing and Publishing
Other Transportation Equipment
Petroleum Refining
Primary Metals

■ Productivity growth rate   ▢ Output growth rate

Source: Virgil H. Ketterling, "Economic Performance of U.S. Industries, 1974–82," Department of Commerce, *U.S. Industrial Outlook 1984*, p. 29.

Note: Growth rates are annual rates of change compounded, based on data for 1974 and 1982. "Output" represents constant dollar gross product originating in each industry (i.e. the industry's contribution to gross domestic product). "Productivity" represents gross product originating per person engaged in production.

[a]Industries and major sectors are ranked in descending order of productivity growth.

Figure 4-3. Output and Productivity Growth Rates in U.S. Industries, 1974–1982

Table 4-5
Output, Employment, and Productivity in U.S. Industries, 1974-1982

Industry title	1972 SIC code	1982 Levels			1974–82 Compound growth rate (percent)		
		Output: gross product originating (millions of 1972 dollars)	Employment: persons engaged in production (thousands)	Productivity: gross product originating per person (1972 dollars)	Output: gross product originating (1972 dollars)	Employment: persons engaged in production	Productivity:[1] gross product originating per person (1972 dollars)
All private industries[2]		$1,290,962	77,482	$16,661	2.4	1.5	0.9
Agriculture, forestry, and fishing	01–09	44,186	3,099	14,258	2.7	−0.7	3.3
Mining		21,607	1,122	19,258	1.5	6.1	−4.3
Coal	11–12	4,231	235	18,004	3.7	3.5	0.3
Oil and gas extraction	13	14,466	704	20,548	1.9	11.1	−8.3
Other mining	10,14	2,910	183	15,902	−2.9	−2.2	−0.7
Construction	15–17	47,669	4,739	10,059	−1.4	0.1	−1.5
Manufacturing		336,120	18,570	18,100	0.9	−0.8	1.7
Nondurable goods		138,708	7,519	18,448	1.3	−0.6	1.9
Food and kindred products	20	35,754	1,587	22,529	2.5	−0.6	3.0
Tobacco manufactures	21	3,947	66	59,803	1.6	−1.9	0.6
Textile mill products	22	9,954	720	13,825	1.6	−3.5	5.2
Apparel and other textile products	23	11,358	1,103	10,297	0.6	−1.9	2.5
Paper and allied products	26	12,626	652	19,365	−0.3	0.7	0.4
Printing and publishing	27	17,050	1,233	13,828	1.6	2.0	−0.4
Chemicals and allied products	28	27,608	1,072	25,754	2.0	0.7	1.3
Petroleum refining	29	7,117	194	36,686	−1.7	0.3	−2.1
Rubber and misc. plastic products	30	11,186	679	16,474	−1.5	−0.2	1.7
Leather and leather products	31	2,108	213	9,897	−0.7	−2.7	2.1
Durable goods		197,412	11,051	17,864	0.7	−0.9	1.6
Lumber and wood products	24	9,177	635	14,452	−0.9	−2.3	1.4

Industry	Code						
Furniture and fixtures	25	4,934	427	11,555	0.8	−1.5	2.3
Stone, clay, and glass products	32	9,263	569	16,279	−1.2	−2.2	1.0
Primary metal industries	33	14,384	905	15,894	−7.0	−4.2	−2.9
Fabricated metal products	34	21,958	1,411	15,562	0.5	−1.6	2.1
Machinery, except electrical	35	42,781	2,256	18,963	2.3	0.2	2.1
Electric and electronic equipment	36	40,294	2,000	20,147	5.6	0.3	5.3
Motor vehicles and equipment	371	19,752	700	28,217	−1.9	−3.1	1.3
Other transportation equipment	372–9	15,827	1,037	15,262	0.3	1.0	−0.8
Instruments and related products	38	13,228	708	18,684	4.5	2.5	2.0
Misc. manufacturing industries	39	5,814	403	14,427	1.6	−1.5	3.2
Transportation		46,832	2,931	15,978	−0.7	0.2	−0.9
Railroad transportation	40	9,110	411	22,165	−2.4	−4.1	1.8
Trucking and warehousing	42	19,313	1,383	13,965	−0.8	0.6	−1.3
Transportation by air	45	9,411	423	22,248	0.7	2.2	−1.5
Other transportation	41,44,46,47	8,998	714	12,602	−0.1	1.6	−1.7
Communication	48	57,159	1,341	42,624	7.0	2.1	4.8
Electric, gas, and sanitary services	49	34,895	847	41,198	2.3	2.0	0.3
Wholesale and retail trade		248,005	19,089	12,992	2.3	2.0	0.3
Wholesale trade	50–51	106,270	5,363	19,815	2.6	2.0	0.6
Retail trade	52–59	141,735	13,726	10,326	2.1	2.0	0.1
Finance, insurance, and real estate	60–67	250,957	5,672	44,245	3.9	3.6	0.3
Services		203,532	20,072	10,140	4.1	3.6	0.4
Business services	73	37,482	3,313	11,314	6.3	6.1	0.2
Health services	80	61,758	5,553	11,122	4.8	4.8	0.1
Other services	70–89, exc. 73,80	104,292	11,206	9,307	3.0	2.5	0.4

Definitions: "Gross product originating" represents each respective industry's contribution to the "gross domestic product" (GDP); "persons engaged in production" represents full-time equivalent employees plus the number of self-employed proprietors and partners who are active in their unincorporated businesses; "productivity" is calculated by dividing gross product originating by the number of persons engaged in production. The industry classification is on an establishment basis. The growth rates are annual rates of change compounded, using data for the 2 end years—1974 and 1982.

[1] These rates of productivity change may differ from the productivity data published by the Bureau of Labor Statistics because of differences in coverage and definition and different techniques for calculating rates of change.

[2] Includes private domestic industries only—the "government sector" and "rest of the world sector" are excluded.

Source: Virgil H. Ketterling, "Economic Performance of U.S. Industries, 1974-82," *1984 U.S. Industrial Outlook* (Washington, D.C.: U.S. Department of Commerce), p. 31.

Table 4-6
Prices, Profits, Compensation, and Unit Labor Costs

Industry title	1972 SIC code	1982 Average compensation per employee	1974–82 Compound growth rates (percent)					
			Average compensation per employee	Total labor compensation	Total profits	Unit[1] labor costs	Unit profits	Implicit price deflator
All private industries[2]		$21,913	8.5	10.2	1.5	7.7	-0.9	7.6
Agriculture, forestry, and fishing	01–09	12,511	10.1	9.4	-7.7	6.5	-10.1	3.4
Mining		34,066	10.6	17.3	-4.9	15.6	3.4	15.7
Coal	11–12	37,645	10.5	14.4	-13.2	10.2	-12.8	5.7
Oil and gas extraction	13	33,873	10.6	22.9	8.6	20.6	6.6	18.7
Other mining	10,14	30,117	10.1	7.7	-16.5	10.9	-14.1	10.9
Construction	15–17	25,187	7.9	8.0	(3)	9.5	(3)	8.9
Manufacturing		26,022	9.5	8.4	0.2	7.4	-0.7	7.0
Nondurable goods		23,702	9.3	8.7	5.2	7.3	3.9	6.9
Food and kindred products	20	23,906	9.0	8.4	17.2	5.8	14.4	6.0
Tobacco manufactures	21	32,909	13.2	11.0	16.2	12.6	17.8	9.4
Textile mill products	22	16,731	8.4	4.6	-1.4	3.0	-2.9	2.8
Apparel and other textile products	23	13,626	7.8	5.8	13.6	5.1	12.9	5.9
Paper and allied products	26	28,185	9.7	9.0	-8.4	9.3	-8.6	7.5
Printing and publishing	27	23,708	7.9	10.1	8.5	8.4	6.8	8.8
Chemicals and allied products	28	32,438	9.8	10.5	-5.7	8.4	-7.6	8.8
Petroleum refining	29	50,016	11.7	12.1	9.3	14.1	11.2	7.3
Rubber and misc. plastic products	30	22,966	8.6	8.4	40.3	6.8	38.3	6.6
Leather and leather products	31	14,981	8.2	5.3	33.4	6.0	34.3	8.3
Durable goods		27,601	9.2	8.2	-19.4	7.4	-19.9	7.1
Lumber and wood products	24	20,087	8.8	6.3	(3)	7.3	(3)	5.1
Furniture and fixtures	25	18,179	8.5	6.9	32.6	6.0	31.5	6.9
Stone, clay, and glass products	32	25,887	9.0	6.6	(3)	8.0	(3)	7.6
Primary metal industries	33	33,814	9.4	4.9	(3)	12.8	(3)	8.6
Fabricated metal products	34	25,727	8.7	6.9	13.0	6.4	12.5	7.6
Machinery, except electrical	35	28,340	9.2	9.4	6.4	7.0	4.0	7.4
Electric and electronic equipment	36	25,466	9.5	9.8	(3)	4.0	(3)	5.9
Motor vehicles and equipment	371	36,944	9.6	6.2	(3)	8.2	(3)	7.2
Other transportation equipment	372–9	33,179	9.7	10.9	(3)	10.6	(3)	8.5
Instruments and related products	38	26,521	9.4	12.1	15.9	7.3	11.0	6.9
Misc. manufacturing industries	39	20,000	9.1	7.4	(3)	5.7	(3)	7.3

Industry	SIC code							
Transportation		28,520	8.5	8.8	(3)	9.5	(3)	9.3
Railroad transportation	40	36,929	9.9	5.4	(3)	8.0	(3)	9.3
Trucking and warehousing	42	25,535	7.9	8.5	(3)	9.4	(3)	8.6
Transportation by air	45	37,138	9.1	11.5	(3)	10.7	(3)	8.0
Other transportation	41,44,46,47	22,976	8.5	10.2	−2.5	10.3	−2.4	11.6
Communication	48	34,374	10.3	12.6	13.3	5.2	2.0	4.3
Electric, gas, and sanitary services	49	33,615	9.9	12.1	33.7	9.6	30.7	10.9
Wholesale and retail trade		17,441	7.5	9.7	0.6	7.2	−1.6	6.8
Wholesale trade	50–51	25,042	8.2	10.3	−0.3	7.5	−2.9	5.9
Retail trade	52–59	14,255	7.1	9.2	19.3	7.0	16.9	7.5
Finance, insurance, and real estate	60–67	22,775	8.9	12.8	−1.9	8.6	−5.6	8.0
Services		18,511	9.1	13.1	−5.1	8.7	−8.8	8.1
Business services	73	19,271	8.6	15.2	−2.2	8.4	−8.0	8.3
Health services	80	21,040	9.9	15.1	5.6	9.8	0.7	8.6
Other services	70–89,exc. 73,80	16,777	8.6	11.3	(3)	8.1	(3)	7.9

Definitions: "Compensation per employee" represents total compensation, including supplements to wages and salaries, per full-time equivalent employee; "total labor compensation" represents the compensation of employees, plus the estimated income of self-employed persons that is attributable to their labor input in unincorporated enterprises; "total profits" include the profits of corporations, plus the estimated profit portion of proprietors' income, and inventory valuation adjustments; "unit labor costs" represent total labor costs per unit of constant-dollar gross product originating; and "unit profits" represent total profits per unit of constant-dollar gross product originating; the "implicit price deflator" represents the ratio of current-dollar to constant-dollar gross product originating. The industry classification is on an establishment basis. Growth rates are compounded annual rates of change, using data for the 2 end years—1974 and 1982.

[1] Rates of change in unit labor costs may differ from data published by the Bureau of Labor Statistics because of differences in coverage and definition, and different techniques for calculating rates of change.

[2] Includes private domestic industries only; the "government sector" and the "rest of the world sector" are excluded.

[3] Meaningful growth rates can not be computed because of losses in the initial or terminal years.

Source: Virgil H. Ketterling, "Economic Performance of U.S. Industries, 1974–82," *1984 U.S. Industrial Outlook* (Washington, D.C.: U.S. Department of Commerce), p. 33.

Evidence for such a view lies in the falling ratio of R&D expenditures to GNP.

Against this negative background, several factors provide grounds for cautious optimism. Important demographic changes will occur. The growth of the labor force, particularly that of young people, will slow down during the next decade as the baby boomers come of age. Health, safety, and environmental regulation appears to have peaked, allowing the proportion of new investment being allocated to productive uses to increase.

Increases in energy prices could outpace growth of other prices in the foreseeable future. These increases will provide incentives for shifting to energy-saving methods of production, thereby stimulating new investment and productivity. Hence, an improvement in the long-run real growth of productivity will take place.

Prospects for a long-term revival of economic growth in the United States are excellent. Rises in employment should continue, and productivity has improved. The long-term growth potential of GNP is anticipated to be about 4% annually from 1985 to 1990.[23] This outlook, according to the *Economic Report of the President*, is based on (1) an anticipated labor force growth of 1.8%; (2) a population growth of 0.9%; (3) a labor participation growth rate of 0.6%; (4) an employment growth of 0.3%, and (5) an expansion in labor productivity of 2%.

Trends in Investment

The fixed investment of U.S. businesses has historically been quite volatile. It has fluctuated both in absolute value and as a percentage of GNP in response to various factors:

Expected output growth

Profits

Capacity utilization

Business confidence

Growth rate of the population and labor force

Relative cost of capital

Amount of innovation.

Since 1946 fixed investment has ranged from 8.1% to 10.7% of GNP. It averaged about 9.5% in the 1950s and early 1960s, moved somewhat above 10% from 1965 to 1975, then averaged almost 11% from 1976 to 1980, and rose to 15% from 1981 to 1982.

Capital investment in the U.S. economy has made a strong recovery since the fourth-quarter recession of 1982. The rapid rise in investment spending during the current recovery was stimulated by surges in total demand and corporate profits, as well as by favorable changes in tax laws, stable prices for capital goods, and moderate interest rates.

The strong international competitive position of the United States also depends on whether fixed investment grows at an adequate pace. An international comparison of investments shows that most industrial countries devote a larger share of their output to investment than does the U.S., and their growth rates in productivity have also been higher than that of the United States.

U.S. demographic factors are likely to favor relatively strong investment growth over the next five years, since the postwar baby boom will continue to cause large increases in the prime home-buying age group of twenty-three- to thirty-five-year-olds. The demand for housing is therefore likely to be robust in the years immediately ahead. A slowing of growth in the labor force and a response to strong competitive pressures, caused by past deregulation and the presently strong dollar, will encourage substituting capital for labor. Finally, a strong rise in fixed investment by business will be required if the goals of reducing unemployment and maintaining low inflation are to be achieved.

Foreign Trade and the Balance of Payments

U.S. exports of goods and services reached $368 billion in 1984, or 10.1% of GNP, while imports reached $430 billion, or 11.7% of GNP. Export volume expanded at an annual average rate of 12.5% between 1970 and 1980, but declined sharply during four subsequent years. Imports increased by 5.6% and 7.7% during this period. U.S. exports of manufactured goods reached $140 billion in 1984, or 69% of total exports of goods, whereas imports of manufactured goods were valued at $171 billion, or 66% of total imports of goods.[24]

The U.S. share of total world mechandise exports was 12.4% in 1983, compared with 10.5% for West Germany, 9.1% for Japan, and 4.7% for Canada. The U.S. share of world exports of manufactured goods was 19.4%, compared with about 19.7% for West Germany, 14.8% for Japan, and 7.8% for the United Kingdom.

The service sector plays a large and important role in U.S. international trade, and the U.S. is becoming more dependent on such trade. Services and investment income constituted 36.3% of all exports of goods and services in 1972, and 39.7% in 1984. From 1972 to 1983, the U.S. showed a positive or favorable balance of trade in services and investment income, suggesting a considerable comparative advantage in international trade in services and investment.

The current account of the balance-of-payments shows a U.S. deficit of $42 billion in 1984, compared with a deficit of $11.8 billion in the previous year.

Direction and Composition of Foreign Trade

The U.S. does not belong to any trading bloc. Western Europe accounts for about 28% of the total U.S. export market, with the U.K. and West Germany accounting for 5.1% and 4.4%, respectively.[25] They are followed by the Netherlands, with about 3.4%; France, with over 2.9%; and Italy, with about 2.2%. The USSR and Eastern Europe buy about 1% to 2% of U.S. exports. Asia, Australia, and Oceania make up 22% of the U.S. export market. Within this region, Japan is the main buyer, accounting for about 11.1% of the total, followed by 2.1% flowing to Australia. Canada, buying 20.9% of U.S. exports, is the largest single market for the U.S., while Latin America accounts for 13.6% of U.S. exports. More specifically, Mexico buys 6.3%; Venezuela, 1.3%; and Brazil, 1.4%.

Agricultural products make up about 18% of total exports, while nonagricultural products account for 82%. Food, feed, and beverages represent over 15%; industrial supplies and materials, 30%; capital goods, 35%; and automotive vehicles, 8.1%.

U.S. imports categorized by trading region and country differ slightly from exports. Asia, Australia, and Oceania are the leading sources of U.S. imports, accounting for 26.5% of the total, followed by Canada, with 19.5%; Western Europe, with 17.5%; Latin America, with 15.7%; and Africa, with 7.1%.

The leading European exporters to the United States are West Germany, accounting for 6.0% of total U.S. imports, and the U.K., with 3.8%. France and Italy are responsible for more than 2% of the imports, while Canada accounts for 19.5% of total imports to the United States. As for Latin America, Mexico accounts for 5.2%, Venezuela for 1.8%, and Brazil for 2.5% of total U.S. imports. Agricultural commodities account for 6.1% of U.S. imports, while nonagricultural goods account for 93.9%. Petroleum and related products account for about 25%. Capital goods, except automotive, are 15.5% of total imports; crude materials, excluding fuels, 17.5%; and automotive vehicles, 14% (see tables 4-7, 4-8 and 4-9).

Controls

Exports are not subject to license, but certain controls are applied. Under the Export Administration Act of 1979, the president of the United States may suspend exports of goods for reasons of national security or foreign policy or because of shortages in the domestic economy. Export-controlled goods require a license from the Department of Commerce.

Controls a high-technology exports to noncommunist countries are designed to prevent unauthorized diversion to communist nations. Engaging in restrictive trade practices or boycotts initiated

Table 4-7
Direction of Trade
(Percentage of Total)

	Exports			Imports		
	1985	*1980*	*1970*	*1985*	*1980*	*1970*
Industrial Countries	61.0	56.8	61.1	62.6	49.9	68.1
Canada	20.9	16.0	21.0	19.5	16.6	27.8
Japan	11.1	9.4	10.8	19.9	13.0	14.7
Belgium	2.3	3.0	2.8	1.0	0.8	1.8
France	2.9	3.4		2.7	2.2	
W. Germany	4.4	5.0	6.3	6.0	5.0	7.8
Netherlands	3.4	3.9		1.2	0.8	
United Kingdom	6.1	5.8	5.9	3.8	4.0	5.5
Oil-Exporting Countries	5.6	7.7	4.4	5.1	21.3	3.9
Saudi Arabia	2.2			0.4	5.3	
Venezuela	1.3			1.8	2.2	
Nonoil-Developing Countries	29.1	31.7		26.9	25.4	
Africa	2.4	2.2	1.4	2.8	3.0	1.7
Asia	11.3	9.9	8.8	12.5	8.0	8.2
Peoples Republic of China	1.4	1.7	1.2	1.1	0.5	1.4
Hong Kong	1.4	1.2	0.9	2.6	2.0	2.4
Korea	2.8	2.1	1.5	2.9	1.8	0.9
Malaysia	0.9	0.5	0.1	0.4	1.1	0.7
Philippines	0.6	0.9	0.9	0.7	0.8	1.2
Singapore	1.7	1.4	0.6	1.3	0.8	0.02
Europe	1.4	1.8		0.6	0.6	
Yugoslavia	0.2	0.3		0.2	0.2	
Middle East	6.0	2.3		1.5	0.6	
Israel	1.3	0.9		0.6	0.4	
Western Hemisphere	13.6	15.5	13.4	14.2	13.1	11.9
Argentina	0.3	1.2		0.3	0.3	
Brazil	1.4	2.0		2.5	1.6	
Mexico	6.3	6.9		5.2	5.1	
USSR, Eastern Europe	2.0	1.4	0.7	0.3	0.5	0.5

Source: Calculated from International Monetary Fund, *Direction of Trade*, various issues.

Table 4-8
U.S. Imports of Manufactured Products

Products	1972 SIC Code	1982 Imports[1]		1974–82[1,2] Growth rate (percent)	Import penetration ratio[1,3]		1974–81 Change in import penetration ratio (percent)
		Value (millions)	Percent of total		1974 (percent)	1981[4] (percent)	
Total manufactured products	—	$170,406[5]	100.0	11.1	7.7	9.1	1.4
Food and kindred products	20	9,561	5.6	4.0	4.7	4.3	– 0.4
Tobacco manufactures	21	227	0.1	27.4	0.7	2.0	1.3
Textile mill products	22	2,225	1.3	5.9	5.3	5.9	0.6
Apparel and other textile products	23	8,432	5.0	16.6	8.3	16.2	7.9
Lumber and wood products	24	3,059	1.8	6.2	8.6	9.8	1.2
Furniture and fixtures	25	1,354	0.8	15.6	3.2	5.0	1.8
Paper and allied products	26	5,468	3.2	8.1	6.1	6.8	0.7
Printing and publishing	27	547	0.3	10.4	1.0	0.9	– 0.1
Chemicals and allied products	28	7,632	4.5	11.5	4.0	4.7	0.7
Petroleum refining	29	15,643	9.2	6.3	16.2	7.3	– 8.9
Rubber and misc. plastic products	30	2,937	1.7	9.5	5.3	6.1	0.8
Leather and leather products	31	4,496	2.6	18.4	20.0	40.3	20.3
Stone, clay, and glass products	32	2,398	1.4	11.7	4.1	5.4	1.3
Primary metal products	33	15,352	9.0	5.9	11.8	15.4	3.6
Fabricated metal products	34	5,186	3.0	10.3	3.4	4.1	0.7
Machinery, except electrical	35	14,994	8.8	14.8	6.3	8.7	2.4
Electrical and electronic equipment	36	20,097	11.8	16.0	10.0	13.9	3.9
Transportation equipment	37	36,657	21.5	12.9	12.6	16.5	3.9
Instruments and related products	38	5,379	3.2	17.2	7.6	12.7	5.1
Miscellaneous manufactures	39	7,111	4.2	17.6	16.9	29.9	13.0
Unclassified products		1,651[5]	1.0				

[1] Import data for 1974 and 1982 are valued on a customs basis; data for 1981 are valued on a f.a.s. basis. Data for all years have been adjusted to include comparable commodities in each group.

[2] Compound annual rate of growth in the value of imports.

[3] Ratio of imports to new supply (domestic product shipments plus imports).

[4] 1982 data are not yet available on a comparable basis.

[5] Includes $1,651 million of gold bullion not allocated to a product group.

Source: Virgil H. Ketterling, "Economic Performance of U.S. Industries, 1974–82," *1984 U.S. Industrial Outlook* (Washington, D.C.: U.S. Department of Commerce), p. 37.

Table 4-9
Imports for 20 Leading 4-digit SIC Product Groups Ranked by Value of Manufactured U.S. Imports in 1982

Products	1972 SIC code	1974[1] Imports (millions)	1982[1] Imports (millions)	1974–82[2] Growth rate (percent)	Percent of total 1981 imports
Motor vehicles and car bodies	3711	$9,106.7[3]	$25,579.0[3]	13.8	15.0
Petroleum refinery products	2911	9,549.3	15,590.4	6.3	9.1
Blast furnace and steel mill products	3312	5,132.2	8,860.5	7.1	5.2
Motor vehicle parts and accessories	3714	2,529.8[4]	6,045.0[4]	11.5	3.5
Radio and TV receiving sets	3651	2,208.6	5,307.0	11.6	3.1
Semiconductors and related devices	3674	944.8	4,100.6	20.1	2.4
Office machines NEC	3579	646.5	3,411.2	23.1	2.0
Paper mill products	2621	1,652.7	3,239.6	8.8	1.9
Radio and TV communication equipment	3662	664.8	2,820.7	19.8	1.7
Primary nonferrous metals NEC	3339	1,876.6[5]	2,746.1[5]	4.9	1.6
Outerwear NEC	2369	687.6	2,122.8	15.1	1.2
Photographic equipment and supplies	3861	470.3	2,106.5	20.6	1.2
Lapidary work	3915	445.0	1,980.6	20.5	1.2
Industrial inorganic chemicals NEC	2819	565.1	1,895.6	16.3	1.1
Sawmill and planing mill products NEC	2421	1,047.9	1,770.3	6.8	1.0
Men's and boys' shirts and nightwear	2321	486.5	1,707.0	17.0	1.0
Meat products	2011	969.5	1,637.7	6.8	1.0
Games, toys, and children's vehicles	3944	231.8	1,621.2	27.5	1.0
General industrial machinery NEC	3569	363.5	1,526.9	19.7	0.9
Pulp mill products	2611	1,097.9	1,493.2	3.9	0.9

NEC—Not elsewhere classified.

[1] Imports are valued on a customs basis. Data have been adjusted to ensure comparability between 1974 and 1982. In some cases, the trade values reported in this table differ from the values in the individual industry chapters. The variation results from the use of trade concordances in the industry chapters which differ from the Census Bureau concordances used for this article.

[2] Compound annual rate of growth in the value of imports.

[3] Includes imports from Canada of $4,110.5 million in 1974 and $9,050.0 million in 1982.

[4] Includes imports from Canada of $1,618.6 million in 1974 and $3,159.9 million in 1982.

[5] Excludes $1,650.7 million of gold bullion.

Source: Virgil H. Ketterling, "Economic Performance of U.S. Industries, 1974–82," *1984 U.S. Industrial Outlook* (Washington, D.C.: U.S. Department of Commerce), p. 37.

by foreign countries is prohibited. The act requires U.S. exporters to report restrictive trade practices by a foreign government against a country friendly to the United States. The law provides civil and criminal penalties for violators and allows certain tax benefits to be revoked.

All exports from Cuba, Democratic Kampuchea, the Democratic People's Republic of Korea, and Viet Nam are prohibited from entering the United States unless individually licensed by the Department of Commerce.

There are also some limits on ports of entry; routing; storage or use; and required treatment, labeling, or processing as a condition of release from customs. Generally, the U.S. does not require licenses for importing except for specific products, mostly drugs and foods.

Tariffs and Quotas

Import tariff duties are quite low. More than half the imports destined for U.S. consumption enter duty free.

The average tariff on industrial products was 6.1% in 1979 and will drop to 4.2% by 1987, according to the tariff reduction negotiated under the Tokyo Round Multilateral Trade Negotiations. Most tariffs are levied ad valorem, but a few are levied on a specific basis. The U.S. tariff is a three-column tariff with full rates applicable only to imports from some communist countries. Imports from all noncommunist countries and some eastern ones are eligible for most-favored-nation treatment. A third column shows the preferential duty rate applicable to products imported from LDCs under the Generalized System of Preferences (GSP).

The GSP went into effect in the United States in January 1976 and it was renewed until 1993 under the Trade and Tariff Act of 1984. The program eliminates tariffs on eligible imports from qualifying developing countries. Some 3,000 products from 140 developing countries are eligible for duty-free entry under the GSP. These products are eligible for preferential treatment under certain criteria. One example of the criteria is that the exporting nation must not account for more than 50% of U.S. imports of that product in one calendar year. Imports must contain at least 35% value added by the exporting country. The GSP list is revised annually.

GSP eligibility may be withdrawn from certain countries on a product-by-product basis. Cumulative treatment under the GSP scheme is extended to members of the Andean Group, of the ASEAN, and of Caricom. Cumulative treatment allows two or more member countries of an eligible association to contribute to a product, so that jointly they can meet the 35% content requirement.

Two types of import quotas are in effect. Tariff-rate quotas allow a reduced rate of duty to be imposed until a certain level of imports is reached. Then higher duties are imposed. Absolute quotas set a fixed quantity and allow no further imports until the next quota period. Only a few items are subject to quotas.

Certain foodstuffs and fabrics are subject to annual quotas, and other voluntary quotas have been negotiated. No general restrictions exist on imports from communist countries—except from Cuba, Democratic Kampuchea, the Democratic People's Republic of Korea, and Viet Nam—but certain items do require licenses.

Import quotas are in effect for cotton, certain cotton waste and products, most dairy products, peanuts, and sugar. There are tariff-rate quotas for certain fish and potatoes. Most of the quantitative import quotas are on a country-of-production basis.

The United States is party to the GATT Multifiber Arrangement (MFA) and to over 25 bilateral textile agreements negotiated in accordance with MFA provisions. These agreements restrict exports of textiles and apparel to the United States.

Export Incentives

Export incentives are offered by the U.S. government under various programs, primarily by the Department of Commerce, the Department of Defense, and the Department of Agriculture. The Department of Defense offers incentives, such as export credit and information, for exports of military equipment and armaments. The Department of Agriculture has a similar program for agricultural products. The Department of Agriculture's Commodity Credit Corporation (CCC) administers export sales and donations of U.S. agricultural commodities and provides export guarantees to foreign buyers.

Export credit insurance is available from the Foreign Credit Insurance Association (FCIA). Export credit is also available from the Eximbank. The Foreign Sales Corporation (FSC) offers tax incentives to certain export companies.

From 1971 to 1984 the government allowed companies to defer income tax on about 50% of the income from U.S.-sourced exports if revenues were channeled through a Domestic International Sales Corporation (DISC). More than 8,000 DISCs have been set up. A typical DISC is a subsidiary of a U.S. manufacturing corporation.

On January 1, 1985, the Foreign Sales Corporation (FSC) replaced the DISC as the primary tax incentive for exporting U.S. goods. To qualify, the FSC must be incorporated and maintain an office in the United States, in a U.S. possession (possessions for this purpose include Guam, American Samoa, the Commonwealth of Northern Mariana Islands, and the U.S. Virgin Islands, but exclude Puerto Rico), or in a foreign country with an IRS-approved program for the exchange of tax information with the United States. Some additional requirements include the nomination of a resident director and maintenance of separate books. The FSC benefits from an approximate 15 percent permanent income tax exemption.

The Export Trading Company Act of 1982 allows banks to invest in export trading companies (ETCs) for the purpose of U.S. export promotion. While a large number of ETCs were established, their success was quite limited.

The U.S. International Cooperation and Development Agency (ICDA) can help U.S. exporters establish and expand their markets overseas through three institutions: (1) the Overseas Private Investment Corp (OPIC), which functions as an insurer of U.S. direct investments abroad; (2) the Agency for International Development (AID) and its Bureau for Private Enterprise, which deals with small-scale investments in developing countries; and (3) the Trade Development Program (TDP), which offers project planning services to those selling U.S. technology for project implementation.

Export credit insurance is available through the FCIA, which is reinsured and guaranteed by the Export-Import Bank. Coverage is generally for political losses and commercial losses on foreign credit.

Eximbank and OPIC provide export, credit, and investment guarantees. OPIC provides insurance against loss caused by such operating risks as currency inconvertibility; expropriation; and war, revolution, or insurrection. OPIC also guarantees private U.S. loan investments against nonpayment by the borrower.

Export credit is also available through commercial banks, and specialized financial institutions.

Foreign Trade Zones

There are over sixty free-trade zones in major ports of entry throughout the United States. These zones provide corporations with manufacturing and warehouse facilities free of customs duties and quotas. Foreign trade zones are used by importers and exporters to warehouse, exhibit, package, label, sort, and manufacture goods. Many zones have industrial subzones in which specialized manufacturing operations are performed.

Duties are paid only on items imported into the U.S. domestic market from the zone. Many of the newest zones are located in industrial parks, which offer the greatest opportunities for using zone benefits. When merchandise enters U.S. territory, the customs appraisal excludes profit and the costs of processing—such as U.S. labor, overhead, and facilities when—determining the duty value of imported goods.

Foreign trade zones are operated by private and public corporations under grants from the Foreign Trade Zones Board. Applications to manufacture in these zones must show that an operation is in the public interest and will have a positive impact on the U.S. balance of payments. (Appendix B describes individual free-trade zones.)

5
Labor and Industrial Relations

L abor and industrial relations have been relatively peaceful in the United States, compared with those in the United Kingdom, Italy, and Canada.

A full 96.8% of the employed labor force in 1984 was in nonagricultural sectors. Only 3.2 million workers, or 2.9%, were in the farm sector. Wage and salary workers in nonagricultural establishments amounted to about 94 million people. Of this total, 19.6 million were employed in the manufacturing sector; about 1.0 million in mining; 4.3 million in construction; 5.1 million in transportation; 21.8 million in wholesale and retail trade; 5.7 million in finance, insurance and real estate, 20.7 million in services; and 16 million in government.

U.S. labor is highly qualified and mobile, and it is composed of skilled, semiskilled, technical, and professional workers. The labor force is distinguished by its academic education and vocational training in the latest technology. Almost 75% of the workers have a high-school education. Approximately 30% of the adult population continues its education at a college or university after high-school graduation. Low growth in the population and labor force, along with general social preferences for white-collar or service work, may induce spot shortages of skilled labor in the manufacturing area. Because wage rates have risen slowly and productivity has improved, the United States has increased its international competitiveness.

An investor should consider the local labor structure when acquiring an existing business or establishing a new one. Some states have weak labor unions or nonunionized workers. Most foreign firms follow local labor practices.

Labor compensation is characterized by a reliance on direct salaries rather than fringe benefits. Because of rising wages and salaries, improved pensions and health-insurance benefits, labor costs have increased substantially. Fringe benefits, for instance, average about

27-30% of total compensation. Hourly compensation and international comparisons for some private nonagricultural industries are listed in tables 5-1, 5-2, 5-3, and 5-4, and in Appendix C, Average Hours and Earnings of Production Workers by State.

U.S. wage scales have traditionally been high, and they have continued to climb substantially in this inflationary era. However, wages in many other countries have risen more steeply. When compensation is measured in U.S. dollars and the effect of the exchange rate is considered, the wage gap is particularly wide when compared with Japan and the LDCs. But U.S. wages are only slightly higher than those of the major countries of Western Europe, where costly fringe benefits are included in any wage contract.

When expressed in U.S. dollars, the cost of production workers is largely affected by prevailing exchange rates. Accordingly, compensation and unit labor costs expressed in U.S. dollars have increased significantly since 1980 in comparison with other industrial countries. Such an increase has been caused by the dollar's sharp appreciation. As the dollar depreciates, the trend in labor costs will reverse, thereby making U.S. labor more competitive internationally.

Labor Law and Organization

Relations between employers and employees are addressed in several federal statutes, ensuring that certain regulations are observed to some extent in all fifty states. Although there is a certain uniformity to labor laws in the various states, disparities exist because of different political and economic environments, the relative strength of organized labor, and the degree of industrialization.

The National Labor Relations Act (NLRA) of 1935 and the National Labor Relations Board (NLRB), which administers and enforces the Act, were designed to define and protect the rights of employers and employees and to help avoid industrial strife. The NLRB conducts representation elections, certifies their results, and prevents employers and unions from engaging in unfair labor practices. Under the law, employees have the right to organize themselves and to join labor organizations, to bargain collectively through their representatives, and to strike. While the law guarantees the right of employees to strike, it places limitations and qualifications on exercising that right. The lawfulness of a strike depends on its purpose and timing, and its legality is often decided by the National Labor Relations Board. To avoid crippling strikes in essential sectors, the NLRA established mechanisms for strike resolution.

Table 5-1
Hourly Compensation Costs for Production Workers: All Manufacturing, 1984

Country or Area	Exchange Rate[a]		Average Hourly Earnings in National Currency	Ratio of Additional Compensation to Hourly Earnings	Hourly Compensation		
	National Currency Unit	National Currency Units per U.S. Dollar			National Currency	U.S. Dollars	Index U.S. = 100
United States	dollar	—	9.17	39.8	12.82	12.82	100
Canada	dollar	1.295	11.59	28.6	14.90	11.51	90
Brazil	cruzeiro	1847	1609	37.7	2216	1.20	9
Mexico[b]	peso	192.3	222.46	44.9	322.34	1.68	13
Japan	yen	237.4	1302	17.1	1525	6.42	50
Korea	non	806.0	907	15–20	1066	1.32	10
Taiwan	dollar	39.69	64.13	15–20	75.35	1.90	15
Austria	shilling	20.00	70.38	86.1	130.98	6.55	51
Belgium	franc	57.75	282.76	82.0	514.62	8.91	70
Denmark	krone	10.35	66.40	20.6	80.08	7.74	60
France	franc	8.736	35.29	79.0	63.17	7.23	56
Germany	mark	2.845	15.49	75.8	27.23	9.57	75
Ireland	pound	.9205	3.80	31.6	5.00	5.43	42
Italy	lira	1761	7007	86.8	13089	7.43	58
Netherlands	guilder	3.208	16.31	69.2	27.60	8.60	67
Spain	peseta	160.8	545	40	763	4.75	37
Sweden	krona	8.271	46.29	64.4	76.10	9.20	72
United Kingdom	pound	.7482	3.33	33.6	4.45	5.95	46

Source: U.S. Department of Labor, Bureau of Labor Statistics, Office of Productivity and Technology, Dec. 1984.
[a]Preliminary annual average; Taiwan, January–September average.
[b]Average of selected manufacturing industries.

Table 5-2
Hourly Compensation in Manufacturing, National Currency Basis
(Indexes: 1977 = 100)

Year[a]	United States	Canada	Japan	Belgium	Denmark	France	Germany	Italy	Netherlands	Norway	Sweden	United Kingdom
1960	36.7	27.1	8.9	13.9	12.6	15.1	18.8	8.3	12.2	15.8	14.7	14.9
1961	37.7	27.8	10.4	14.7	14.1	16.7	21.1	9.2	13.9	17.3	16.1	15.9
1962	39.2	28.6	11.8	15.8	15.5	18.4	23.9	10.9	14.8	19.0	18.0	16.7
1963	40.3	29.6	13.2	17.5	16.8	20.1	25.5	12.9	16.3	19.9	19.9	17.5
1964	42.0	30.8	14.9	19.5	18.2	21.8	27.6	14.4	18.9	21.3	21.7	18.7
1965	42.8	32.3	16.7	21.6	20.2	23.7	30.3	15.4	21.2	23.3	23.9	20.5
1966	44.8	34.8	18.5	24.0	22.9	25.1	32.9	16.1	23.8	25.3	26.2	22.2
1967	47.0	37.5	20.7	26.2	25.7	27.0	34.7	17.9	26.3	28.4	29.1	22.9
1968	50.4	40.2	24.1	28.0	28.3	30.5	37.3	19.1	29.4	31.1	31.5	24.5
1969	53.9	43.3	28.5	30.7	31.8	32.5	40.9	21.8	33.3	34.3	34.3	26.7
1970	57.6	46.5	33.9	34.7	36.3	36.5	48.1	26.1	38.5	37.9	38.5	30.9
1971	61.1	50.1	39.3	39.8	41.8	41.3	53.8	30.2	44.0	43.3	43.3	35.7
1972	64.4	53.7	45.4	46.2	46.2	45.4	59.8	34.6	50.5	48.2	48.4	40.2
1973	69.0	59.2	55.7	53.6	56.1	52.1	67.6	43.7	60.1	54.6	54.2	45.0
1974	76.4	68.5	73.0	65.4	67.9	61.9	77.1	54.5	71.7	63.7	63.8	57.2
1975	85.5	78.2	85.4	79.0	81.0	76.6	84.8	70.2	81.9	77.2	77.3	75.1
1976	92.3	89.9	91.1	89.4	90.4	88.8	91.4	84.1	92.1	88.9	91.5	88.9
1977	100.0	100.0	100.0	100.0	100.0	100.0	100.0	100.0	100.0	100.0	100.0	100.0
1978	108.3	106.7	105.9	107.9	110.2	113.7	107.7	114.5	108.7	110.0	111.4	116.8
1979	118.8	118.3	112.8	117.5	123.2	129.7	115.4	134.7	117.3	116.0	120.1	137.1
1980	132.7	130.6	121.2	130.2	140.6	148.1	125.0	160.2	123.5	128.0	133.6	162.8
1981	145.2	151.5	130.2	144.7	155.5	171.7	133.8	197.1	130.3	142.8	148.1	185.4
1982	158.0	167.2	136.8	152.9	172.1	202.4	141.0	236.1	139.4	158.8	158.9	201.6
1983	163.4	178.5	140.7	163.9	181.4	228.4	146.1	277.8	147.3	172.5	173.2	216.4

Source: U.S. Department of Labor, Bureau of Labor Statistics, Office of Productivity and Technology, December 1984.

Note: The data relate to all employed persons (wage and salary earners, the self-employed, and unpaid family workers) in the United States and Canada, and all employees (wage and salary earners) in the other countries.

[a]Preliminary estimates for latest year.

Table 5-3
Hourly Compensation in Manufacturing, U.S. Dollar Basis, Competitors Indexes
(Indexes: 1977 = 100)

Year[a]	United States	Canada	Japan	Belgium	Denmark	France	Germany	Italy	Netherlands	Norway	Sweden	United Kingdom
1960	13.7	27.9	19.2	12.8	14.1	13.8	15.0	13.9	13.7	13.6	15.0	14.6
1961	15.0	29.3	20.8	14.5	15.6	15.4	16.4	15.5	15.2	15.1	16.6	16.1
1962	16.3	31.0	22.4	16.1	17.2	17.0	18.0	17.1	16.8	16.6	18.1	17.7
1963	17.6	32.3	23.9	17.4	18.6	18.4	19.5	18.3	18.1	17.9	19.5	19.1
1964	19.2	34.0	25.6	19.0	20.2	20.0	21.3	19.8	19.7	19.5	21.0	20.8
1965	20.9	35.4	27.3	20.8	22.0	21.7	23.1	21.6	21.4	21.2	22.8	22.4
1966	22.6	37.3	29.1	22.3	23.7	23.4	24.8	23.3	23.0	23.1	24.6	24.0
1967	24.4	39.4	31.0	23.9	25.5	25.1	26.8	24.8	24.6	24.9	26.3	25.9
1968	26.3	42.2	33.0	25.8	27.2	26.7	28.8	26.7	26.4	26.6	28.0	28.3
1969	29.1	45.6	35.7	28.2	29.9	29.8	31.5	29.4	28.9	29.4	30.8	31.0
1970	33.7	49.8	40.4	32.9	34.6	35.1	35.3	34.3	33.7	34.0	35.6	35.5
1971	39.1	54.1	45.4	38.2	39.9	40.6	40.5	39.5	38.8	39.2	41.0	40.4
1972	47.0	59.1	52.0	45.9	47.5	48.3	48.2	47.0	46.5	46.9	48.4	47.8
1973	59.0	66.2	62.3	59.3	59.3	60.7	59.7	59.5	59.2	58.9	60.3	60.1
1974	69.4	74.4	71.3	68.6	69.2	70.8	69.0	69.5	68.7	69.1	70.3	69.2
1975	83.6	85.1	85.5	84.6	84.5	84.3	85.9	83.1	83.7	84.0	84.6	83.3
1976	88.8	91.1	89.9	87.8	88.5	87.5	89.2	87.4	87.5	88.7	88.3	88.2
1977	100.0	100.0	100.0	100.0	100.0	100.0	100.0	100.0	100.0	100.0	100.0	100.0
1978	120.4	112.1	116.8	123.4	121.0	121.7	121.0	122.5	122.6	121.4	121.4	119.5
1979	137.7	124.6	135.2	145.3	140.3	140.6	140.3	141.3	142.8	139.5	140.4	135.8
1980	154.2	139.6	153.3	163.6	159.2	157.9	159.4	158.1	160.8	156.7	158.4	150.2
1981	150.4	147.7	149.2	149.6	151.3	150.5	153.9	149.8	150.4	150.6	152.4	144.2
1982	146.8	155.5	150.2	146.3	145.9	147.6	149.9	146.2	145.6	144.2	150.1	142.7
1983	148.1	159.0	149.7	144.5	143.2	147.9	149.4	145.3	144.0	142.1	150.0	143.5

Source: U.S. Department of Labor, Bureau of Labor Statistics, Office of Productivity and Technology, December 1984.

Note: Competitors indexes are a geometric average.

The data relate to all employed persons (wage and salary earners, the self-employed, and unpaid family workers) in the United States and Canada, and all employees (wage and salary earners) in the other countries.

[a]Preliminary estimates for latest year.

Table 5-4
Output per Hour in Manufacturing, Competitors Indexes
(Indexes: 1977 = 100)

Year[a]	United States	Canada	Japan	Belgium	Denmark	France	Germany	Italy	Netherlands	Norway	Sweden	United Kingdom
1960	37.7	53.3	46.6	38.7	41.1	40.3	39.2	40.0	39.7	38.8	41.0	39.9
1961	40.0	55.2	48.4	40.8	43.1	42.4	41.2	42.0	41.7	41.0	43.1	42.1
1962	42.1	57.7	50.9	43.1	45.3	44.8	43.4	44.1	44.0	43.1	45.3	44.4
1963	44.2	61.6	53.7	45.2	47.7	47.1	45.7	46.5	46.2	45.5	47.6	46.8
1964	47.7	65.1	57.1	48.8	51.4	50.7	49.0	50.3	49.8	49.2	51.2	50.4
1965	50.3	67.5	60.0	51.8	54.2	53.6	51.8	52.8	52.6	51.8	53.9	53.2
1966	53.2	69.0	62.2	54.6	56.8	56.1	54.8	55.4	55.2	54.5	56.5	55.8
1967	56.9	70.3	64.6	58.0	60.4	59.5	58.0	58.8	58.6	58.4	59.8	59.0
1968	62.1	73.7	69.0	63.2	65.4	64.2	63.0	63.6	63.5	63.5	64.5	63.7
1969	66.8	76.0	72.2	67.4	69.7	68.5	67.2	67.8	67.7	67.9	68.5	68.0
1970	70.4	76.9	74.2	70.6	72.7	71.5	70.8	70.9	70.7	71.4	71.5	71.1
1971	74.2	81.4	78.0	74.0	76.2	74.9	74.6	74.4	74.2	75.1	75.1	74.7
1972	79.6	86.1	83.0	79.1	81.6	80.5	80.1	79.8	79.6	80.6	80.6	80.0
1973	85.8	91.2	88.6	84.9	87.5	86.8	86.5	85.4	85.3	86.7	86.5	86.0
1974	88.9	90.4	90.2	88.2	90.3	89.4	89.1	88.0	88.0	89.4	88.8	88.2
1975	89.7	92.7	91.7	89.8	91.7	90.6	90.3	90.2	90.2	91.4	90.6	90.3
1976	96.3	97.4	97.3	96.5	97.4	97.0	96.8	96.4	96.5	97.1	96.7	96.5
1977	100.0	100.0	100.0	100.0	100.0	100.0	100.0	100.0	100.0	100.0	100.0	100.0
1978	103.9	101.7	102.5	103.8	103.3	103.2	104.1	103.5	103.6	103.6	103.3	103.6
1979	108.9	103.4	105.7	108.5	108.0	107.7	108.7	107.8	108.1	108.6	107.4	108.3
1980	111.3	104.3	106.8	110.5	110.0	110.3	111.7	109.9	110.4	111.4	109.6	111.1
1981	115.1	107.7	110.1	113.8	113.4	114.1	115.9	113.5	114.0	115.2	113.5	114.5
1982	118.3	110.4	112.9	117.4	117.1	117.3	120.6	117.0	117.7	119.0	116.9	118.1
1983	124.6	115.4	118.3	123.4	123.4	122.8	126.6	123.0	123.6	125.4	122.5	123.7

Source: U.S. Department of Labor, Bureau of Labor Statistics, Office of Productivity and Technology, December 1984.

Note: Competitors indexes are a geometric average.

The data relate to all employed persons (wage and salary earners, the self-employed, and unpaid family workers) in the United States and Canada, and all employees (wage and salary earners) in the other countries.

[a]Preliminary estimates for latest year.

A presidential emergency board may be appointed to prevent a strike if it threatens to substantially interrupt state commerce.

Collective bargaining is a keystone of the Act and is usually governed by it, and is administered by the National Labor Relations Board. The law requires that the employees' representative and their employer discuss and negotiate, in good faith, issues concerning wages and other conditions of employment. Any agreement must be put into writing if requested by either party. It is unfair labor practice for either party to refuse to bargain collectively with the other.

The Fair Labor Standards Act of 1938 (FLSA), also known as the Wage and Hour Law, is administered by the U.S. Department of Labor's Wage and Hour Division. The act regulates minimum wage, overtime pay, and child labor. It also requires equal pay for the same work, regardless of sex. The act applies to all employees of large enterprises engaged in interstate or foreign commerce. State governments have also enacted minimum wage regulations.

The Department of Labor's Labor–Management Services Administration works with state and local governments in providing assistance to employers and unions in solving problems. The Employment Standards Administration handles employment programs concerning minimum wage and overtime standards and determines wage rates to be paid on government contracts. The agency also monitors nondiscrimination and affirmative action programs.

The Equal Employment Opportunity Commission (EEOC) was created to eliminate discrimination based on race, color, religion, sex, national origin, and age in hiring, promoting, firing, testing, training, and paying of employees. The commission is responsible for all compliance and enforcement activities that relate to discrimination connected with employment. Employers of 100 or more people are subject to the EEOC.

The Occupational Safety and Health Act (OSHA) of 1970 is a labor-standards law designed to ensure that employees have safe and healthful working conditions. This act gives the U.S. Secretary of Labor the authority to promulgate occupational safety and health standards applicable to most businesses.

Social Security

Social Security was established by the Federal Insurance Contributions Act in 1935 to alleviate financial hardships caused by retirement, disability, or death of a wage earner. The Social Security program is administered by the Social Security Administration. It is self-financed by taxes levied at equal rates on both employers and employees for the future benefit of employees. Eligibility for retirement (old-age) benefits is based on a retiree's age and the length of time he or she has contributed to Social Security. The required employer contribution to Social Security, which includes old-age and survivor pensions as well as Medicare, is now 7%, applied to a maximum $37,800 of earnings.

The unemployment insurance program is jointly administered by state agencies and the U.S. Department of Labor through the Unemployment Insurance Service under the Social Security Act and the Federal Unemployment Act of 1935. The U.S. Department of Labor assists state employment security agencies in developing and operating the joint federal–state unemployment insurance program and related wage and lost income maintenance programs.

Unemployment insurance contributions vary from state to state and are based on the "experience rating" of employers. Lower rates are charged to employers whose benefit claims from former employees have been low. This practice discourages employers from hiring seasonal employees who will then be subsidized by unemployment insurance.

Unemployment benefits are not granted to former agricultural and domestic workers, those dismissed from work because of misconduct, those who stopped working without a justifiable reason, and those unable or unwilling to work. Benefit payments vary by state, but the majority of states determine size and duration of benefit based on a person's past employment record and salary.

Workers compensation benefits are designed to protect wage earners who are injured, become ill, or die in the course of or because of their employment by providing them or their dependents with financial assistance. This program is entirely a state responsibility. In more than half the states, small employers are not required to contribute to workers compensation. In some states contributions are noncompulsory for employers, although most companies find it advantageous to contribute.

Labor Unions

The relative power of the various national and local unions varies substantially. Union membership has been declining in recent years and is concentrated in the manufacturing, transportation, and service industries. The AFL–CIO, the principal labor federation in the U.S., was established in December 1955 through a merger of the American Federation of Labor and the Congress of Industrial

Organizations. This federation is composed of 106 national and international labor unions in the United States. It represents most American labor unions whose membership is about 15 million. The total labor force in the United States is 115 million people. The largest nonaffiliated unions are the Teamsters, the United Auto Workers, and the United Mine Workers.

Each member union of the AFL–CIO remains autonomous, and its affairs are conducted in a manner determined by its own members. AFL–CIO operations are financed primarily through regular dues, known as per capita taxes. These dues are about $2 per member per year, and they are paid by the affiliates on behalf of each member. The AFL–CIO is not affiliated with a political party, which is in sharp contrast with European labor unions, but it does conduct lobbying activities in Congress.

The AFL–CIO's 106 affiliated unions have more than 60,000 local unions, through which day-to-day business is conducted with several hundred thousand employers. The National Labor Relations Act bans the closed shop, which allows only union members to be hired. The act allows the union shop agreement in labor contracts, but requires all workers to become members of the union after being hired. Generally, a union shop arrangement determines whether labor union membership is a precondition for hiring or employment in a unionized plant. Union shop agreements are illegal in twenty southern states which have enacted right-to-work legislation.

Collective bargaining on behalf of their employers is the most significant activity of the local unions. Collective bargaining is conducted on a plant-by-plant or company-by-company basis, with the exception of the steel, glass, coal, and railroad industries. Most contracts contain a no-strike, no-lockout clause for the term of the agreement. The unions play a key role in determining wages and employment conditions for their members and for the rest of the economy. Specific provisions, such as those concerning union shops, overtime pay, strike procedures, and fringe benefits, affect the cost and productivity of labor-union contracts.

About 98% of all negotiated contracts run their course of two to three years without a strike or other work interruption. The majority of strikes usually coincide with the expiration date of a contract and are part of the bargaining process.

Working Conditions and Labor Cost

The typical workweek in manufacturing is 40 hours; in offices, 35 hours. Usual work hours during the five workdays are 7 or 8 A.M.

to 3:30 or 4:30 P.M. with a half-hour lunch break in factories; 8 or 9 A.M. to 4 or 5 P.M., with an hour lunch break in offices.

The legal minimum wage under the Fair Labor Standards Act is $3.35 per hour for all workers. However, actual wages are usually much above the minimum. Average hourly earnings for workers in manufacturing are listed in appendix C. Wage levels tend to be highest in the West and lowest in the South. Employees other than those on supervisory and administrative staffs must be paid at least 150% of their regular rate of pay for all hours over 40 in a work week.

The general retirement age is 65, but early retirement after age 62 is common, and working until age 70 is allowed by law. Some union contracts allow retirement after 20 to 30 years of employment. Company-paid pension plans are often provided under labor contracts, and can range from about 7% to 12% of the annual payroll.

There are eight or nine annual public holidays, usually with pay. Paid annual vacations are customary. Vacation time is generally one or two weeks after one year of service, increasing to three weeks after five or ten years and four after twenty years.

Dismissal is not regulated by the federal government, but notification and compensation procedures are defined in private collective agreements or in wage contracts. For employees not so covered, two or more weeks notice of dismissal and some severance pay is customary.

In conclusion, the United States has a highly trained and dedicated labor force. Peaceful labor-industrial relations improved productivity, and a lower dollar exchange rate have reduced the effective labor cost in the United States.

6
U.S. Energy

Energy Demand, Imports, and Efficiency

The U.S. energy situation has improved substantially in the past few years. Energy efficiency has increased, more domestic energy resources are being developed, dependence on foreign energy sources has declined, and vulnerability to supply disruption has been reduced. However, oil imports in 1983 cost over $53 billion, accounting for about 21% of total merchandise imports in the United States. By comparison, in 1973 oil imports cost $8 billion and accounted for 10% of total imports.

Domestic energy consumption has declined and has become more efficient. U.S. energy demand expanded by 4.1% per year from 1960 to 1973, then slowed sharply to 0.3% from 1973 to 1983 (see tables 6-1 and 6-2). The ratio of total primary energy to GDP, an energy efficiency indicator, declined from 1.12 in 1973 to 0.92 in 1983. During the same period, Europe's ratio went from 0.71 to 0.60, and Japan from 0.69 to 0.48. The United States seems to have gained most in achieving energy efficiency and the outlook suggests further improvements.

U.S. National Energy Policy

A National Energy Policy was originally formulated by the Carter administration in 1979 and partially implemented during 1980. The Reagan administration has reformulated U.S. energy policy, based on free-market principles, within the context of its overall economic program. President Reagan's National Energy Policy establishes several basic objectives:

1. To provide an adequate supply of energy at reasonable cost

Table 6-1
U.S. Energy Supply and Demand
(Mtoe)

	1973	1981	1982	1985	1990	2000
			1. GENERAL			
Energy Demand (TPER)	1741.7	1822.0	1750.1	1894.0	2008.0	2167.0
Energy Production	1465.1	1614.3	1599.3	1654.0	1759.0	1985.0
Production/TPER	0.84	0.89	0.91	0.87	0.88	0.92
Net Oil Imports	298.9	283.5	229.8	303.0	294.0	261.0
Total Oil Requirements	770.2	732.5	702.0	726.0	719.0	648.0
TPER/GDP Ratio	1.12	0.97	0.96	0.92	0.85	0.72
Per Capita TPER	8.22	7.93	7.54	7.92	7.91	8.09
Oil Requirements/GDP	0.49	0.39	0.38	0.35	0.30	0.22
Oil Requirements/TPER	0.44	0.40	0.40	0.38	0.36	0.30
			2. SUPPLY			
PRODUCTION						
Solid Fuels	381.4	545.0	552.1	564.0	642.0	875.0
Oil	486.6	485.1	486.4	458.0	446.0	408.0
Gas	514.5	459.5	422.9	435.0	419.0	375.0
Nuclear	19.9	64.6	67.0	116.0	164.0	199.0
Hydro/Geothermal	62.7	60.2	70.9	81.0	86.0	103.0
Other [1]	-	-	-	-	2.0	25.0
Electricity (tWh)	2086.9	2437.0	2419.4	2630.0	2950.0	3670.0
TRADE						
Coal Exports	- 32.3	- 73.6	- 69.5	- 65.0	- 77.0	- 127.0
Imports	.7	1.0	0.6	1.0	1.0	1.0
Oil Exports	- 12.5	- 19.8	- 32.8	- 30.0	- 30.0	- 30.0
Imports	311.3	303.3	262.6	333.0	324.0	291.0
Bunkers	- 9.2	- 25.2	- 20.3	- 21.0	- 21.0	- 21.0
Gas Exports	- 1.8	- 1.4	- 1.4	- 2.0	- 2.0	- 2.0
Imports	24.5	21.5	23.0	36.0	52.0	68.0
			3. DEMAND			
TFC	1326.7	1328.8	1266.5	1340.0	1392.0	1431.0
Share of TFC (%):						
Oil	52.2	51.1	51.7	48.5	47.1	42.7
Solid fuels	9.8	10.2	9.9	10.5	10.9	12.8
Gas	27.2	25.3	24.7	25.4	25.2	24.1
Electricity	10.8	13.4	13.7	15.6	16.9	20.4
Heat	-	-	-	-	-	-
Other [1]	-	-	-	-	-	-
END USE BY SECTOR:						
INDUSTRY [2]						
Total	481.3	451.3	393.5	485.0	531.0	561.0
Oil	127.0	126.9	114.5	131.0	155.0	130.0

Table 6-1   *(continued)*

	1973	1981	1982	1985	1990	2000
Solid Fuels	115.5	109.4	97.8	117.0	126.0	148.0
Gas	183.2	153.7	126.6	156.0	162.0	165.0
Electricity	55.5	61.4	54.5	81.0	88.0	118.0
Heat	-	-	-	-	-	-
Other [1]	-	-	-	-	-	-
OTHER SECTORS [3]						
Total	436.8	443.8	445.1	438.0	463.0	467.0
Oil	157.0	118.2	113.0	102.0	102.0	81.0
Solid Fuels	14.5	25.8	27.0	24.0	25.0	35.0
Gas	177.8	182.9	186.4	184.0	189.0	180.0
Electricity	87.5	116.8	118.7	128.0	147.0	171.0
Heat	-	-	-	-	-	-
Other [1]	-	-	-	-	-	-
TRANSPORT						
Oil	408.2	433.3	427.7	417.0	398.0	400.0
Total	408.6	433.6	428.0	417.0	398.0	403.0
ELECTRICITY GENERATION [4]	474.1	601.3	591.4	684.0	772.0	951.0
Oil	84.2	50.7	36.1	56.0	49.0	32.0
Solid Fuels	221.7	339.5	340.8	356.0	412.0	554.0
Gas	85.6	86.4	76.7	75.0	61.0	42.0
Nuclear	19.9	64.4	67.0	116.0	164.0	199.0
Hydro/Geothermal	62.7	60.2	70.9	81.0	86.0	103.0
Other [1]	-	-	-	-	-	21.0

4. REFERENCE ITEMS

	1973	1981	1982	1985	1990	2000
GDP (1975 US$ billion)	1559.8	1870.4	1826.3	2048.4	2363.2	2995.7
Population (million)	211.9	229.9	232.1	239.0	254.0	268.0

5. GROWTH RATES [5]

	1973-81	1981-82	1982-85	1985-90	1990-2000
TPER	0.6	-3.9	2.7	1.2	0.8
GDP	2.3	-2.4	3.9	2.9	2.4
TFC	0	-4.7	1.9	0.8	0.3
TPER/GDP Ratio	-1.7	-1.6	-1.2	-1.7	-1.6
Elasticity [6]	0.25	1.67	0.68	0.41	0.32
Energy Production	1.2	-0.9	1.1	1.2	1.2
Net Oil Imports	-0.7	-19.0	9.7	-0.6	-1.2
Oil Requirements	-0.6	-4.2	1.1	-0.2	-1.0

1. Data for other energy sources (solar, wind, tidal, etc.) are shown for forecast years only.
2. Includes non-energy use.
3. Includes residential, commercial, public and agricultural sectors.
4. Fuel inputs.
5. Percent per year.
6. TPER growth rate divided by GDP growth rate.

Source: International Energy Agency, *Energy Policies and Programmes of IEA Countries, 1983 Review* (Paris: OECD, 1984), p. 479.

Table 6-2
Historical Energy and Oil Requirements per Unit of GDP

	1973	1980	1981	1982	1983 [1]	Average Annual Growth Rate (%)			
						1973-80	1980-81	1981-82	1982-83
TPER/GDP [2]									
IEA Total	0.90	0.81	0.78	0.76	0.74	-1.4	-4.3	-2.4	-2.8
North America	1.12	1.04	0.99	0.97	0.94	-1.1	-5.1	-1.4	-3.8
Europe	0.71	0.63	0.61	0.60	0.59	-1.7	-2.9	-2.2	-0.8
Pacific	0.69	0.59	0.56	0.54	0.52	-2.2	-5.4	-3.9	-4.4
TFC/GDP									
IEA Total	0.67	0.58	0.56	0.54	0.52	-2.0	-4.5	-3.2	-2.8
North America	0.85	0.75	0.71	0.70	0.67	-1.7	-4.9	-2.3	-3.8
Europe	0.53	0.46	0.44	0.43	0.43	-2.2	-3.5	-2.9	-0.8
Pacific	0.50	0.40	0.38	0.36	0.35	-2.9	-6.5	-4.3	-4.4
Oil/GDP [2]									
IEA Total	0.46	0.38	0.35	0.33	0.32	-2.8	-8.6	-3.8	-4.0
North America	0.50	0.43	0.39	0.39	0.37	-1.9	-9.3	-2.2	-4.5
Europe	0.41	0.32	0.30	0.28	0.27	-3.4	-7.5	-4.2	-3.3
Pacific	0.49	0.36	0.33	0.31	0.29	-4.1	-9.5	-6.7	-4.6

1. IEA Secretariat estimate.
2. Measured in toe per US$ 1000 of GDP at 1975 prices and exchange rates.

Source: International Energy Agency, *Energy Policies and Programmes of IEA Countries, 1983 Review* (Paris: OECD, 1984), p. 24.

2. to reduce U.S. dependence on foreign oil, thereby diminishing the economic and political cost of oil-import dependence

3. to develop domestic energy substitutes and renewable supplies.

These objectives are to be achieved through minimized federal control and involvement in energy markets as well as through promotion of a balanced and mixed energy resource system. Energy policies were designed to reduce energy consumption through decontrol of domestic energy prices; increased conservation; and an increased domestic supply of energy through increased production of domestic oil, natural gas, and coal. Energy policies also promoted rapid development of alternative energy supplies, including synthetic fuel, coal, shale oil, and solar energy.

Decontrol of U.S. oil prices, which began in mid-1979 and was completed by President Reagan's executive order on January 28, 1981, was designed to encourage conservation and domestic production. Decontrol was meant to improve the balance of payments and reduce vulnerability to possible oil market disruptions. Decontrol has increased the price of domestically produced oil to the world market price level. The Natural Gas Policy Act of 1978 and the Natural Gas Consumer Regulatory Reform Amendment of 1983 provide for an increase in natural gas wellhead prices and deregulation of some post-1977 gas by 1985.

Three energy programs of particular importance are concerned with conservation, research and development, and energy security. The Reagan administration places a high priority on legislation designed to remove controls on natural gas wellhead prices and legislation reforming the nuclear licensing and regulatory process.

Energy conservation efforts have been successful to date. Evidence shows that since the Arab oil embargo, energy use per dollar of GNP has declined steadily. Oil imports now constitute about 28% of total oil consumption, down from 46% in 1977. Yet there is still great dependence on international supply and, consequently, vulnerability to world market shocks.

The Synthetic Fuels Program

The United States has enormous hydrocarbon resources in the form of coal, oil shale, tar sands, and heavy oil. Existing processes can extract those resources and transform them into synthetic substitutes for conventional oil and gas. Improved processes are also being developed. However, since world conditions have changed and projections suggest no shortages or large price increases, incentives for these projects have diminished.

The Reagan administration was initially committed to development of a commercial synthetic-fuel industry, whose product will be price competitive and capable of replacing imported oil. However, the oil glut reduced significantly the economic feasibility of this program. As part of the general effort to employ market forces instead of bureaucratically administered programs, greater emphasis is now being placed on the private sector in meeting this task. Accordingly, the private sector is expected to devote more of its own financial resources to such projects. Decontrol of conventional fuel prices, revitalization of the economy, and removal of regulatory uncertainties will improve the growth climate for synthetic fuels.

The synthetic energy program has been restructured. Commercialization and demonstration activities have been removed from the Department of Energy and given to the Synthetic Fuels Corporation. The Department of Energy will, however, continue to support the long-range, high-risk research and development that the private sector has traditionally stayed away from. This restructuring in responsibilities was designed to eliminate duplicate programs at the Department of Energy and to reduce future risks of a budget burden.

As a result of this change, arrangements for direct government funding of coal liquefaction and gasification projects will be terminated. Projects selected by the Department of Energy for feasibility studies, cooperative agreements, and loan guarantee awards will not be funded.

The synthetic fuels program is to be helped by revenues from the windfall profits tax. Passed on March 27, 1980, the windfall profits tax recoups a portion of the profits oil companies receive under domestic oil and gas decontrol. Revenues are placed in the Energy Security Corporation (ESC) for use in developing energy sources, improving mass transit, and assisting low-income families adversely affected by high energy costs. The ESC can also provide financial assistance for private synthetic fuel projects and participate in joint ventures with private companies.

Renewable Sources

Renewable energy sources include solar, wind, ocean systems, biomass, and urban wastes. Technologies that convert renewable resources into usable energy offer great potential for helping to meet power demand. Development of these sources is, in the main, undertaken by the private sector. However, direct and indirect government assistance is provided through several channels: (1) decontrol of domestic oil and gas prices, which enhances the competitive position of renewable fuels, (2) tax credits, and (3) government research and development.

The Reagan administration has terminated feasibility studies, cooperative agreements, and loan guarantees for alcohol fuels and biomass energy development as part of its general effort to adopt market principles to achieve national energy goals. The change in the government's budget policy reduces the level of subsidies for alcohol fuels and biomass programs, but tax credits will continue. In the case of alcohol fuels, these credits will result in a subsidy of more than $18 per barrel. The administration has also proposed a reduction in government subsidies to programs in geothermal, energy storage, electric energy systems, energy impact assistance, environmental studies, uranium resource assessments, and hydropower. The Energy Mobilization Board is charged with expediting the establishment of high-priority energy projects by cutting red tape. Through tax credits and other incentives for shale oil and solar energy, the Board will accelerate development of new energy sources. The goal is to get one-fifth of U.S. energy from the sun and other renewable energy sources by the year 2000.

The Reagan administration eliminated the Solar Energy and Energy Conservation bank, primarily intended to promote residential energy conservation and solar technology investments through subsidies. The government maintains that substantial economic incentives already exist for such investments. These incentives include rising energy prices and significant tax credits for residential energy conservation improvements and solar technology measures.

The market for solar energy products is expanding rapidly because of federal tax credits. Deregulation of oil and increasing natural gas prices have contributed to market expansion. Under the president's plan total federal support for solar energy will remain extremely high because of continued tax credits. The administration will continue direct government support for solar programs, focusing on advanced research concepts and exploratory development. The Department of Energy's solar activities will be shifted away from near-term development, demonstration, and commercialization efforts and toward long-range research and development projects that are too risky for private firms to undertake.

Federal Leasing

The federal government owns one-third of all U.S. onshore land and all of the outer-continental shelf, which contains about 50% of all U.S. prospective oil and natural gas resources. Moreover, about 75% of all oil shale and tar sand resources are in the outer-continental shelf. To encourage exploration and development of energy resources, the government leases federal offshore and onshore resources to companies.

Reduced Regulations

The administration has concluded that some federal conservation programs are no longer necessary, while others may impede private initiative by imposing an excessive regulatory burden on the public. Reductions were therefore proposed for three conservation programs conducted by the Department of Energy: technology development, regulation and information, and financial assistance to state and local governments. These changes will allow the Department of Energy to diminish its regulatory activities, which were designed to compensate for marketplace imbalances caused by price controls on oil. Examples include: price and allocation functions of the Economic Regulatory Administration, intervention in state public utility proceedings, mandatory fuel-use restrictions, and coupon-rationing.

Stockpiles, Oil Sharing, and Emergency Preparedness

The federal government intends to enhance energy security through private and public efforts. The administration has taken a new approach to emergency preparedness. Instead of relying on price and allocation controls, its approach is based on allowing market forces to determine the price and allocation of energy supplies, even during an emergency. Large petroleum stockpiles may reduce the adverse effect of some future oil supply interruption. To ensure optimal stockpiling of oil, the administration is working toward having a Strategic Petroleum Reserve (SPR) of 750 million barrels by 1989.

Additional mechanisms available to meet this task include: (1) encouraging emergency oil-stockpile building by private firms; (2) encouraging manufacturers and utilities to use dual-fuel capability for installations and equipment, which will allow them to switch to the most widely available fuels during a disruption; and (3) encouraging international coordination.

The United States is a member of the International Energy Agency (IEA) and is committed to cooperation with other member countries under IEA emergency oil-sharing systems in the event of major oil supply disruptions.

The Energy Outlook

According to the energy plan, the U.S. economy should gradually become less dependent on foreign oil and, thus, less vulnerable to disruptions in supply. The decontrol of domestic oil and gas prices and the production of energy from shale oil and solar energy are likely to reduce oil requirements per GDP from 0.38 in 1982 to 0.30 in 1990. Whether the particular projections prove to be optimistic or pessimistic, the United States remains vulnerable to shifts in the world oil market.

According to recent U.S. energy studies (see tables 6–1 and 6–2), total primary-energy requirements (TPER) are projected to diminish from a rate of 2.7% per year between 1982 and 1985 to about 1.2% per year between 1985 and 1990. Between 1990 and 2000 TPER should rise about 0.8% per year (see table 6–1).

Total consumption of petroleum products is thought to have bottomed out. Oil's share of total energy consumption is forecasted to decline from about 44% in 1973 to 30% in 2000. Natural gas has represented one-quarter of the total energy consumption in the United States in recent years.

Electricity currently provides about 15% of total energy consumption in the United States, compared with approximately 11% in 1973. Coal production has increased continuously over the past decade, reaching about 10% of total energy demand. Electric utilities account for 70% of total coal demand and have provided the main growth area, with their coal requirements increasing by about 60% over the past decade. Nuclear power's share of total electric generation increased from 4.2% in 1973 to 11.3% in 1982, and it is projected to increase to over 20% in the 1990s.

Current projections provide for about 136 million tons oil equivalent (MTOE) to be supplied from renewables other than hydro and geothermal sources by the end of the century, which is more than double the 1982 level of 59 MTOE. Significant increases are projected in wind power (21 MTOE) and solar energy, including photovoltaic (16 MTOE). In summary, in the 1990s radical changes in the pattern of energy supply are projected, with oil and gas declining, and coal, nuclear, hydro, and other renewables increasing their contributions.

7
The U.S. Banking System

The U.S. banking system is the largest and most sophisticated in the world. It consists of 35,000 depository institutions, including about 14,500 commercial banks with $1.9 trillion in assets, as well as savings banks and savings and loan associations. Banking follows the dichotomous nature of the U.S. legal system. The establishment and operation of a U.S. bank is subject to either the regulations of the Federal Reserve or the respective state banking departments of the fifty states. The banking system is based on a statutory framework that limits how different classes of depository institutions may function and constrains their geographic expansion.

Characteristics and Trends

In recent years competition among various financial institutions has led to a proliferation in the type of services and products they provide. Technological developments are affecting the structure of banking, while deregulation and the market forces are changing the character of the financial services industry. A dominant feature of the financial services industry is an increasing number of banklike competitors with banklike powers. These competitors offer services similar to banks, but on a more flexible geographic basis than is permitted to commercial banks. While deregulation of the banking industry has been a slow process, several important pieces of legislation were adopted in recent years.

The Depository Institutions Deregulation and Monetary Control Act of 1980 and the Garn–St. Germain Depository Institutions Act of 1982 diminished the differences in lending and deposit services offered by banks and thrift institutions. The Garn–St. Germain Act also allowed existing state-chartered savings banks to become federal savings banks regulated by the Federal Home Loan Bank Board but insured by the Federal Deposit Insurance Corporation. These changes have blurred any distinction between the savings and loan industry and the savings bank industry.

Savings institutions suffer from a maturity mismatch in their assets and liabilities. Their future is affected by interest-rate levels and fluctuations. Since regulations have diminished the differences between commercial banks and savings institutions, the latter could be attractive acquisitions for commercial banks and foreign investors.

Proposals to reform the regulatory framework of the U.S. banking system have long been discussed in Congress and by the Task Group on Regulation of Financial Services headed by Vice-President George Bush. One of this group's recommendations is the consolidation of the regulatory responsibilities that rest with the Federal Reserve, the FDIC, the Comptroller of the Currency, and the state banking departments.

Similarly, banks are advocating access to markets and services previously denied to all depository institutions. Bank holding companies already provide such services as insurance and data processing that are outside the traditional scope of banking activity. Under the Glass-Steagall Act, banks are also attempting to eliminate some restrictions on their securities dealings.

Regulations established by the McFadden Act and the Douglas Amendment to the Bank Holding Company Act prohibit interstate branch banking. Statewide branch banking is permitted in some states. In other states limited branch banking is allowed only in one city or county; a number of states even forbid it. Yet all major commercial banks do business throughout the country.

Strict federal antitrust laws also limit bank mergers within a state. This, in turn, has preserved the independence of many banks. Still, the dominant banks are the money-center banks in the big industrial states. Of the ten largest banks, six are located in New York, two in California, and two in Illinois.

Another important characteristic of the U.S. banking system is its duality. About 70% of its commercial banks are state banks, having obtained their charters to do business from a state, while the remaining 30% are national banks, with a charter from the federal comptroller of the currency.

Since the mid-1950s, bank holding companies—corporations that control one or more banks in the United States—have become significant elements in the banking system. There are about 2,500 bank holding companies, accounting for 70% of commercial banking deposits.

Recently, financial markets have experienced fundamental changes, and financial institutions have expanded their geographic reach. The financial service industry is inherently an interstate business, and banking activities on the wholesale side are increasingly conducted on an interstate basis. This development is helping transform the financial system into a nationwide market, while the statutory approach toward geographic expansion by banks has remained virtually unaltered for nearly half a century.

Since the mid-1960s, the United States has experienced a massive movement toward internationalization of its banking system. By the end of 1983, 163 member banks were operating 890 branches in foreign countries and overseas areas of the United States.

Effective December 1981, the Federal Reserve Board began allowing international banking facilities (IBFs) in the United States. IBFs may be established by U.S. depository institutions, by Edge and Agreement corporations, and by U.S. branches and agencies of foreign banks. With some exceptions these facilities provide Eurocurrency market capabilities.

To promote U.S. exports, the Bank Export Services Act was passed in 1982, permitting bank holding companies and their subsidiary Edge or Agreement corporations to participate in financing and developing export trading companies. Since then, many export trading companies have been established by banks.

In summary, present developments and underlying forces suggest that during the 1980s, depository institutions will experience a liberalized statutory environment. The number of financial institutions in the United States is expected to shrink because of consolidation through mergers and acquisitions and the emergence of a nationwide banking system.

The Federal Reserve System

The Federal Reserve System—the nation's central bank—is composed of member banks, the Federal Reserve Banks, the Board of Governors, the Federal Open Market Committee, and the Federal Advisory Council. The system was created by the Federal Reserve Act of 1913.

The Federal Reserve System has a pyramidal structure: at its base are about 5,425 member commercial banks; in the middle is a nationwide network of twelve Federal Reserve Banks and twenty-five branches; and at the apex of the organization is a seven-member Board of Governors, with headquarters in Washington, D.C.

The chief responsibilities of the Federal Reserve System, like those of other central banks throughout the world, are to regulate the flow of money and credit; to promote stability of the financial system; and to provide services for depository institutions, the Treasury, and the public. Almost 90% of the nation's cash is issued by the Federal Reserve Bank in the form of Federal Reserve notes.

All national banks must be members of the Federal Reserve, while state banks may join if they meet certain requirements. Although the 5,425 member banks account for only about 36% of the nation's commercial banks, they hold about 77% of all commercial bank assets and deposits.

Member banks are subject to various regulations, of which the most important obligations are to: (1) hold reserves against deposits; (2) subscribe to capital stock of the district's Federal Reserve Bank; (3) comply with various requirements of the federal banking law; and (4) complete necessary system reports. State member banks are also examined and supervised by the Federal Reserve Banks. Federal Reserve members have access to:

Borrowing under certain conditions from a district Federal Reserve Bank

Using the system's check collection and wire-transfer facilities

Obtaining currency and coin, free of transportation costs

Using the facilities of the Reserve banks for safekeeping of their securities.

Uniform reserve requirements are imposed on all depository institutions, including commercial banks, savings banks, savings and loan associations, credit unions, and industrial banks with transaction accounts or nonpersonal time deposits. Under provisions of the International Banking Act of 1978, the same reserve requirements are also imposed on U.S. agencies and branches of foreign banks. By the same token, all U.S. depository institutions have access to the services of the Federal Reserve System.

Federal Reserve Banks are operating arms of the system, and they serve as a link between the Board of Governors and the banking system. The country is divided into twelve Federal Reserve districts, with Federal Reserve Banks in Boston, New York, Philadelphia, Cleveland, Richmond, Atlanta, Chicago, St. Louis, Minneapolis, Kansas City, Dallas, and San Francisco. There are also twenty-five branches of these banks to serve areas within each district.

Federal Reserve Banks provide many banking services to the banking community, the public, and the government. They supervise state-chartered member banks and bank holding companies, examining member banks for safety and soundness. They also help shape monetary policy.

Reserve Banks hold the cash reserves of depository institutions and make loans to them. Federal Reserve Banks perform a major role in the nation's payments mechanism by distributing coin and currency, processing checks, and transferring funds electronically. They are part of the Federal Reserve Communications System, or "Fedwire," an electronic network through which member banks can transfer funds and securities nationwide within minutes. Federal Reserve Banks and their branches operate automated clearing houses (ACHs). These computerized facilities allow payments to be electronically exchanged between participating banks, making an actual check unnecessary. ACHs are primarily used to effect recurring transactions, such as direct deposits of payrolls or mortgage payments. The twelve Federal Reserve Banks act as the government's fiscal agents, handling transactions of Treasury securities vis-a-vis the public and assisting the Treasury and other government agencies in many other ways. The Federal Reserve Banks collect and process checks, provide safekeeping facilities, and act as the government's banker.

Each of the twelve Federal Reserve Banks is managed by a board of nine directors. Similarly, the twenty-five Reserve Bank branches are managed by five to seven directors, who represent the interests of the branch territory. The board of directors oversees the operations of each bank under the general supervision of the board of governors.

Each Reserve Bank has three Class A directors, three Class B directors, and three Class C directors. Member banks elect three Class A directors to represent member banks and three Class B directors to represent the public in each Reserve Bank's district. Three Class C directors, also representing the public, are appointed by the board of governors of the Federal Reserve System. The chairperson and deputy chairperson of each board are selected from the C directors by the board of governors and serve one-year terms.

The board of governors of the Federal Reserve System is composed of seven members. Appointed by the president of the United States and confirmed by the Senate, they serve fourteen-year terms. Members serving their full terms may not be reappointed. Terms are staggered, with a term expiring every two years. A governor who serves a partial term may be reappointed to a full term of office. The president designates one member of the board to be chairperson and another to be vice-chairperson for terms of four years. These two officers may be reappointed.

The prime responsibility of board members concerns monetary policy. The seven board members constitute a majority of the twelve-member Federal Open Market Committee (FOMC), the group that makes key decisions on money and credit. The board:

Establishes reserve requirements

Issues regulations concerning how and when the twelve Reserve Banks may make discount loans

Determines the discount rate

Establishes ceiling rates on interest banks may pay on time and savings deposits

Sets margin requirements for use of credit in securities markets.

The board has broad supervisory and regulatory authority over the domestic and foreign activities of its member banks, and is authorized to collect reports from all depository institutions. The board also supervises operations of such federal consumer-credit laws as Truth in Lending and Equal Credit Opportunity.

Monetary policy is implemented through the following methods:

1. Changes in the discount rate
2. Reserve requirements and changes thereof
3. Open-market operation
4. Margin requirements for loans secured by securities.

The Federal Open Market Committee (FOMC) is the most important monetary policy-making arm of the Federal Reserve System. It is composed of the seven members of the board of governors and five Reserve Bank presidents. Presidents of the Federal Reserve Banks serve one-year terms on a rotating basis. Traditionally, the chairperson of the board of governors is elected chairperson of the FOMC, and the president of Federal Reserve Bank of New York is elected vice-chairperson.

FOMC meetings are held every four to six weeks in the offices of the board of governors in Washington, D.C., according to a schedule tentatively agreed on at the beginning of each year. If circumstances require, members may be called on to participate in a special meeting or a telephone conference or to vote on a recommended action by telegram or telephone.

At each regular meeting the FOMC votes on a policy concerning the purchase and sale of government securities in the open market. These decisions affect the availability of money and credit in the economy. At least twice a year, the committee also votes on certain longer-term policy objectives.

After adopting a policy, the committee issues a directive on monetary targets and interest rate levels to the trading desk of the Federal Reserve Bank of New York. The trading desk serves as the committee's agent in making actual purchases and sales. Similarly, the foreign department of New York's Reserve Bank acts as the committee's agent in foreign exchange transactions.

The interest rate most directly affected by open-market operations is that of federal funds—the rate at which member banks lend reserves to one another, usually on an overnight basis. That rate is determined by the supply and demand for funds.

The board of governors issues several reports on action taken by the FOMC. A *Record of Policy Actions* is prepared after each meeting and released to the press and the public a few days after the next regularly scheduled FOMC meeting. At the same time another report, *Minutes of Action,* which lists policy and nonpolicy actions, is issued for public inspection.

The twelve-member Federal Advisory Council performs significant roles in the system's operations. It is composed of bankers, one from each Federal Reserve district, who have been elected by the board of directors of the Federal Reserve Banks in their districts. The Council meets in Washington, D.C., four times a year and advises the board of governors of the Federal Reserve on important current developments.

Enhanced Federal Reserve System Authority

The Depository Institutions Deregulation and Monetary Control Act of 1980 was designed to improve the effectiveness of monetary policy. It applies new reserve requirements set by the Federal Reserve Board on all depository institutions. Among its other key provisions, the Act: (1) authorizes the Federal Reserve to collect reports from all depository institutions; (2) extends Federal Reserve discount and borrowing privileges and other services to nonmember depository institutions; (3) requires the Federal Reserve to set a schedule of fees for Federal Reserve services; and (4) provides for the gradual phaseout of deposit interest-rate ceilings, while providing broader powers for thrift institutions.

The Comptroller of the Currency and the FDIC

The comptroller of the currency has primary supervisory authority over national banks. State banking supervisors have similar jurisdiction over banks organized under state laws.

The Federal Deposit Insurance Corporation (FDIC) was established in the 1930s to insure deposits. Federal insurance covers deposits up to $100,000. Almost all commercial banks are now insured, subjecting them to FDIC regulations. Insured state banks that are members of the Federal Reserve System are controlled by the Federal Reserve, the FDIC, and state regulatory agencies.

Foreign Banking

The number of foreign bank offices in the United States reached 562 in mid-1984. Branches numbered 289; agencies, 177; subsidiaries, 53; Edge Act corporations, 34; and investment companies, 9. Nearly half of these offices were located in New York, followed by California, Florida, and Illinois. The four most represented countries were Japan, the United Kingdom, Canada, and France.

The International Banking Act (IBA) of 1978 created a federal regulatory structure for agencies and branches of foreign banks in the United States. The Act permits the comptroller of the currency to license federal branches and agencies of foreign banks in the United States, providing their establishment is not prohibited by state law. The Act also permits foreign banks to establish Edge and Agreement corporations.

The main thrust of the International Banking Act was to equalize the competitive environment by placing restrictions similar to those placed on domestic banking institutions on the U.S. activities of foreign banks. Limitations were also enacted on interstate banking.

The IBA authorized the board of governors to impose Federal Reserve regulations on U.S. agencies and branches of foreign banks (Regulation D) whose consolidated worldwide banking assets exceed $1 billion. The board may also limit the maximum interest rate such agencies and branches may pay on time deposits to the rate member banks are permitted to pay. Agencies and branches are made eligible for services provided by the Federal Reserve Banks. The law also allows federal insurance on deposits in foreign banks operating in the U.S. and permits such banks to form Edge Act corporations.

8
Regulation and the Legal Framework

Basic Principles

The U.S. has a long tradition of free private enterprise, and there has been an absence of nationalization of private companies. However, certain industry- and nonindustry-specific regulations have been enacted, particularly during the era of the Great Depression. These regulations have sought to preserve free competition, to prevent monopolies, to provide a stable economic environment, to assure environmental control, and to create equal opportunities for all citizens.

Government agencies regulate such industries as banking, insurance, securities, transportation, and utilities. These agencies deal with numerous issues, including those concerning antitrust, consumer protection, food and drugs, environmental control, and labor relations. The Food and Drug Administration (FDA), for instance, must test and approve all new pharmaceuticals and cosmetics before they can be marketed. Imported food and drugs must meet the same standards as U.S. products.

Since the late 1970s deregulation has proliferated in many industries, such as airlines, trucking, and communications. However, reform has been slow. The government still exercises considerable influence and control on business operations in the U.S. Environmental laws and regulations exist at all levels of government in the United States. Air and water pollution, noise pollution, pesticides, and radiation are all controlled. Toxic waste disposal is an environmental issue of increasing importance.

All entities, foreign or domestic, doing business in the United States are subject to federal, state, and local regulations. There is no federal corporate law, so each of the fifty states and the District of Columbia has its own corporate law.

A corporation is considered to be foreign owned if more than one-fifth of its capital stock is owned by aliens, a foreign government, or a corporation organized under the laws of a foreign country. A corporation is considered to be foreign controlled if it is directly or indirectly controlled by a corporation whose capital stock is at least one-quarter owned by foreign interests.

The foreign investment policy of the United States reorganizes the growing importance of international direct investment in the world economy. The government has a liberal attitude toward foreign investment, both direct and portfolio, admitting and treating foreign capital on an equal basis with domestic capital. No general federal law governs new investments or expansions by either domestic or foreign firms in the U.S., nor is there a federal company law. There are no laws of general application restricting direct investments by foreigners, but there are many of specific application.

Generally, there are no limitations on foreign investors. However, restrictions on acquisitions are applicable without regard to the nationality of the potential acquirer. Most important are the federal antitrust laws forbidding specific anticompetitive practices. Although these laws may prevent a particular acquisition by a domestic or foreign investor, they do not prevent entry into an industry or business.

Federal restrictions on foreign investments are primarily in the areas of: communications, defense contracting, air transport, coastal and freshwater shipping, fishing, atomic energy, hydroelectric power, and mining on government property. Under federal law, aliens and foreign-owned corporations are prohibited from holding and operating such businesses. Most states prohibit foreign control of insurance companies. Some states do not grant charters to foreign banks.

Various state laws place restrictions on foreign investment. Among the most common concern ownership of land, particularly agricultural land. These restrictions usually do not prohibit outright investment in real estate and agricultural land. Rather they limit the size of the land holdings or the duration of ownership. The Agricultural Foreign Investment Disclosure Act of 1978 requires that any foreign individual or entity acquiring or transferring interest in agricultural land submit a report to the secretary of agriculture within ninety days after acquisition or transfer. Ownership of U.S. farmland by foreign nationals or by U.S. corporations whose ownership is at least 5% foreign, must also be reported to the U.S. Department of Agriculture.

The U.S. will continue to pursue liberal policies, but it will also continue its monitoring to ensure that investment transactions are consistent with national security and other interests. No foreign investment registration or approval procedure exists, but foreign investors must file various reports with the government, while a Treasury Department Committee on Foreign Investment monitors acquisitions by non-U.S. interests.

The U.S. does not impose exchange restrictions on the inflow or outflow of capital, except on transactions involving Cuba, Democratic Kampuchea, Iran, and North Korea. A foreign investor is not restricted on repatriation of capital, loans, profit, dividends, and royalties. However, federal income tax on certain types of income payable to nonresident aliens, nonresident partnerships, and foreign corporations is withheld at the source. The United States applies licensing controls prohibiting the entry of capital from Cuba, Democratic Kampuchea, North Korea, and Vietnam.

Legal Organizations

The U.S. legal system is complicated by its federal nature, since either federal or state laws or both may be applicable to particular situations. However, some provisions governing capital investment contain elements similar to those found in the legal systems of other countries involved in international business.

The U.S. as well as each of the fifty states has a constitution, a set of statutory laws and regulations issued thereunder, and a body of court interpretations. Under the U.S. Constitution the states have general jurisdiction except in matters expressly reserved for the federal government. Even in cases in which federal laws are applicable, a state may enact legislation to supplement federal law. Since there is no federal corporate law, a substantial portion of the jurisdiction over enterprises doing business in the United States rests with the individual states. Each of the fifty states may enact, administer, and enforce its own regulations on business and commerce within its boundaries, so long as these regulations do not violate the federal constitution.

Although each state issues and administers its own corporate laws, these laws reflect common principles. One of these principles is that individual shareholders assume no personal liability because of their involvement in a corporation. Nevertheless, laws vary in such details as formalities for incorporation and mechanics for operating a corporation. Separate and distinct state laws give rise to the possibility of legal conflicts when activities involve interstate boundaries and when no uniform law or federal statutes are applicable.

Generally, it is desirable to incorporate in the state where most business activity will occur. However, certain advantages may suggest another state as the most appropriate. Indeed, it is a common practice to incorporate in the state with the most favorable laws, rates, and incorporation costs. Delaware, Maryland, and New York are often selected for incorporation of new enterprises. Delaware is among the most favorite states for incorporation of publicly held companies because of its flexible corporate laws and low corporate income and franchise taxes.

A company may incorporate in any one of the fifty states and set up offices or plants in other states. A corporation may also conduct business through several corporations operating under the laws of different states.

Any resident alien, nonresident alien, or any foreign legal entity may incorporate in the U.S. under the various state laws. A corporation formed within a state is a citizen of that state. Legally, a corporation is considered a domestic corporation only in the state in which it is incorporated. It is a foreign corporation in all other states and must comply with certain requirements to do business in those states.

Any of the following legal entities may serve as a vehicle for investment:

Corporation

Partnership

Joint venture

Branch of a foreign corporation

Sole proprietorship.

The most common form of business for foreign investors starting a firm in the U.S. is the corporation. Foreign capital investments in the United States may be made through existing or newly created American entities. They may also be made through the American offices, agencies, or branches of companies created and existing under a foreign law.

Stock Corporations

A corporation is formed by obtaining a corporate charter, also known as a certificate of incorporation, from the authorities of the chosen state. The corporation must have bylaws stating the rules under which it operates. Generally, such issues as corporate formation, management, and capitalization vary between the states.

A U.S. corporate entity offers several advantages to investors: (1) shareholder liability is limited to the amount invested; (2) ownership is easily transferred; and (3) continuity of the business is assured despite changes in or the death of managers or owners. As a business structure the corporation allows more flexibility in income distribution for tax purposes than any other structure. U.S. corporations may be either private corporations or public corporations. Therefore, the corporation is the most viable structure for the resident or nonresident alien.

The corporation's board of directors, which is elected by the shareholders, is charged with such duties as managing the corporation, appointing officers, and declaring dividends. A number of states require that a portion of the incorporators or directors be U.S. citizens or state residents. The day-to-day running of a corporation is done by officers, whose authority is stated in the by-laws and resolutions of the board of directors.

Closely Held Corporations

A closely held corporation is owned by a relatively small number of shareholders. Closely held corporations choose not to issue public shares and are managed directly by shareholders.

The purpose of creating and operating a closely held corporation is usually to avoid the reporting requirements of a full-fledged stock corporation, while preserving the limited liability of the shareholders. Such corporations are relatively new in the United States and are confined to small business operations.

Partnerships

State laws generally recognize two kinds of partnerships: general and limited. In a general partnership the liability of all partners is unlimited. In a limited partnership the partners are prohibited from actively participating in the operation of the partnership and, thus, are liable for operation of the partnership only to the extent of their contribution. A limited partnership has at least one "general" partner who is active in the business. That person's liability for the partnership is unlimited. This structure is normally not attractive to foreign investors because of the difficulty of raising capital, the unlimited legal liability, and the high individual income-tax rates.

The organization, operation, and termination of a partnership is governed by state laws. It is easier to operate this type of legal entity than others because fewer government regulations and restrictions apply to it. The purpose of a partnership, as well as the duties and rights of the partners, is stated in the partnership agreement.

Joint Ventures

In the United States the term *joint venture* is loosely used to cover the association of two or more entities for the purpose of accomplishing a business objective. It may take the form of a partnership or a corporation. If two unrelated businesses, either incorporated or unincorporated, agree to conduct a joint venture, it will probably be considered a partnership for legal and tax purposes.

Since there are very few statutes or legal precedents concerning joint ventures, both parties should clearly state, in a written agreement, their understanding of the purpose of their venture. They should also write their concomitant rights and responsibilities into the agreement. A joint venture between a foreign and a U.S. company is sometimes appropriate for clearly defined projects or goals. The advantages include spreading the financial risks and benefiting from capital and know-how.

Sole Proprietorships

The majority of sole proprietorships require no license or permit. Relatively few enterprises are required to obtain a license to conduct business under state laws. Generally, there are few formalities in operating a sole proprietorship. Individuals operating sole proprietorships have unlimited liability for debts incurred in conducting business. Investment in the United States may also be made as a sole proprietor, with very few formalities in its operation. With this form of investment the proprietor's liability is unlimited. Generally, the trade name under which the business of sole proprietorship is conducted must be recorded.

Foreign Entities

Corporations created and existing under the laws of a foreign country may establish a representative office, agency, or branch in the United States, if they do not wish to make U.S. investments through a corporation organized under the laws of a state. Before starting operations in some states, the representative office, agency, or branch of certain foreign corporations must obtain permission from and register in the states where it intends to operate. However, in many states, such permission is not required.

A branch subjects the foreign parent company to liability for the branch's debts. Most foreign investors prefer to operate in the United States through a local subsidiary rather than through a branch of the foreign parent company for reasons of convenience or because of legal or tax considerations.

Specific Federal Laws

Although the creation and operation of a U.S. corporation and the offices, agencies, and branches of foreign corporations doing business in the United States are governed by state laws, there are also many important federal laws concerning foreign investment in the United States.

Securities Laws

Federal securities laws apply to all publicly held companies. Public offerings of securities raise intricate legal problems, which might involve the filing of extensive reports and disclosures. Registration may also be necessary. To comply with these laws, one may need expert guidance. Many states also have their own securities laws.

Securities offered publicly in the United States must be registered with the U.S. Securities and Exchange Commission (SEC) and must conform with state security laws, known as "blue-sky" laws, unless they are listed on the New York or American Stock Exchange. The SEC is an independent government agency, established in 1934 to regulate the selling and trading of securities. Its responsibilities are set primarily by the Securities Act of 1933, the Securities Exchange Act of 1934, and the Foreign Corrupt Practices Act of 1977.

A public offering of securities requires that a detailed registration statement be filed with the SEC before a public offering is made. This statement, which must include a prospectus containing historical financial and other data, is made available to the public. Most states exempt securities listed on the New York or American Stock Exchanges from registration.

Antitrust Laws

Antitrust laws are designed to avoid restraint of trade and to encourage competition. Two federal agencies—the Department of

Justice and the Federal Trade Commission—administer the laws under overlapping authority. The main statutes include: the Sherman Antitrust Act, which prohibits agreements restraining trade or commerce; the Clayton Act, which prohibits corporate acquisitions that diminish competition; and the Robinson–Patman Act, which requires customers in a given category to be treated equally. Firms doing business in and trading with the U.S. must be aware of the requirements and prohibitions of antitrust laws. Under antitrust laws an interlocking directorship among competitors is prohibited. Individuals damaged by violations of antitrust laws may demand damages equal to three times their losses.

Antitrust laws are intended to restrict mergers and acquisitions that may substantially reduce competition. A corporation contemplating a merger or acquisition should seek the opinion of either the Justice Department or the FTC about its legality. In some cases prior notification to the FTC is mandatory.

Antitrust laws give substantial power to government agencies and courts to restrain the activities of domestic and foreign corporations inside and outside the U.S. However, enforcing antitrust provisions when foreign corporations are concerned may be limited by foreign laws.

Patents, Trademarks, and Copyrights

Obtaining a U.S. patent can be difficult and time-consuming, and the cost depends on the complexity of the invention. U.S. patent applicants must establish their item's usefulness, novelty, and utility and also specify, document, and corroborate the inventor's claim. The United States is signatory to the International Convention for the Protection of Industrial Property, known as the Paris Union. The U.S. patent is granted for seventeen years and is not renewable. Patent laws apply equally to residents and nonresidents.

Trademark rights are acquired in the United States by use in interstate commerce, and registration is not necessary to acquire exclusive rights. However, registration with the principal registrar of the U.S. Patent Office normally provides a clearer case for ownership. Registration, which runs for twenty-year terms, is renewable.

Copyright protection is granted from the time a work is created and runs the life of the individual author, plus fifty years. With works created for hire, the period is for up to 100 years from creation. The United States has copyright agreements with over sixty countries.

Commercial Law

Once an investment is in place and operating within the United States, local laws apply to its transactions. Rules governing the various contracts are those included in applicable state laws. Although laws differ from state to state, most states have adopted "uniform" business laws such as the Uniform Commercial Code and the Uniform Limited Partnership Act.

One paramount principle of U.S. law should be observed by foreign investors. This is the requirement of providing equal treatment to all customers. Concessions to specific customers, which may impede free competition, is prohibited.

Legal Guidance

Before making a final decision about investing in the United States, the foreign investor should consult various federal and state authorities with jurisdiction in the area of interest. Most authorities have helpful, informative pamphlets readily available.

Business in the United States has become increasingly affected by litigation and complex laws. Therefore, it must be emphasized that only by consulting an attorney can a foreign investor fully understand the U.S. laws that could affect an investment and its operations. Expert legal guidance should prove invaluable.

9
Financing Direct Foreign Investment

Very large and highly developed domestic financial markets have significantly contributed to the dynamic growth of the U.S. economy. These financial markets have maintained an open-door policy toward direct foreign investment, treating foreign-controlled and domestic companies alike. Foreign companies find U.S. capital markets receptive to financing acquisitions, start-up, expansion, and current operation. Various financing methods are adaptable to specific needs, and the cost of financing compares favorably with other world financial markets. Methods of financing and sources of capital for foreign investments are varied enough to accommodate the special needs of foreign firms doing business in America.

Financing is primarily determined by the mode of investment, relative costs, and the parent company's financial conditions and objectives. Once a foreign company is established in the United States, various types of commercial bank and commercial finance loans will be as readily available as they are to a U.S.-owned company.

Traditionally, foreign investors have financed their operations primarily by equity inflows. Reinvested earnings have fluctuated widely according to business cycles and have provided a relatively smaller fraction of financial resources. The incidence of mergers and acquisitions has declined, from about 720 in 1980 to about 240 in 1983. The level of Eurodollar sources as a substitute for U.S. sources is subject to interest rate and currency fluctuations and outlook.

Types of Direct Foreign Investment and Methods of Financing

To date, foreign companies have most commonly established operations in the U.S. through mergers and acquisitions. This method of investment achieves smooth entry into the market over a relatively short time. Historically, mergers and acquisitions have been made using cash for stock transactions. However, this method of financing is subject to business conditions, and its use is expected to decline during economic slowdowns, when fewer funds are available from internal sources. If an acquisition exceeds 80% of the total equity and is funded through domestic sources, substantial tax benefits may be realized. A major problem with cash transactions, however, is that shareholders of acquired companies are subject to capital gains tax. Methods used to avoid this tax include installment sales, formation of mutual funds, cash options, and creation of redeemable preferred stock.

New ventures, or new plant construction, are another form of foreign direct investment in the United States that has increased in recent years. Undertaken largely by mature parent companies with specialized technology or products, new ventures are initially capitalized with cash from the parent company and with guaranteed commercial bank loans. Local and state authorities also issue industrial revenue bonds to provide inexpensive, long-term credit for financing new plant construction, subject to a $10 million ceiling on each municipal issue.

Direct foreign investment has also been undertaken in the form of joint ventures by two or more companies that need to pool their complementary resources and know-how but do not seek to establish wholly owned subsidiaries in the United States. This type of foreign investment, if undertaken with a domestic firm, may help foreign investors reduce the transportation costs incurred by operating away from the home country. Joint ventures are most often facilitated by purchasing stocks and assets, and financed by both parties' initial capitalization.

Recent data show over one-third of DFI projects in the United States to be done through acquisitions. New establishments account for the remainder. In terms of investment outlays, acquisitions makes up about 60 to 65% of total investment, while new establishments constitute the remaining 35 to 40%. The bulk of DFI projects (41% of the projects and 67% of the funds) are carried out by U.S. affiliates, while the balance are carried out by parents.

As table 9–1 shows, in 1983 outlays by foreign investors were $7.0 billion, down from $10.8 billion in 1982. The number of investments fell in 1983 to 629, down from 1,108 in 1982. Most outlays— $4.5 billion—were for acquiring existing U.S. businesses, while the remainder—$2.5 billion—were for establishing new U.S. businesses. By type of investor, $4.9 billion in outlays were by U.S. affiliates, while the balance was by foreign direct investors themselves.[26]

Sources of Funds

The primary methods of corporate finance are through debt and equity. The capital structure of the corporation—the mix between equity and debt—is determined by: (1) maintaining the appropriate debt/equity ratio, which corresponds with cost and risk minimization; (2) preventing ownership delution; and (3) obtaining optimum tax advantages. Table 9-2 shows the sources of funds of large U.S. corporations.

The most popular and practical forms of U.S. financing for foreign firms include:

Commercial bank financing
Commercial paper
Asset-based financing
Long-term leasing
Public and private debt and equity financing
Industrial revenue bonds

Commercial banking, commercial financing, commercial paper, and commercial leasing provide medium- and short-term funding; equity markets supply long-term. Short- and medium-term bank financing are handled by commercial banks; long-term financing is handled by investment banking firms or investment banking divisions of commercial banks.

Funds used to facilitate foreign direct investment, including short- and long-term capital, have been obtained through domestic and foreign sources. Business loans are provided by commercial banks, commercial finance companies, suppliers of capital equipment

Table 9-1
Direct Foreign Investment in the U.S. by Acquisitions, Start-ups, and Investors

	Number					Investment outlays (millions of dollars)				
	1979	1980	1981	1982ʳ	1983ᵖ	1979	1980	1981	1982ʳ	1983ᵖ
Investments, total	1,568	1,659	1,332	1,108	629	15,317	12,172	23,219	10,817	6,962
Acquisitions	666	721	462	395	242	13,159	8,974	18,151	6,563	4,473
Establishments	902	938	870	713	387	2,158	3,198	5,067	4,254	2,489
Investors, total	1,770	1,833	1,521	1,218	682	15,317	12,172	23,219	10,817	6,962
Foreign direct investors	1,072	1,188	979	720	365	3,440	4,129	6,158	3,954	2,113
U.S. affiliates	698	645	542	498	317	11,876	8,043	17,060	6,863	4,849

ʳ Revised.
ᵖ Preliminary.

Source: U.S. Department of Commerce, Bureau of Economic Analysis, "U.S. Business Enterprises Acquired or Established by Direct Investors in 1983," *Survey of Current Business*, May 1984.

Table 9-2
Financing Large U.S. Corporations:
Sources of Funds

Funds	Percentage
Composition of Total Funds	
Internal Funds	77
External Funds	23
Total	100%
Composition of External Funds	
Net new bond issues	32.9
Private placements	5.5
Net new equity	6.9
Bank term loans	12.8
Bank short-term loans	13.7
Commercial paper	27.2
Other	1.0
Total	100%

Source: The Conference Board, *Financial Indicators and Corporate Financing Plans: A Semiannual Survey,* April 1985.

and other goods, certain specialized lenders, and state and federal agencies. Most foreign companies bring some funds into the United States as starting capital, although a few are able to raise most of their starting capital on the basis of the parent company's credit.

Until 1981 U.S. sources were traditionally employed because of the depressed value of the dollar, which made dollar investments attractive on a purchasing power parity basis. U.S. financial markets have offered relatively inexpensive capital to large and mature multinational corporations, thereby increasing the attractiveness of financing through domestic sources. Another factor is that foreign investors have begun to realize the importance of establishing relations with U.S. lenders to meet their needs for early working capital. U.S. sources of funding are usually used when the home country of the foreign investor imposes stringent capital outflow restrictions. Many such regulations are expected to be relaxed in the future when economic conditions improve.

Funding through the Eurodollar market has been prevalent because the funds have been relatively inexpensive and available. However, contributions from the Eurodollar market toward investment funds depends on economic and policy developments as well as cost considerations.

Funding from foreign sources is currently the largest contributor toward the financing of foreign direct investment. Foreign investors tend to use foreign sources when no established relations exist with a U.S. lending institution. Foreign sources are also used to avoid disclosing sensitive information to U.S. regulatory agencies. The major factor affecting foreign investors' use of foreign-source capital, however, has been the attractive financial packages that home governments offer as a means of increasing country exports. In the intensely competitive export market, preferential home-country financing will continue to encourage foreign-source funding.

Although foreign investment in the United States is funded through various methods, commercial banks have remained a primary source of funds, particularly for working capital. Commercial banks provide short-, medium-, and some long-term financing to foreign investors, ranking as the primary source of short-term capital. Credit is provided to U.S. subsidiaries of foreign companies, particularly with the guarantee of the foreign parent, for a wide variety of corporate purposes, including acquisitions. Short- and medium-term credit lines are most likely to be used by the foreign investor in the early stages of operation in the United States.

The overdraft facility used in other countries is not customary in the United States. Short-term credit, of which the most common form is the ninety-day loan, is obtained from commercial banks and is arranged through a credit line. A customer is allowed to draw down a prespecified amount of funds at any time, subject to certain repayment conditions and the bank's power of immediate revocation. The loan is normally and indefinitely renewable as long as it is fully paid off once a year. This line is subject to a commitment fee on the unused portion and interest on the borrowed funds.

The revolving credit loans offered by commercial banks provide financing for periods ranging from one to five years. Essentially, the company borrows, pays back, and then reborrows as needed, up to a ceiling amount set by the bank.

Another source of short-term credit is commercial paper. It consists of unsecured notes issued by well-known companies. These notes are sold through banks and brokers specializing in such paper. It is the least expensive form of short-term financing. Commercial-paper financing is not feasible for newly established U.S. operations of foreign companies.

Commercial finance companies are a major source of secured financing for small- and medium-size firms. Loans from commercial finance companies are an alternative form of financing for firms not qualifying for commercial bank loans. Interest rates are above the U.S. prime rate, reflecting the higher risk of the borrower. The commercial finance company provides revolving working capital, which is usually secured by the borrowing company's accounts receivable, inventory, plant and equipment, real estate, or other assets. Commercial finance companies also provide financing for leveraged buy-out acquisitions. In such cases the buyer of a company finances the purchase by arranging a loan collateralized by the assets of the company being acquired.

Other sources of financing include accounts receivable and inventory financing, factoring, and leasing. These sources are available through commercial banks, commercial financing companies, and factoring firms. Accounts-receivable financing consists of loans secured by a company's accounts receivable. Inventory financing is similar to account receivable financing except that the borrower's inventory serves as collateral. Factoring is still another form of receivables financing except that the lender assumes responsibility for the company's credit and collection and bad-debt losses. When the factoring method is used, account receivables may be sold at a discount to the commercial finance company.

Leasing is an alternative to borrowing funds to purchase assets with considerable flexibility. Long-term leasing has become an important method of financing fixed assets including plant and equipment, ships, aircrafts, railroad stock, and real estate such as office buildings and warehouses. Leasing is available from leasing companies, manufacturers and distributors of equipment, commercial finance companies, and commercial banks. The two basic types of long-term leasing are financial leasing and leveraged leasing.

Established businesses should also consider trade suppliers as possible sources of financing. Vendors finance equipment purchases on installment plans. In such cases the seller assumes the role of financing agent or works through a financing company. This form of financing, which is more applicable to the purchasing of new equipment, usually requires a down payment of 25 to 33%. The balance is divided into equal monthly or quarterly installment payments. This method is attractive because of the tax advantage and because it frees up working capital.

Banks also provide investment consulting services, credit facilities for short-term working capital needs, and many other related financial services. U.S. commercial banks with large international operations are particularly sensitive to the financial needs of a foreign investor, and they can coordinate a global banking relationship from their headquarters or regional offices in the U.S. and abroad.

Other sources of long-term financing in the United States are life and casualty insurance companies; foundations; state and local authorities; pension funds; and the U.S. securities market, the largest capital market in the world. Commercial banks provide relatively little long-term financing.

The Securities and Exchange Commission requires that all public issues of securities be registered. This involves a thorough and detailed disclosure of a company's audited financial statement and business activities. Because many foreign companies do not wish to undergo this disclosure, stock and bond issues provide only a small percentage of the financing for direct foreign investors.

If a public offering is feasible, the foreign company will retain an investment banking firm to underwrite the issue at a stated price. The size of the issue will determine the size of the investment banker to be hired. Large investment banking firms will not work with issues of less than $1 million, nor will they work with speculative issues. Going public is initially expensive and time-consuming. Also, maintaining a public corporation involves recurring expenses which do not occur in the private corporation. The investment banking firm, with the help of accounting and law firms, will assist the company in preparing its registration statement and filing it with the SEC.

The underwriter's fee for a new issue is borne by the issuing corporation, and ranges from 7.5 to 12.5% of the offering, depending on the size of the offering (a large offering being less expensive), and the company's creditworthiness. The legal and accounting fees for going public will probably be about $50,000 to $100,000, and a portion of these fees will be recurring. When the underwriting fee—which is typically around 10% of the offering and which will be withheld from the offering—is added to various other expenses, such as printing costs, taxes, and transfer agent fees, a $1,000,000 offering could end up costing $200,000.

Financing through bonds issued at a public offering may be subject to the Trust Indenture Act of 1939. This act requires that bonds and notes be issued under an indenture that meets the qualifications of the act and that the indenture be qualified by the SEC.

Private placement of long-term debt obligations avoids the complications of a public debt offering. Although it is an option available only to large, well-known companies, it provides funds tailored to the borrower's needs and avoids some of the costs and delays of a public offering. Private placements involving interstate commerce must be registered with the Securities and Exchange Commission. Private placements are usually arranged by investment bankers. It generally takes two or three months to complete a private placement.

The most viable approach for foreign companies is private debt financing, because the disclosure requirements are less stringent. Securities offered publicly must be registered with the SEC and must also conform with the states' blue-sky laws. This involves substantial public disclosure of all information on the operations of the issuer.

A private debt financing issue can be arranged for as little as $1 million. The interest rate to be paid by the foreign borrower could be twenty-five to 100 basis points higher than rates on similarly rated public securities. Usually, the noninterest costs of issuing public securities will exceed the costs associated with a comparable sale of private securities.

Municipal bonds are tax-exempt debt securities issued by state and local governments on behalf of companies to cover the cost of a new industrial installation. The bonds are secured by the installation. Interest costs are about two to four percentage points below comparable debt interest rates in the United States. Most of the fifty states provide industry financing through bonds at either the state or city level.

Industrial development bonds are underwritten in the same way as municipal bonds, which are placed directly with banks or other financial sources. Also called revenue bonds, industrial development bonds are special obligation bonds payable solely from the revenues pledged to each project. The U.S. Internal Revenue Service limits industrial revenue bonds to the financing of plant and equipment at a specific location for one company. Investment in the facility may not exceed $10 million over a prescribed period, which extends three years backward and three years forward from the date the bonds were issued. Issuance of the bonds is not subject to registration under the Securities Act of 1933, but the full disclosure provisions of section 10 of the Securities Exchange Act of 1934 apply.

Principal and interest are paid by the industrial company to the issuer, who in turn pays the industrial revenue bond holder. These bonds may have serial maturities or sinking funds if the issue is large enough. This form of financing is usually as flexible as other forms of bonds. The investor using industrial revenue bonds retains all the tax advantages of an ordinary debt issue.

Government Sources

Financial assistance from government sources, primarily at state and local levels, is available in the form of loans, loan guarantees, and leases. The foreigner and the U.S. citizen are treated equally when trying to obtain federal and state financial aid. Federal sources of financial aid include the Small Business Administration, Department of Housing and Urban Development, Economic Development Administration, Agricultural Stabilization and Conservation Service, Farm Credit Administration, and Export-Import Bank. Chapter 11 details the sorts of incentives government agencies provide.

In summary, there are various options for financing direct foreign investment in the United States. These include loan financing, debt financing through bond issues, and equity financing through stock issues. The cost of equity is much higher than the cost of debt, and it dilutes ownership. Credit markets do not discriminate between domestic and foreign investors, but foreign investors must carefully consider many factors in order to obtain the most appropriate and least expensive financing that is also conducive to the initiation and operation of the U.S. investment.

10
Taxation

This chapter highlights basic principles of the U.S. tax system. However, for further planning purposes, companies should consult tax experts and accountants. Careful tax planning by foreign investors can significantly reduce the tax burden of conducting business in the United States. Planning is necessary to avoid the pitfalls of a multitiered tax system with complicated laws and administrative procedures. Thoughtful tax planning can lessen the overall tax expense during both the start-up and operating phases of the new investment.

Taxes in the United States are levied by federal, state, and local authorities. A corporation operating nationwide may be subject to income, franchise, property, license, sales, and use taxes in each state, and it may have to file many tax returns.

Federal Corporate Taxation

Almost all domestic corporations in the United States are subject to federal income tax. Foreign corporations are subject to tax on the portion of their income connected with a U.S. trade or business and on fixed income from U.S. sources. Federal income tax is applied equally in the various states and on a worldwide basis. Double taxation is avoided through bilateral tax treaties and foreign-tax credits.

The maximum federal income tax rate on a U.S. or foreign corporation with business income from U.S. operations is 46%. In accordance with the Economic Recovery Tax Act of 1981, corporate rates since 1982 are:

Taxable income		Tax rate (%)
Over	*Not Over*	
0	$ 25,00	15
$ 25,000	50,000	18
50,000	75,000	30
75,000	100,000	40
100,000		46

Other federal taxes include security and unemployment insurance, which are based on wages and salaries paid to employees. (The social security tax rate for 1985 was 7.05%, payable by both the employee and the employer on an employee's salary of up to $39,600.) Excise taxes are imposed on the purchase or use of a product regardless of whether profit is derived from its sale. Among the major excise taxes levied by the federal government are those on special motor fuels and gasoline.

A foreign corporation is subject to U.S. tax on income from U.S. sources and from certain foreign sources if the income is effectively connected with a trade or business in the United States. Other income, such as interest and dividend income, from U.S. sources are also subject to U.S. tax, even if they are not effectively connected with a trade or business in the United States.

U.S. branches of foreign corporations are generally taxed only on income effectively connected with their U.S. branches. Exceptions occur when, under certain treaties, business income is taxable only if it is attributable to a permanent establishment in the United States. In either event under some circumstances taxable business income may include business income from sources outside the United States. The advantage of using a U.S. branch rather than a U.S. subsidiary is that there is no U.S. withholding tax imposed on branch remittances of profits to a foreign home-office. A U.S. subsidiary, on the other hand, must usually withhold tax on dividend remittances to its foreign parent. In addition, operation as a branch might be advantageous when start-up losses are involved, since U.S. losses could be used to offset head-office profits. The branch would be treated as a separate company, but the determination of arm's-length profits will sometimes cause controversy. Operating through a separate corporate entity will reduce the controversy with the Internal Revenue Service over an appropriate basis for allocation of income and expenses.

A non-U.S. subsidiary is subject to the same tax liability as a U.S. branch of the foreign investor; however, it may minimize disputes with the tax authorities about allocation of income. Profits of the non-U.S. subsidiary remitted to the foreign parent may be subject to the withholding tax imposed on U.S.-source income. A U.S. subsidiary is subject to the taxes imposed on a regular U.S. corporation. There is no tax justification for a non-U.S. investor to operate in the United States through a U.S. subsidiary rather than a foreign subsidiary.

When a U.S. corporation is acquired, the foreign investor may organize a U.S. holding company to carry out the acquisition. The main advantage is that interest cost incurred on funds borrowed by the holding company to finance the acquisition may be used to offset the profits of the operating company on a consolidated return filed by the companies. However, if the parent has guaranteed the loan, interest cost may be treated as nondeductible dividends or as payments by the parent.

In 1980 in order to prevent tax avoidance on real estate transactions, the U.S. passed the Foreign Investment in Real Property Tax Act (FIRPTA). This act requires significant reporting on foreign investors in real estate.

Generally, each corporation is taxed as a separate entity. A consolidated return may be filed when there is a common U.S. corporate parent owning, directly or indirectly, 80% or more of the U.S. subsidiaries. With a consolidated return, losses incurred by one corporation may offset income earned by other corporations.

Gross taxable income includes income from the sale of goods, commissions, royalties, interest, dividends, and service fees, as well as gains on the sale of assets and investments, plus income from all other sources. The total figure may be adjusted by deducting ordinary and necessary business expenses and depreciation, and by considering inventory valuation. Corporations may deduct various taxes paid to federal, state, local, and foreign governments. Deductible taxes are state and local income taxes, real property and personal property taxes, and employment taxes. Federal income taxes are not deductible, but federal taxes on payroll, such as social security tax and federal unemployment insurance tax, may be deducted. If deductible expenses exceed taxable income for a taxable year, the net operating loss may be carried back three years and forward fifteen years to reduce the amount of income subject to U.S. tax. The tax code permits companies with leftover tax benefits to sell them to firms that want to lighten their tax burden.

Under the Accelerated Cost Recovery System, business or investment assets may be depreciated using statutory recovery periods shorter than the actual useful lives of the business or investment assets. The cost of an eligible asset is recovered over a three-year, five-year, ten-year, fifteen-year, or twenty-year period, depending on the type of asset. The cost of depreciable real property may be recovered over twenty years.

An investment tax credit is provided to companies that construct or purchase depreciable tangible property, exclusive of buildings and their structural components. The tax credit grants a dollar-for-dollar reduction in federal tax liability for 10% of the value of investments in new property. The investment tax credit is limited to 85% of tax liability exceeding $25,000 for tax years beginning after 1982. Excess investment tax credits may be carried backward three years and forward fifteen years. The Economic Recovery Tax Act allows an income tax credit, limited to 25% of the current year's research expenditures, for qualified research expenses incurred after June 30, 1981, and before January 1, 1986.

Accelerated depreciation and investment tax credits substantially reduce the effective tax rate of corporations. In November 1985, the House Ways and Means Committee approved a bill that would slow down depreciation schedules and eliminate the investment tax credit.

Dividends paid by one U.S. corporation to another qualify for a special intercorporate dividend deduction equal to 85% of the amount of the dividend. When the recipient owns 80% or more of the corporation paying the dividend, the deduction is 100% of the dividend.

A U.S. corporation with income from foreign sources pays tax on that income in foreign countries. A foreign tax credit is allowed for foreign income taxes paid by a U.S. corporation. The credit is allowed regardless of whether the foreign country has a tax treaty with the U.S.

The foreign tax credit for any year may not exceed the amount of foreign tax paid or accrued, and is subject to an overall income limitation, which is computed as follows:

$$\text{Maximum credit} = \frac{\text{Total foreign-source taxable income}}{\text{Worldwide taxable income}} \times \text{U.S. income tax before the credit}$$

If part of the credit cannot be used because of the overall limitation, the unused portion may be carried backward two years and forward five years.

Foreign corporations' taxes may be affected by a tax treaty, convention, or agreement. U.S. income tax treaties usually provide tax exemptions or tax reductions only to persons without a permanent establishment in the United States. Tax treaties also deal with such issues as profit allocation as well as taxation of capital gains, dividends, and royalties. The U.S. has tax treaties with over fifty countries.

Unless tax treaties provide for lower rates, U.S. withholding tax of 30% applies to dividends, rents, salaries, wages, premiums, annuities, and any "fixed or determinable annual or periodical income" paid to foreign persons not engaged in a trade or business in the U.S. ("Foreign person" is broadly defined by U.S. tax regulations, to include people and corporate entities.) The 30% withholding tax on interest paid to nonresident aliens on financial obligations issued after the date of the bill's enactment in 1984 was repealed. This repeal does not affect withholdings on dividends paid to nonresident aliens. Withholding taxes can be substantially reduced if the foreign corporate shareholder is located in a country that has a favorable tax treaty with the United States.

No federal tax is imposed on capital assets. But a 28% tax is imposed on gains arising from the sale or exchange of capital assets held by corporate taxpayers for more than one year. Gains on the sale of capital assets held for less than six months are taxed at ordinary income tax rates. Losses on the sale of capital assets may be deducted only against capital gains, but no part of the losses may be used to offset ordinary income.

Capital gains realized by a foreign corporation, including capital gains on the sale of stock in a U.S. corporation, are not subject to U.S. taxes. This rule does not apply if the gains are effectively connected with the foreign entity's U.S. branch or arise from the sale of U.S. real property interests.

Inventory valuation should be consistent from year to year, but permission may be obtained to change the method. Inventory may be valued under the last-in, first-out (LIFO) method or the first-in, first-out (FIFO) method.

The Financial Accounting Standards Board (FASB) establishes standards for financial accounting and reporting that are officially recognized by the SEC and the American Institute of Certified Public Accountants (AICPA). The accounting standards and disclosure requirements established by the FASB and the SEC are more extensive than those in most countries. U.S. accounting practices distinguish between private companies and publicly held companies with respect to certain disclosures. Supplemental disclosures are sometimes necessary from large, publicly held companies.

State and federal laws do not require that a company publish financial information. Usually, privately owned businesses do not disclose financial data to the public. However, companies that are publicly owned must generally prepare financial statements that are provided to shareholders and filed with the SEC. In addition, companies operating in certain regulated industries are required by regulatory agencies to publish financial information. The SEC and the national securities exchanges generally require that financial statements filed with them be audited.

Taxes are payable in quarterly installments during the year in which the income is earned. Final payment is due on March 15 or the fifteenth day of the third month following the close of the company's fiscal year. Tax payments include withholdings from employees' wages and salaries and quarterly estimated tax payments. 90% of the final tax bill must be paid before the final due date. Each person or entity subject to U.S. tax must annually report actual income, compute the tax, and file tax returns with the IRS. Any tax due after withholding and estimated tax payments is payable with the tax return.

The Internal Revenue Service has broad discretion to restructure transactions between commonly owned corporations to reflect armslength pricing. Reallocation of gross income, deductions, credits, and other allowances between organizations owned directly or indirectly by the same interest is permitted.

State and Local Taxation

States and localities impose various taxes on income, capital, property, and sales. The method used to determine the taxable base varies from state to state. There are no uniform rules on the definition of taxable income or on allocation of income among the various tax jurisdictions. State corporate income taxes are usually assessed on total taxable income, but a few states assess on net income after federal taxes. Some states retain the federal definition of taxable income as a base for taxation, but many southern and western states do not follow federal rules. Each state is required to apportion the taxable base inside and outside the state in a reasonable manner. Only the amount apportioned to the state may be taxed. Thus, even though only activity within the state is taxable, apportionment methods do vary from state to state. In some instances activities that initially appear unrelated to a state may be apportioned to that state.

Comparisons of tax rates levied by the various states are not entirely meaningful because the definition of taxable income varies from state to state. Many states apply taxes at a flat rate—usually 3 to 12%—but some have graduated rates (see appendix E on state tax).

Most states use a three-factor apportionment formula consisting of real and tangible personal property, payroll, and gross receipts. First, the ratio for each factor derived within the state to the worldwide total is determined. Then, the three ratios are averaged. Some states use only one or two factors or double-weigh a factor. Gross receipts are normally derived at the location of the buyer. Some states, such as California, treat commonly controlled corporations as one in applying the three-factor allocation formula. In doing so, the states may include the income of corporations that transact no business and have no property or employees in the state. There is a growing trend by the states to repeal use of the worldwide unitary tax method.

Tax liability will vary substantially depending on the state and the activities conducted in that state. In some states corporate entities earning no net income can incur significant tax liabilities.

Unique provisions in the laws of various states may deny carry-backs or carryovers of net operating losses, deny deductions for intercorporate interest expenses, prohibit filing consolidated returns to offset one corporation's losses against another corporation's income, or as in California, require filing combined returns including the income and apportionment factors of U.S. and foreign parents, subsidiaries, and affiliates. Since state taxes are deductible against federal taxes and often do not exceed 10% of income, they do not constitute a prohibitive cost. Yet, avoidable costs may be incurred if one does not think about the impact of taxes.

Local, or municipal, income tax rates generally vary from 1 to 2%, while corporate rates vary from 1 to 9%. Other state and local taxes include inheritance and estate tax, gift tax, use tax, and property tax.

State governments generally impose a sales tax, which is similar to a value-added tax except that sales tax is imposed only on a final sale. Sales tax, with local variations in many cases, ranges from approximately 3 to 8%. Local jurisdictions levy annual real and personal property tax on the assessed value of property. Rates, assessment methods, and exemptions vary by locality.

Individual Income Taxes

U.S. citizens and resident aliens are taxed on their worldwide incomes. Nonresident aliens are taxed on U.S.-source income, which includes payments for personal services performed in the United States. Federal personal income tax rates are progressive, with a maximum rate of 50% since 1982. Deductions are permitted for business and investment expenses, interest expenses, certain medical expenses, charitable contributions, and taxes other than federal taxes. A credit for foreign tax payments is also permitted. Many states and a few local jurisdictions impose additional individual income taxes at rates of up to 15%.

Closing Comments

U.S. taxation is complicated. Corporations are subject to federal, state, and local tax, with income tax applied on a worldwide basis. Consulting with tax experts might be necessary in the early stages of planning before coming to America.

The Department of the Treasury has developed a comprehensive proposal to simplify and reform the federal tax system. This proposal, by substantially broadening the tax base, would significantly reduce marginal tax rates; increase fairness; and stimulate future savings, investment, and growth. The Treasury proposal calls for reductions in the corporate tax rate (from 46% to 33%) and in the personal tax rate (from 50% to 35%), and the elimination of most tax shelters. The recently adopted Gramm–Rudman Act, which calls for a balanced federal government budget, may lead to an increase in taxes.

The U.S. objective of unrestricted capital flow is evidenced by the 1984 removal of the withholding tax on interest earned by nonresidents on U.S. bonds and other financial instruments. The new tax rules now make it feasible for U.S. corporations to issue securities directly to foreigners without having to issue an offshore shell subsidiary, a procedure that was both costly and cumbersome.

11
Investment Incentives

I n the United States, federal, state, and local governments offer
investment incentives to new foreign and domestic investors in
all types of industry. The most active promotion of new investment is carried out on the state and local levels through development
programs designed to stimulate local economies and aid target
groups or industries. Many state and local governments significantly help foreign businesses locate in the United States by assisting with site selection, and providing financial or tax incentives.
Many states operate representative offices abroad to help foreign
investors investigate direct investment opportunities. The Department of Commerce provides information on investing in the United
States, primarily through publications.

Federal Incentives

Unlike many other central governments around the world, the U.S.
government plays only a minor role in providing inducements to
investors. It believes that economic stimulus is more effectively ac-
complished through the free-enterprise system and local and state
authorities. The federal government has traditionally relied on fiscal
and monetary policies rather than specific financial incentives to
stimulate business activities. The U.S. opposes government practices that distort, restrict, or place unreasonable burdens on direct
investment.

The federal government sponsors some incentives designed to
assist state and local development agencies and individual corporations in reducing operating expenses or capital requirements. The
main incentive programs include corporate tax credits and some
loan and guarantee schemes for certain eligible areas and sectors
suffering from cyclical or structural problems.

State and local governments provide various tax incentives and sources of financial assistance. These incentives include exemption from or reduced assessment of property tax, exemption from sales tax, and liberal rules for tax-deductibility of expenses in determining state corporate income tax. In addition, state and local governments issue industrial development bonds whose proceeds may be used to help foreign investors finance new ventures.

Federal aid is channeled through federal economic development programs. The Economic Development Administration (EDA) of the Department of Commerce guarantees loans and provides technical, planning, and research assistance to investors starting new businesses in poverty or high-unemployment areas. The EDA is no longer accepting loan applications, since its operations are being phased out because of federal budget cuts. The Small Business Administration (SBA) is providing loans to small businesses at significantly reduced levels because of recent budget cuts. The SBA offers financial assistance, guarantees, and marketing expertise to small companies under several programs.

An important federal program utilized by cities to attract investment is the Urban Development Action Grant (UDAG), which is administered by the Department of Housing and Urban Development. Under this program older cities meeting certain "distress criteria" are eligible for federal funds covering 15 to 20% of a project's cost.

The Farmers Home Administration, a division of the Department of Agriculture, runs the Business and Industrial Loans and Grants Program, which provides loans to both locally owned firms and those with up to 49% foreign-ownership which are interested in setting up operations in rural areas.

Eligibility for assistance often depends on the benefits that will accrue to a geographic area from the proposed investment. Applications to federal programs usually require disclosure of a company's financial data and information concerning the economic and environmental impact of the proposed investment.

State and Local Incentives

Most state and local government authorities offer various incentives to attract new investors to their regions. These incentives are generally designed to facilitate the establishment of new business operations. Incentives range from providing industry feasibility studies to industrial revenue bonds, which can be used by companies to finance the construction of warehouses, plants, or other industrial facilities.

The major significant features of investment promotion in the U.S. are the incentives granted by the state and local governments. Indeed, nearly all the planning and executing of regional economic-development programs and projects is done by state and local governments. States have about 6,000 economic-development groups and spend large sums each year to stimulate foreign investment.

More specifically, state and local governments may offer the following types of incentives:

financial aid—direct loans, industrial revenue or development bond financing, and loan guarantees

state and local tax breaks—property tax abatement, tax increment financing, and general tax relief

state regulatory reliefs (environmental quality) and nonfinancial incentives (site location)

Financial Assistance

Most states offer some type of financial aid to new industries within their borders. Many states have established loan funds and mortgage guarantee programs to help firms locating or expanding within the state.

Four types of state industrial financing are commonly used: (1) industrial revenue bonds and mortgages, (2) loan guarantee programs, (3) direct loan programs, and (4) development credit corporations. These programs are implemented at the state, county, or municipal level. Not all states offer each of these programs, and the incentives vary considerably from state to state. Funding under some of these programs is limited.

As explained in chapter 9, industrial development or revenue bonds are issued by state, county, and city governments to buy or build plants and equipment for leasing to particular firms. In some states, sale-and-leaseback arrangements are common. A company that constructs a plant sells it to the town or municipality, and simultaneously leases the property back. The seller, or lessee, obtains the use of funds and attractive tax benefits (for example, exemption from property taxes).

Today most states allow the issuing of industrial revenue bonds. Some states allow state-chartered pools of funds to guarantee revenue bonds when the bonds are not fully backed by the state.

Many states have industrial finance institutions that channel state funds and credit to local development corporations to help them build plants for new industry. State loan-guarantee programs usually insure development loans for up to 90% of the acquisition cost of land and buildings. Sometimes loans for equipment and machinery may also be provided. Some state programs guarantee repayment to the private financial institutions making the loans if default occurs.

Some local governments have industrial development agencies (IDAs) that issue their own revenue bonds to finance the establishment of new manufacturing, commercial warehousing, and research facilities. Financing depends on the company's contributions to local economic development or employment.

Tax Incentives

Various state and local tax incentives are commonly available on a negotiated or case-by-case basis. Among them are tax reductions and exemptions, tax credits and preferential assessment. These are usually offered as exemptions or deferrals from property, inventory, sales, or income tax.

Many states have enacted legislation to exempt new companies from various state taxes for specified periods. Some states provide a corporate income tax exemption for qualified companies. Preferred property tax assessment is commonly applied to machinery, equipment, furniture, and fixtures in addition to real estate. In-transit inventories, may also be exempted from property tax. Business purchases may be exempted from sales tax. Reduced income tax is sometimes provided for out-of-state sales, and preferential income tax write-offs may be given for selected types of investment.

Nonfinancial Incentives

Nonfinancial incentives include public services, such as rail and highway connections and water and sewage facilities, as well as:

Site location assistance, including the possibility of free land for industrial development or a low-cost site in a state-prepared industrial park

Improved land, industrial parks, or custom-built plants, and stores leased at lower rates

Sale-and-leaseback arrangements

State and local training programs to meet specialized needs

Assistance in conducting market and feasibility studies, and joint venture partnership searches.

Enterprise Zones

Enterprise zones are specially designated areas in which states and local governments reduce taxes, ease regulations, and provide various incentives to stimulate private business activities. Among the zones' tax incentives are exemption from sales taxes on material used for construction within the zones, real property tax abatement, and tax credit or deductions for structural improvements or employee training. The authorities also provide various loans and credit programs. Each enterprise zone might have its own staff of planners, marketing, and government-relations experts.

Some 1,300 enterprise zones in 525 local communities in 25 states have been established to date. The zones are designed to provide an impetus to inner-city and distressed rural areas. While strongly promoted by President Reagan, Congress has yet to pass enterprise legislation.

In summary, only a sampling of investment incentives are cited above, and many more exist on the state, local, and federal levels. New investors may benefit greatly from a thorough examination of investment incentives offered in the United States (See appendix G for more information on state incentives.)

12
How Banks Can Be of Assistance

Because banks such as the Bank of America view direct investment in the United States as a stimulus to the national and world economies, they are willing and able to facilitate business transactions that might promote such investment.

Banks deliver their corporate banking services from units around the world. These services are directly available through a client's corporate headquarters or through more geographically remote offices. A bank coordinates global corporate financing for its client through branches of its international financial network or through representative offices, subsidiaries, or affiliates. This network allows the bank to assist customers in finding and financing investment opportunities. Because of the banks' contacts with companies around the world, they are well positioned to assist both the investment buyer and the investment seller. Major banks are usually organized both geographically and by industry specialization through their world banking divisions to maximize their ability to provide such services.

To effectively serve the special requirements of foreign corporations investing in the United States, many banks have established direct foreign investment sections. These specialized teams of bankers combine the knowledge of international corporate finance with the banks' prominence and demonstrated expertise in the United States.

The DFI section at the Bank of America, for instance, represents the bank both to subsidiaries of foreign corporations with established U.S. operations and to corporations considering U.S. investments. At the Bank of America's New York and Los Angeles corporate offices, DFI officers arrange all types of commercial banking services in the United States. With their broad experience in the foreign investment field, they are particularly well qualified to provide guidance and introductions to new investors. Established foreign operations in the United States can rely on these bankers to help them expand their businesses.

Conclusion

The relative importance of direct foreign investment inflows in the U.S. economy has continued to increase in the 1980s. These investments are expected to expand further in the future, as large- and middle-market corporations seek to position themselves in the United States. The integration of both the global economy and financial markets made investment abroad a necessary condition for corporate success.

Operating in the U.S. provides many advantages, including a reduction in vulnerability to exchange-rate movements and protectionism, and the ability to benefit from the largest and most affluent market in the world. The United States maintains an open-door policy toward foreign companies operating here, and the 50 states provide substantial incentives to foreign investors.

While this book provides background information on doing business in the United States, companies that plan to invest here should thoroughly evaluate the issues concerning location, corporate organization, staffing, financing, and taxation, and prepare a strategic and operating plan. Success would then be more certain.

Appendix A
Growth of Manufacturing Industries

Source: U.S. Department of Commerce, International Trade Administration, "Highlights of the 1985 U.S. Industrial Outlook," *1985 U.S. Industrial Outlook*, January 1985, pp. 9–12.

Growth in Constant Dollar Industry Shipments for 209 Manufacturing Industries Listed by 1985 Rank Order[1]

1985 Rank[2] Order	SIC Code	Industry Title	Annual Growth Rate 1984-85	Annual Growth Rate 1983-84	Compound Annual Growth Rate 1972-82
1	3674	Semiconductors and Related Devices	37.4	44.2	34.1
2	3332	Primary Lead	28.0	-27.0	-3.8
3	3721	Aircraft	21.1	-6.6	2.8
4	3764	Space Propulsion Units and Parts	18.0	9.6	1.4
5	3573	Electronic Computing Equipment	17.0	20.5	19.2
6	3334	Primary Aluminum	15.6	-17.0	-2.2
7	3693	X-ray Apparatus and Tubes	15.4	15.4	15.4
8	3761	Guided Missiles and Space Vehicles	14.7	12.6	0.2
9	332	Iron and Steel Foundries	13.6	12.8	-4.3
10	3714	Motor Vehicles Parts and Accessories	12.3	16.1	-4.0
11	3769	Space Vehicle Equipment, n.e.c.	11.7	10.8	-0.8
12	336	Nonferrous Foundries	10.8	5.0	-2.1
13	2819	Industrial Inorganic Chemicals, n.e.c.	10.0	10.7	0.1
14	3825	Instruments To Measure Electricity	10.0	19.1	8.4
15	3331	Primary Copper	10.0	-2.4	-2.3
16	3448	Prefabricated Metal Buildings	10.0	18.4	4.2
17	3451	Screw Machine Products	9.6	11.6	-0.1
18	3544	Special Dies, Tools, and Jigs	9.6	16.3	-0.9
19	2812	Alkalies and Chlorine	9.6	1.9	-5.4
20	3623	Electric Welding Apparatus	9.4	7.8	-1.0
21	3662	Radio and TV Communication Equipment	9.1	7.5	8.0
22	2891	Adhesives and Sealants	8.9	9.3	1.8
23	2893	Printing Ink	8.7	8.5	-0.2
24	3567	Industrial Furnaces and Ovens	8.6	16.7	-1.4
25	3465	Automotive Stampings	8.1	22.5	-2.6
26	2831	Biological Products	8.0	10.0	12.2
27	3661	Telephone and Telegraph Apparatus	8.0	10.0	4.3
28	2879	Agricultural Chemicals, n.e.c.	7.9	4.1	2.8
29	2038	Frozen Specialties	7.6		1.2
30	3724	Aircraft Engines and Engine Parts	7.4	-11.2	2.7
31	3841	Surgical and Medical Instruments	7.2	7.2	7.1
32	3494	Valves and Pipe Fittings	7.1	6.1	2.0
33	3519	Internal Combustion Engines, n.e.c.	7.0	8.0	0.9
34	2647	Sanitary Paper Products	7.0	6.5	4.1
35	2611	Pulpmills	7.0	4.9	3.4
36	3546	Power Driven Handtools	7.0	7.4	2.6
37	3679	Electronic Components, n.e.c.	6.9	16.3	8.8
38	3842	Surgical Appliances and Supplies	6.8	6.6	6.7
39	3533	Oilfield Machinery	6.7	5.4	10.1
40	3532	Mining Machinery	6.7	5.6	-1.4
41	3643	Current-carrying Wiring Devices	6.5	10.0	0.2
42	3621	Motors and Generators	6.5	10.0	

1985 Rank[2] Order	SIC Code	Industry Title	Annual Growth Rate 1984-85	Annual Growth Rate 1983-84	Compound Annual Growth Rate 1972-82
43	331A	Steel Products (3312, 3315, 3316, 3317)	6.4	2.6	-4.8
44	3542	Metal-Forming Machine Tools	6.2	39.6	-4.4
45	3861	Photographic Equipment and Supplies	6.2	7.0	5.4
46	3631	Household Cooking Equipment	6.1	12.9	3.3
47	3622	Industrial Controls	6.0	8.0	2.9
48	3579	Office Machines and Typewriters, Etc.	6.0	6.5	7.4
49	3574	Calculating and Accounting Machines	6.0	6.0	13.0
50	3811	Engineering and Scientific Instruments	6.0	12.6	4.0
51	3562	Ball and Roller Bearings	6.0	8.9	-2.9
52	2771	Greeting Card Publishing	5.9	7.0	2.7
53	3678	Electronic Connectors	5.9	11.9	10.6
54	2816	Inorganic Pigments	5.9	12.6	-3.9
55	2821	Plastics Materials and Resins	5.8	6.5	1.3
56	3944	Games, Toys, and Childrens' Vehicles	5.6	6.8	2.9
57	3272	Concrete Products, n.e.c.	5.5	14.2	-2.5
58	3715	Truck Trailers	5.5	50.1	-3.6
59	3541	Metal-Cutting Machine Tools	5.5	12.3	1.4
60	371A	Truck and Bus Bodies (3713, 3716)	5.3	17.4	-0.2
61	2086	Bottled and Canned Soft Drinks	5.1	5.4	2.0
62	3911	Jewelry and Precious Metal	5.1	-8.9	-5.2
63	3829	Measuring and Controlling Devices, n.e.c.	5.1	11.4	7.7
64	2875	Fertilizers, Mixing Only	5.0	13.0	-1.1
65	3531	Construction Machinery	5.0	8.8	-3.2
66	2761	Manifold Business Forms	5.0	6.0	4.1
67	3651	Radio and Television Receiving Sets	5.0	12.2	3.4
68	2022	Natural and Processed Cheese	5.0	11.1	3.8
69	3523	Farm Machinery and Equipment	5.0	3.1	0.0
70	2824	Organic Fibers—Noncellulosic	4.8	1.8	2.9
71	3942	Dolls	4.7	13.0	2.0
72	3563	Air and Gas Compressors	4.5	4.3	5.3
73	2653	Corrugated and Solid Fiber Boxes	4.5	7.8	1.5
74	2017	Poultry and Egg Processing	4.5	3.6	4.2
75	2731	Book Publishing	4.5	5.1	2.5
76	2052	Cookies and Crackers	4.5	5.7	0.6
77	3561	Pumps and Pumping Equipment	4.5	3.5	2.0
78	3711	Motor Vehicles and Car Bodies	4.4	19.5	-1.5
79	2741	Miscellaneous Publishing	4.4	5.4	-1.5
80	3832	Optical Instruments and Lenses	4.4	21.8	16.7
81	2721	Periodicals	4.3	6.0	5.3
82	2869	Industrial Organic Chemicals, n.e.c.	4.3	17.5	-0.3
83	2843	Surface Active Agents	4.1	3.9	6.3
84	2621	Papermills, Except Building Paper	4.1	9.3	3.4
85	2492	Particleboard	4.1	6.0	-1.3
86	2833	Medicinals and Botanicals	4.0	4.2	13.9

87	3524	Lawn and Garden Equipment	4.0	12.0	0.7
88	2631	Paperboard Mills	4.0	4.8	-0.2
89	3555	Printing Trades Machinery	4.0	4.8	3.5
90	3636	Sewing Machines	4.0	8.7	-2.1
91	3613	Switchgear and Switchboard Apparatus	4.0	7.0	0.2
92	275A	Commercial Printing (2751, 2752, 2754)	4.0	5.8	-2.8
93	2655	Fiber Cans, Drums, and Similar Products	4.0	5.0	-0.8
94	2874	Phosphatic Fertilizers	4.0	13.0	1.9
95	2511	Wood Household Furniture	4.0	9.7	-1.6
96	3949	Sporting and Athletic Goods, n.e.c.	4.0	7.0	1.1
97	2873	Nitrogenous Fertilizers	4.0	12.7	3.8
98	2512	Upholstered Household Furniture	4.0	9.9	-0.6
99	2654	Sanitary Food Containers	4.0	5.9	-1.9
100	3823	Process Control Instruments	4.0	4.5	8.9
101	3635	Household Vacuum Cleaners	4.0	8.3	0.4
102	3273	Ready-mixed Concrete	4.0	14.0	-1.7
103	2448	Wood Pallets and Skids	3.9	10.0	8.3
104	2016	Poultry Dressing Plants	3.8	3.0	6.2
105	2795	Lithographic Platemaking Services	3.8	6.1	9.8
106	3241	Hydraulic Cement	3.8	12.9	-2.6
107	3728	Aircraft Equipment, n.e.c.	3.7	-3.9	4.1
108	3554	Paper Industries Machinery	3.6	-0.8	-0.9
109	3751	Motorcycles, Bicycles, and Parts	3.6	8.1	-1.9
110	3644	Noncurrent-carrying Wiring Devices	3.5	6.0	0.1
111	3632	Household Refrigerators and Freezers	3.5	12.4	-2.9
112	2641	Paper Coating and Glazing	3.5	4.6	1.1
113	2732	Book Printing	3.5	4.5	1.4
114	2842	Polishes and Sanitation Goods	3.3	3.1	-0.1
115	3675	Electronic Capacitors	3.3	5.8	3.0
116	3271	Concrete Block and Brick	3.3	12.0	-3.8
117	2711	Newspapers	3.2	4.1	0.8
118	3552	Textile Machinery	3.2	4.9	-5.8
119	3551	Food Products Machinery	3.2	6.8	0.2
120	2861	Gum and Wood Chemicals	3.1	1.8	5.7
121	2892	Explosives	3.1	5.6	-2.9

1985 Rank² Order	SIC Code	Industry Title	Annual Growth Rate 1984-85	Annual Growth Rate 1983-84	Compound Annual Growth Rate 1972-82
122	2515	Mattresses and Bedsprings	3.1	4.9	0.0
123	2037	Frozen Fruits and Vegetables	3.0	-10.1	2.3
124	3079	Miscellaneous Plastics Products	3.0	4.5	4.5
125	3452	Bolts, Nuts, Rivets, and Washers	3.0	3.9	-1.5
126	364A	Lighting Fixtures (3645, 3646, 3648)	3.0	5.6	-0.8
127	2643	Bags, Except Textile Bags	3.0	4.0	0.5
128	3639	Household Appliances, n.e.c.	3.0	13.1	1.3
129	2813	Industrial Gases	3.0	2.9	5.1
130	2899	Chemical Preparations, n.e.c.	3.0	6.9	2.9
131	3634	Electric Housewares and Fans	3.0	5.4	1.5
132	3585	Refrigeration and Heating Equipment	3.0	2.9	-0.7
133	3612	Transformers	3.0	5.5	-1.0
134	2651	Folding Paperboard Boxes	3.0	3.5	1.1
135	3633	Household Laundry Equipment	3.0	10.2	-2.1
136	3564	Blowers and Fans	2.9	1.2	0.3
137	2649	Converted Paper Products, n.e.c.	2.9	4.0	4.0
138	2865	Cyclic Crudes and Intermediates	2.9	5.6	-0.5
139	3843	Dental Equipment and Supplies	2.9	2.5	2.6
140	2141	Tobacco Stemming and Redrying	2.9	6.9	-1.9
141	2851	Paints and Allied Products	2.8	13.4	0.8
142	3961	Costume Jewelry	2.8	1.0	3.9
143	2834	Pharmaceutical Preparations	2.8	3.1	3.1
144	2514	Metal Household Furniture	2.8	7.9	-0.9
145	2642	Envelopes	2.5	2.0	2.9
146	2841	Soap and Other Detergents	2.5	2.5	1.5
147	3069	Fabricated Rubber Products, n.e.c.	2.4	9.9	-0.2
148	2844	Toilet Preparations	2.3	2.4	2.1
149	2051	Bread, Cake, and Related Products	2.1	2.4	-0.8
150	3041	Rubber and Plastic Hose and Belting	2.1	9.7	-1.7
151	2065	Confectionery Products	2.0	9.5	3.6
152	2895	Carbon Black	2.0	11.8	-2.2
153	2645	Die-cut Paper and Board	2.0	2.0	0.4
154	3161	Luggage	2.0	0.0	0.7
155	3824	Fluid Meters and Counting Devices	1.9	19.8	3.1
156	2035	Pickles, Sauces, and Salad Dressing	1.9	3.0	5.6
157	2084	Wines, Brandy, and Brandy Spirits	1.9	1.8	4.7
158	2034	Dehydrated Fruits, Vegetables, and Soup	1.7	1.9	1.4
159	3441	Fabricated Structural Metal	1.5	5.0	-0.9
160	2043	Cereal Breakfast Foods	1.4	-1.1	-3.2
161	3411	Metal Cans	1.4	3.5	-0.4
162	2823	Cellulosic Manmade Fibers	1.2	7.8	0.6
163	3011	Tires and Inner Tubes	1.2	10.6	-3.6
164	3172	Personal Leather Goods, n.e.c.	1.2	0.4	0.2
165	3676	Electronic Resistors	1.1	3.9	1.9
166	3221	Glass Containers	1.1	-0.2	-0.7
167	2033	Canned Fruits and Vegetables	1.0	-6.1	-0.1
168	3931	Musical Instruments	1.0	-0.9	-2.8
169	3677	Electronic Coils and Transformers	1.0	3.6	0.6

Rank	SIC Code	Industry			
170	2822	Synthetic Rubber	1.0	9.7	-0.4
171	2032	Canned Specialties	0.9	0.8	0.1
172	2024	Ice Cream and Frozen Desserts	0.5	-3.0	0.6
173	3111	Leather Tanning and Finishing	0.3	-5.7	-3.0
174	3171	Women's Handbags and Purses	0.2	5.9	-0.3
175	2435	Hardwood Veneer and Plywood	0.1	7.0	-1.9
176	2082	Malt Beverages	0.1	0.2	4.8
177	2013	Sausages and Other Prepared Meats	0.1	0.8	2.5
178	2021	Creamery Butter	0.0	1.0	-0.8
178	2491	Wood Preserving	0.0	4.0	3.0
178	2648	Stationery Products	0.0	1.5	0.2
178	2652	Setup Paperboard Boxes	0.0	-1.5	-6.7
183	3151	Leather Gloves and Mittens	-0.5	0.7	-4.4
184	3251	Brick and Structural Clay Tile	-0.8	9.1	-6.5
185	2131	Chewing and Smoking Tobacco	-0.9	0.8	2.8
186	2911	Petroleum Refining	-0.9	2.5	1.4
187	2026	Fluid Milk	-1.0	-0.3	0.9
188	3262	Vitreous China Food Utensils	-1.0	2.9	2.5
189	2439	Structural Wood Members, n.e.c.	-1.0	5.5	0.1
190	3021	Rubber and Plastics Footwear	-1.1	-1.1	-3.6
191	3275	Gypsum Products	-1.7	5.7	-1.1
192	2111	Cigarettes	-1.8	-0.2	1.2
193	2121	Cigars	-1.8	-1.9	-7.5
194	2431	Millwork	-2.0	3.2	-3.0
195	3822	Environmental Controls	-2.0	15.3	1.6
196	2011	Meatpacking Plants	-2.4	0.1	0.3
197	3263	Fine Earthenware Food Utensils	-2.9	-5.6	-6.3
197	2411	Logging Camps and Log Contractors	-3.0	3.6	5.3
199	2646	Pressed and Molded Pulp Goods	-3.0	-1.4	-4.8
200	2023	Condensed and Evaporated Milk	-3.4	2.6	0.7
201	3671	Electron Tubes	-3.6	2.1	-0.8
202	2085	Distilled Liquor, Except Brandy	-3.9	0.4	-0.2
203	2426	Hardwood Dimension and Flooring	-4.0	5.0	-3.2
204	3731	Ship Building and Repairing	-4.0	-3.3	3.6
204	2386	Leather and Sheep Lined Clothing	-4.0	-22.8	-5.6
204	2661	Building Paper and Board Mills	-4.0	-0.3	-9.5
206	3333	Primary Zinc	-4.9	14.7	-8.7
207	2436	Softwood Veneer and Plywood	-7.4	11.3	-1.0
208	2421	Sawmills and Planing Mills—General	-10.4	17.1	-1.9
209	3511	Turbines and Turbine Generator Sets	-21.9	0.8	-4.4

1 All calculations in Tables 1 and 2 are based on industry shipments expressed in 1972 dollars. The 1972 constant dollar data provide a basis for calculating real rates of change in shipments. The percent change figures provide a measure of changes in the volume of industry shipments and allow interindustry comparisons without the distorting influence of price change.

2 Industries with the same rank have the same growth rate. Due to rounding, industries may have identical printed rates and different ranks. The rank order reflects the unrounded growth rates.

Appendix B
U.S. Foreign Trade Zones

Source: U.S. Department of Commerce, International Administration.

U.S. Foreign Trade Zones

Zone No. 1, New York City
Brooklyn Navy Yard, Brooklyn, NY 11205
Sol Braun, (212) 834-1300
Warehouse and processing facility in bldg. 77 of the navy yard with approved zone area of 240,000 square feet; sponsored by New York City's Department of Ports and Terminals.

Zone No. 2, New Orleans
P.O. Box 60046, New Orleans, LA 70160
Robert Dee, (504) 897-0189
Wharf on the Mississippi at Napoleon Avenue with 19 acres, containing warehouse and processing facilities; sponsored by the Port of New Orleans.

Zone No. 3 and Subzone 3-A, San Francisco
Foreign Trade Services, Inc., Pier 23, San Francisco, CA 94111
Ed Osgood, (415) 391-0176
Piers 19 and 23 on the Embarcadero, consisting of over 225,000 square feet of covered space and a special-purpose subzone for Lilli Ann's textile apparel production facilities; sponsored by the San Francisco Port Commission.

Zone No. 5, Seattle
P.O. Box 1209, Seattle, WA 98111
R.C. McQuigg, (206) 382-3275
Warehouse with 49,500 square feet at terminal 106; sponsored by the Port of Seattle.

Zone No. 7 and Subzone 7-B, Mayaguez, Puerto Rico
G.P.O. Box 2350, San Juan, PR 00936
Jose Cobian, (809) 765-2784
Industrial park of 44 acres and a special-purpose subzone for the Commonwealth Oil Refining Company, Inc.; refinery and petrochemical complex near Penuelas; sponsored by the Puerto Rico Industrial Development Company, Inc.

Zone No. 8, Toledo
3332 St. Lawrence Drive, Toledo, OH 43605
Frank E. Miller, (419) 698-8026
Warehouse/processing facility with 130,000 square feet, in the Port of Toledo's 135-acre general cargo facility on Lake Erie; sponsored by the Port.

Zone No. 9 and Subzone 9-A, Honolulu
Pier 2, Honolulu, HI 96813
Homer Maxey, (808) 548-5435
Pier 2/Fort Armstrong, adjacent to the harbor's main foreign cargo discharge area, covering 20 acres; facility has 300,000 square feet of warehousing and processing space and a special-purpose subzone; sponsored by Hawaii's Department of Planning and Economic Development.

Zone No. 12, McAllen, Texas
6401 South 33rd Street, McAllen, TX 78501
Frank Birkhead, (512) 682-4306
Industrial park with 40 acres near Mexican border; sponsored by McAllen
Trade Zone, Inc., a nonprofit economic development corporation.

Zone No. 14 and Subzone 14-A, Little Rock, Arkansas
Little Rock Port Authority, 7500 Lindsey Road, Little Rock, AK 72206
Robert Brave, (501) 490-1468
Industrial park of 28 acres and subzone for the Sanyo Manufacturing Cor-
poration's production and assembly plant, consisting of 162 acres; spon-
sored by the Little Rock Port Authority.

Zone No. 15 and Subzone 15-A, Kansas City, Missouri
920 Main Street, 600 CharterBank Center, Kansas City, MO 64105
R. Chris Wyatt, (816) 421-7666
Zone consists of 2 sites. *Site 1* is warehouse of 250,000 square feet; *Site 2* is
underground warehouse/processing facility of 2.8 million square feet; *Site 3*
is warehouse complex with 75,000 square feet of warehouse processing space
near the Kansas City Int'l Airport. Subzone at Ford Motor Corp.'s auto
assembly plant, which covers 155 acres in Claycomo, MO; sponsored by
Greater Kansas City Foreign-Trade Zone, Inc., a nonprofit corporation.

Zone No. 16, Sault Ste. Marie, Michigan
Economic Development Corp., 1301 Easterday West Industrial Park, Sault
Ste. Marie, MI 49783
James F. Hendricks, (906) 635-9131
A 17-acre zone in 57 acre industrial park; sponsored by Michigan Depart-
ment of Commerce.

Zone No. 17, Kansas City, Kansas
Greater Kansas Foreign-Trade Zone Inc., 920 Main Street, 600 CharterBank
Center, Kansas City, MO 64105
R. Chris Wyatt, (816) 421-7666
Underground warehouse/processing facility of 405,000 square feet; same
sponsor as Zone No. 15.

Zone No. 18, San Jose, California
801 North First Street, San Jose, CA 951XX
Ted Daigle, (408) 277-4744
Industrial park facility of 30 acres in the 500-acre International Business
Park; sponsored by the City of San Jose.

Zone No. 19, Omaha, Nebraska
Omaha Douglas Civic Center #304, 1819 Farnam Street, Omaha, NB 68183
Irvin H. Smith, (402) 444-5921
Warehouse/processing facility of 20,000 square feet in the City's 18-acre
municipal dock complex; sponsored by the Omaha Dock Board.

Zone No. 20, Suffolk, Virginia
Virginia Port Authority, 600 World Trade Center, Norfolk, VA 23510
John Hunter, (804) 623-8080
Warehouse facility of 105,000 square feet on a 20-acre site; sponsored by the
Virginia Port Authority.

Zone No. 21, Dorchester County, South Carolina
2725 West 5th North Street, Summerville, SC 29483
A.M. Quattlebaum, (803) 871-4870
Warehouse/processing facility of 20 acres in the 200-acre Tri-County Industrial Park; sponsored by the South Carolina State Ports Authority.

Zone No. 22 and Subzone 22A, Chicago, Illinois
Industrial America Corp., 4343 W. Ohio Street, Chicago, IL 60624
Mike Swade, (312) 722-6600
Industrial park of 25 acres with 116,000 square feet warehouse located on the
Lake Calumet Harbor sea channel; sponsored by the Chicago Regional Port
District. The special-purpose subzone covers 46 acres on 2 parcels at the
steel-tube manufacturing plant of the UNR-Leavitt Division of UNR Indus-
tries, Inc., located at 1717 West 115th Street, Chicago.

Zone No. 23 and Subzone 23A, Buffalo, New York
901 Fuhrmann Blvd., Buffalo, NY 14203
George K. Keitner, (716) 856-4436
Zone of 84 acres, including sites at the Buffalo Marine Terminal, Buffalo
International Airport, and at 2 industrial and commercial sites in Buffalo;
sponsored by the County of Erie. The special-purpose subzone is at the Xerox
Corporation's 465-acre photocopier manufacturing plant, located at 800
Phillips Road in the Village of Webster. The subzone covers 102 acres.

Zone No. 24 and Subzone 24A, Pittston, Pennsylvania
Eastern Distribution Center, Inc., P.O. Box 31, Avoca, PA 18641
James Pettinger, (717) 655-5581
Zone of 42 acres in the 265-acre Eastern Distribution Center, located midway
between Scranton and Wilkes-Barre, PA, adjacent to the Wilkes-Barre/Scran-
ton International Airport; sponsored by Eastern Distribution Center, Inc.
The special-purpose subzone is at the typewriter assembly plant of Olivetti,
located on a 100-acre tract at 2800 Valley Road, Harrisburg, PA.

Zone No. 25, Port Everglades, Broward County, Florida
P.O. Box 13136, Port Everglades, FL 33316
Albert J. Redlhammer, (305) 523-3404
Warehouse facility on 82 acres in a 260-acre area of the port authority;
sponsored by the Board of Commissioners of the Port Everglades Authority.

Zone No. 26 and Subzone 26A, Shenandoah, Coweta County, Georgia
Atlanta Foreign-Trade Zone, 50 Amlajack Blvd., Shenandoah, GA 30265
Richard Naspinski, (404) 581-0790
Industrial park of 33 acres in a 1200-acre industrial park in Shenandoah (a
new town adjacent to Newnan, GA), Coweta County, which adjoins the

Atlanta Customs port of entry; sponsored by the Georgia Foreign Trade Zone, Inc. The special-purpose subzone covers 85-acres at General Motors Corportation's auto assembly plant in Altanta and at the company's 139-acre Doraville plant.

Zone No. 27 and Subzone 27A

Massport, 99 High Street, Boston, MA 02110
Carolyn Yee Wong, (617) 482-2930
Zone consisting of 3 sites, all located in South Boston very close to each other and to the airport and seaport facilities and within one mile of downtown Boston. Each site has existing rail access as well as close proximity to major highways. The special-purpose subzone is located at the textile manufacturing plant of the Sterlingwale Corp., 168 Stevens Street, Fall River, MA; sponsored by the Massachusetts Port Authority.

Zone No. 28, New Bedford, Massachusetts

Industrial Development Commission, 1213 Purchase Street, New Bedford, MA 02740
Norman A. Bergeron, (617) 997-6501
Industrial park of 22 acres within a 52-acre industrial park complex in the northwestern section of the city, adjacent to the New Bedford Municipal Airport and 2.5 miles from the New Bedford port facilities; sponsored by the City of New Bedford.

Zone No. 29, Louisville, Kentucky

6310 Cane Run Road, Louisville, KY 40258
James Kellow, (502) 935-6024
Zone of 12 acres in an industrial park adjacent to the port; sponsored by Louisville and Jefferson County Riverport Authority.

Zone No. 30, Salt Lake City, Utah

Rm. 314, City and County Building, Salt Lake City, UT 84111
Shizuko K. Zupon, (801) 535-7902
Zone of 33 acres in the 740-acre Salt Lake International Center business park, located in Salt Lake City adjacent to the Salt Lake International Airport; sponsored by Salt Lake City Corporation.

Zone No. 31 and Subzone 31-A, Granite City, Illinois

2801 Rock Road, Granite City, IL 62040
Oscar Nazetta, (618) 877-8444
General-purpose zone of 47 acres in the 127-acre Tri-City Industrial Center, located on the western limits of Granite City, adjacent to the Chain of Rocks Canal and within 10 miles of downtown St. Louis. The subzone is for Chrysler's St. Louis Assembly Plant, located at 1001 North Highway Drive, Fenton, MO. The subzone covers 107 acres of the main manufacturing area within the 341-acre complex; sponsored by Tri-City Regional Port District.

Zone No. 32, Miami, Florida

1601 Biscayne Boulevard, Miami, FL 33132
Sandra Gonzalez, (305) 350-7700
General-purpose zone on a 73-acre tract west of the Miami International Airport; sponsored by Greater Miami Foreign Trade Zone, Inc.

Zone No. 33 and Subzone 33A, Pittsburgh, Pennsylvania
534 Union Trust Building, Pittsburgh, PA 15219
Frank Brooks Robinson (412) 471-3939
Industrial park of 36 acres in RIDC Park West in Allegheny County near the Greater Pittsburgh International Airport; sponsored by Regional Industrial Development Corporation of Southwestern Pennsylvania. The special-purpose subzone encompasses a 147-acre portion of the new Volkswagen Manufacturing Corporation of America assembly plant in Westmoreland County, some 35 miles southeast of Pittsburgh.

Zone No. 34, Niagara County, New York
County Office Bldg., 59 Park Avenue, Lockport, NY 14094
Theodore J. Belling, (716) 439-6033
A 19-acre site in a multipurpose industrial development project at the Niagara Falls International Airport in the Town of Wheatfield. A 30,000 square feet multiuser bldg. will be constructed by the county for initial zone use; sponsored by the County of Niagara.

Zone No. 35 and Subzone 35A, Philadelphia, Pennsylvania
DVFTZ, Inc., 3440 Bartram Avenue, Philadelphia, PA 19153
Harold E. Cash, (215) 365-5010
72 acres adjacent to Philadelphia International Airport with Bldg. A a 40,000-square-feet multitenant, warehouse/processing/manufacturing facility with 5,000 square feet modules available. Warehouse/processing/manufacturing facilities at Pier 78 South; sponsored by The Philadelphia Port Corporation. The subzone is located at the electronic automative products plant of Ford Electronics and Refrigeration Corp., a 485,000 square-feet facility located on 36 acres at Church Road and Wissahickon Avenue in Lansdale.

Zone No. 36, Galveston, Texas
Galveston Wharves, P.O. Box 328, Galveston, TX 77550
John Massey, Jr., (409) 766-6112
Zone encompasses 884 acres adjacent to the Galveston Ship Channel on Pelican and Galveston Islands; sponsored by the City of Galveston.

Zone No. 37, Orange County, New York
Foreign Trade Development Company of Orange County, Inc., P.O. Box 6147, Stewart Airport, Newburgh, NY 12550
Albert Randall, (914) 564-7700
Two zone sites, one being in the Sage Building at Stewart Airport (a former military facility now owned by the State) and the other in a planned 65-acre industrial park about 1 mile away, adjacent to the New York City Customs port of entry; sponsored by the County of Orange.

Zone No. 38, Spartanburg County, South Carolina
2725 West 5th North Street, Summerville, SC 29483
A.M. Quattlebaum, (803) 871-4870
Warehouse/processing facility, located on a 20-acre tract in 10 miles of Spartanburg; sponsored by the South Carolina State Ports Authority.

Zone No. 39, Dallas/Fort Worth, Texas

Dallas/Fort Worth Airport, P.O. Drawer DFW, Dallas/Fort Worth Airport, TX 75261
James Alderson, (214) 574-6720
Zone of 250 acres in the northeastern portion of the Dallas/Fort Worth Airport at Radio Road and State Highway 114 in Dallas County; sponsored by Dallas/Fort Worth Regional Airport Board.

Zone No. 40, Cleveland, Ohio

101 Erieside Avenue, Cleveland, OH 44114
John Desmond, (216) 241-8004
Warehouse type facility on a 14-acre parcel in the Cleveland Harbor area at Access Road and West 9th Street; sponsored by Cleveland-Cuyahoga County Port Authority.

Zone No. 41 and Subzones 41A & 41B, Milwaukee, Wisconsin

Foreign Trade Zone of Wisconsin, Ltd., 8512 West Bradley Road, Milwaukee, WI 53224
Vincent J. Boever, (414) 354-4404
General-purpose zone of 46 acres in the Northwestern Industrial Park, owned by the City and located at North 87th Street and West Bradley Road, Milwaukee; a special-purpose subzone at the American Motors Corporation automobile assembly plant in Kenosha; and a special-purpose subzone at a manufacturing facility of the Muskegon Piston Ring Company in Manitowoc; sponsored by Foreign Trade Zone of Wisconsin, Ltd.

Zone No. 42, Orlando Florida

Orlando International Airport, 4101 East 9th Street, Orlando FL 32812
William Blood, (305) 859-9485
Zone encompasses 201 acres at the Orlando International Airport, about 8 miles south of downtown Orlando; sponsored by Greater Orlando Aviation Authority.

Zone No. 43, Battle Creek, Michigan

BC/CAL/KAL Inland Port Authority of South Centeral Michigan Development Corp., P.O. Box 1438, Battle Creek, MI 49016
Marilyn E. Parks, (616) 968-8197
Cargo facility of 23 acres in the 2400-acre Fort Custer Industrial Park in Battle Creek; sponsored by City of Battle Creek.

Zone No. 44 and Subzone 44-A, Morris County, New Jersey

Office of International Trade, 744 Broad Street, Room 1709, Newark, NJ 07102
Joesph Brady, (201) 648-3518
Industrial park of 76 acres in the 650-acre Lakeland Industrial Park in the Township of Mt. Olive, Morris County, NJ. The special-purpose subzone for the Ronson Corporation is located at One Ronson Drive, Woodbridge, NJ. The subzone is housed in a 100,000-square-foot building, of which 50,000 square feet have been activated. The zone and subzone are sponsored by the Department of Labor and Industry of the State of New Jersey.

Zone No. 45 and Subzone 45A, Portland, Oregon
P.O. Box 3529, Portland, OR 97208
Elaine Lycen, (503) 231-5000
Industrial park of 66 acres, located in the Rivergate industrial district immediately north of the City of Portland, adjacent to the port's Terminal 6 on the Columbia River. The subzone is at the steel pipe manufacturing facility of the Beall Pipe and Tank Corp. at 12005 North Burgard Road in Portland; sponsored by the Port of Portland.

Zone No. 46 and Subzones 46A & 46B, Cincinnati, Ohio
120 West Fifth Street, Cincinnati, OH 45202
Joe Kramer, (513) 579-3143
Industrial park of about 100 acres, located about 25 miles north of Cincinnati in the southern portion of Butler County. The subzones are at the General Electric aircraft assembly plant in Evendale, OH, and at the Honda motorcycle plant near Columbus, OH; sponsored by Greater Cincinnati Foreign-Trade Zone, Inc.

Zone No. 47, Campbell County, Kentucky
Northern Kentucky Port Authority, 400 Licking Pike, Wilder, KY 41071
Robert Vogt, (606) 581-1444
Industrial park at 2 separate sites in Campbell County, about 10 miles south of Cincinnati; same sponsor as Zone No. 46.

Zone No. 48, Tucson, Arizona
San Xavier Development Authority, P.O. Box 11246, Mission Station, AR 85734
William Tatom, (602) 792-6862
Industrial park of 23 acres located in the San Xavier Industrial Park adjacent to the Tucson International Airport and the City of Tucson; sponsored by Papago-Tucson Foreign-Trade Zone Corporation.

Zone No. 49, Newark/Elizabeth, New Jersey
One World Trade Center, Room 64 West, New York, NY 10048
Catherine Durda, (212) 466-7985
General-purpose zone covering some 2100 acres within the Newark/Elizabeth-Port Authority Marine Terminal seaport complex in Newark and Elizabeth, New Jersey; sponsored by the Port Authority of New York and New Jersey.

Zone No. 50 and Subzone 50A, Long Beach, California
Board of Harbor Commissioners of the Port of Long Beach, P.O. Box 570, Long Beach, CA 90801
Michael R. Powers (213) 437-0041
General-purpose zone of 10.5 acres in an 82-acre undeveloped industrial tract in northwest Long Beach, near the intersection of the San Diego and Long Beach freeways. Two structures of 60,000 and 80,000 square feet will be the zone's first buildings. The subzone is located on 19 acres at Toyota's pick-up truck cargo body production plant; sponsored by the Board of Harbor Commissioners of the Port of Long Beach.

Zone No. 51, Duluth, Minnesota
Seaway Port Authority of Duluth, 1200 Port Terminal Drive, P.O. Box 6877, Duluth, MN 55808
Jerome Marks, (218) 727-8525
Zone of 1.3 acres in the 120-acre Arthur M. Clure Public Marine Terminal on Superior Bay. The construction of a 10,000-square-foot, general-purpose warehouse facility is planned.

Zone No. 52, Suffolk County, New York
Suffolk County Department of Economic Development, 4175 Veterans Memorial Hwy., Ronkonkoma, NY 11779
Joseph C. Giacalone, (516) 588-1000
Zone of 52.6 acres on land owned by the Township of Islip on the south boundary of the Long Island MacArthur Airport. Two 50,000-square-foot multiuser warehouse structures will be the zone's first facilities.

Zone No. 53, Rogers County, Oklahoma
Tulsa Port of Catoosa, 5350 Cimarron Road, Catoosa, OK 74105
Robert W. Portiss, (918) 266-2291
Zone on a 112-acre tract in the 2,000-acre port terminal and industrial park at the Tulsa Port of Catoosa in Rogers County. The zone will be initially activated at one of the existing warehouse/processing structures on the port's channel.

Zone No. 54, Clinton County, New York
Clinton County Area Development Corporation, Box 19, Plattsburgh, NY 12901
Francis A. Lapham, (518) 561-8800
Zone consists of 2 sites. Site 1 includes the entire 123-acres of the Clinton County Air Industrial Park in Plattsburgh. Site 2 involves an 11-acre distribution center at the U.S.-Canadian border in the Town of Champlain; sponsored by Clinton County, New York.

Zone No. 55 and Subzone 55-A, Burlington, Vermont
Greater Burlington Industrial Corporation, 135 Church Street, Burlington, VT 05402
C. Harry Behney, (802) 862-5726
Zone covers 13 acres in a 104-acre industrial park being developed by GBIC at the airport. An existing warehouse facility is being used for zone operations. The special-purpose subzone is for the St. Albans plant of Pedigree USA, Inc., located at a 3.4-acre facility on St. Albans Town Highway at Highway Road. The company is a manufacturer and distributor of quality ski wear, most of which is currently made and imported from the Far East. The subzone would be used to perform a manufacturing, stitching, and labeling operation here rather than offshore. Zone and subzone sponsored by Greater Burlington Industrial Corporation.

Zone No. 56, Oakland, California
Oakland International Trade Center, Inc., 633 Hagenburger Road, Oakland, CA 94607
Dayton Ballenger, (415) 639-7405
Zone on a 13-acre site being developed as an International Trade Center. An

existing 126,000-square-foot building on the site will be modified to serve as the zone's initial facility; sponsored by the City of Oakland.

Zone No. 57, Mecklenburg County, North Carolina
Piedmont Distribution Center, P.O. Box 7123, Charlotte, NC 28217
Richard Primm, (704) 588-3277
Two general-purpose zone sites located at existing warehouse/distribution facilities about 10 miles southwest of downtown Charlotte. A total of 225,000 square feet of space is available for immediate use, and plans call for expansion based on the needs of the community for zone services; sponsored by the North Carolina Department of Commerce.

Zone No. 58, Bangor, Maine
City of Bangor, Economic Department, City Hall, Bangor, ME 04401
Edward McKeon, (207) 947-0341
The zone consists of 2 adjacent parcels of 1.7 and 24.8 acres at the Bangor International Airport. An existing structure of 21,800 square feet for warehouse/processing is immediately available for the zone's first operations on the smaller parcel. The larger one is planned for zone activity as part of the airport's industrial park development plans; sponsored by the City of Bangor.

Zone No. 59 and Subzone 59A, Lincoln, Nebraska
Lincoln Chamber of Commerce, 1221 N Street, Suite 606, Lincoln, NE 68508
Duane Vicary, (402) 476-7511
Zone on a 250,000-square-foot tract at the Lincoln Airpark West industrial park, a new air-cargo center adjacent to the Lincoln Municipal Airport. Operations will begin in an existing 37,000-square-foot building and adjacent open yard. The special-purpose subzone is located at the Lincoln plant of Kawasaki Motors Corp., U.S.A., a domestic subsidiary of Kawasaki Heavy Industry, Ltd., of Japan, located at 5600 N.W. 27th Street in Lincoln near the Municipal Airport; sponsored by the Lincoln Foreign-Trade Zone, Inc.

Zone No. 60, Nogales, Arizona
Nogales Foreign-Trade Zone, 3600 Tucson-Nogales Highway, Nogales, AR 85621
Robert Lawler, (602) 281-9101
The 28-acre zone site is located in the City of Nogales, adjacent to the Nogales West Customs Compound, the area's commercial crossing point on the U.S.-Mexico border. Initially, 2 20,000-square-foot warehouses will be constructed with industrial facilities to be constructed as demand arises; sponsored by Border Industrial Development, Inc.

Zone No. 61, San Juan, Puerto Rico
Puerto Rico Commercial Development Co., Commonwealth of Puerto Rico, P.O. Box 4943, San Juan, PR 0093X
Sandra Quinones (809) 725-1279
Consists of 60 acres in a 203-acre Int'l Trade Center being developed by CDC in the City of San Juan. Two warehouse facilities will be constructed, containing about 125,000 square feet for initial operations; sponsored by the Commercial Development Co. of P.R.

Zone No. 62, Brownsville, Texas

Brownsville Navigation District, Port of Brownsville, P.O. Box 3070, Brownsville, TX 78520

Al Cisneros, (512) 831-4592

Zone at the Port of Brownsville, a deepwater port near the U.S.-Mexico border, consists of several sites on 2,000 acres in the 42,000-acre Brownsville Navigation District and at the nearby Brownsville International Airport.

Zone No. 63, Prince George's County, Maryland

Prince George's County, State of Maryland, County Administration Building, Upper Marlboro, MD 20870

Frank Sheehan, (301) 952-3402

Zone consists of 77.5 acres in county-owned 1,281-acre Collington Center industrial park, located immediately south of the City of Bowie at the intersection of U.S. Route 301 and Maryland 214 (Central Avenue) in Prince George's County. A 50,000-square-foot multipurpose structure will be constructed as the zone's first facility.

Zone No. 64, Jacksonville, Florida

Jacksonville Port Authority, P.O. Box 30X, 2701 Talleyrand Avenue, Jacksonville, FL 32206

M. Fred Whelan, (904) 633-5250

Zone on a 143-acre parcel owned by the applicant and located near the Jacksonville International Airport, about 8 miles north of downtown Jacksonville. Initially, a general-purpose warehouse facility of about 30,000-square-feet was to be constructed for zone operations in a 5-acre portion of the zone with the remainder to be developed as needed.

Zone No. 65, Panama City, Florida

Panama City Port Authority, P.O. Box 150X, Panama City, FL 32406

Tommy L. Berry, (904) 763-8471

Zone of 15.9 acres in the 120-acre Port Panama City industrial park on St. Andrew Bay on the Gulf of Mexico intracoastal waterway. Consisting of contiguous tracts of 2.4 and 13.5 acres, the sites are owned by the City and under lease to the applicant. The smallest tract is undeveloped land on which a general-purpose storage/processing facility will be constructed, while a large diameter steel-pipe plant is under construction by the Berg Steel Pipe Corp. on the larger tract.

Zone No. 66, Wilmington, North Carolina

North Carolina State Ports Authority (operator), P.O. Box 3248, Wilmington, NC 28406

Don Fishero, (919) 763-1621

Two sites in the Wilmington terminal area, which covers 350 acres in the City of Wilmington. Site 1 covers 24 acres and is adjacent to ocean vessel berths. It contains 11 acres of warehouses and cargo shelter and 13 acres of open space. Site 2 is on 12 acres at the north end of the terminal area on land available for expansion and industrial development.

Zone No. 67, Morehead City, North Carolina

North Carolina State Ports Authority (operator), P.O. Box 3248, Wilmington, NC 28406

Don Fishero, (919) 763-1621

Site 1 is located in the 154-acre Morehead City terminal, in the Customs port of entry. It consists of a 92,600-square-foot warehouse and an additional 4 acres of open space. The second site is a 40-acre tract of undeveloped port land 4 miles west of the port near the intersection of U.S. Route 70 and State Route 24, Carteret County, NC.

Zone No. 68, El Paso, Texas
El Paso International Airport, El Paso, TX 79925
Robert C. Jacob, Jr., (915) 772-4271
Zone in the 530-acre Butterfield Industrial Park, an expansion of the El Paso International Airport Board's growing industrial and trade complex. The zone consists of 60 acres and is located near the El Paso International Airport.

Zone No. 70 and Subzone 70A, 70B and 70C, Detroit, Michigan
Greater Detroit Foreign-Trade Zone, Inc., 100 Renaissance Center, Suite 1370, Detroit, MI 48243
Joseph T. Auwers, (313) 259-8077
A dual-site general-purpose zone with a 5 acre parcel at the Clark Street Port facility in downtown Detroit, and a 5.5-acre tract at the Woodfab Company's distribution complex, located at 6700 Chase Road, Dearborn; 10 miles from Detroit Metropolitan Airport. A 10,000-square-foot warehouse is proposed for the downtown site. A 75,000-square-foot structure is available at the Dearborn site for initial operations. Subzone 70A is located at Ford Motor Company's tractor assembly plant in Romeo, MI. Subzone 70B is for Chrysler's 120-acre Jefferson Assembly Plant, located at 12200 East Jefferson Avenue, Detroit. Recently renovated to assemble front-wheel-drive automobiles. Subzone 70C is at Ford Motor Corporation's Wayne Assembly Plant, located at 37625 Michigan Avenue, Wayne. The 141-acre facility has recently been renovated for the assembly of the company's new front-wheel-drive subcompact cars. Greater Detroit Foreign-Trade Zone, Inc., the sponsor, is affiliated with the City of Detroit Chamber of Commerce.

Zone No. 71, Windsor Locks, Connecticut
Industrial Development Commission of Windsor Locks, Town Office Building, Church Street, Windsor Locks, CT 06096
Richard Blackburn, (203) 623-3458
Zone is adjacent to Bradley International Airport and provides zone services for the Greater Hartford area. The 17.5-acre zone will be located in the 38.5-acre Crown Industrial Park, located at 399 Turnpike Road, Windsor Locks. A 28,000-square-foot general-purpose warehouse, currently under construction, will be available to initial zone users.

Zone No. 72, Indianapolis, Indiana
Indianapolis Airport Authority, 2500 South High School Road, Indianapolis, IN 46251
Daniel C. Qrcutt, (317) 248-9594
A 15.3-acre zone at the Indianapolis International Airport on 2 separate parcels. Parcel A is a .5-acre site on Pearson Road adjacent to the airport's international cargo apron. It contains a 20,000-square-foot warehouse, which has been designated for initial zone operations. Parcel B, also on airport property, is located at the intersection of Washington Street and Girls School Road. This 14.8-acre parcel has been designated for future zone growth and development.

Zone No. 73, Baltimore/Washington International Airport, Maryland

Maryland Department of Transportation, BWI Airport, P.O. Box 8766, BWI Airport, MD 21240

T. James Truby, (301) 859-7060

Zone within BWI's Air Cargo/Industrial Park Complex, which covers 500 acres on airport property. The zone consists of 2 sites on 38 acres to be developed in successive stages. Site 1 is a 16-acre parcel on Maryland Route 170 near Taxiway A. It contains 3 existing air cargo buildings, totaling 103,000 square feet of floor space to be used for initial zone operations. Site 2, located on Maryland Route 176 near Taxiway T, would be developed to accommodate the needs of anticipated processing and manufacturing users.

Zone No. 74, Baltimore, Maryland

Baltimore Economic Development Corp., 36 South Charles Street, Baltimore, MD 21201

Paul Gilbert, (301) 837-9305

A 20-acre zone in Holabird Industrial Park, a new 170-acre industrial and commercial complex being developed by the City in southwestern Baltimore.

Zone No. 75, Phoenix, Arizona

City of Phoenix, Community and Economic Development Administration, 8th Floor, Municipal Bldg., 251 West Washington, Phoenix, AZ 85003

Brian Aby, (602) 262-6004

Zone at the Freeport Center industrial park, a new project of the Phoenix Aspen Group. Located at Buckeye Road and 55th Avenue in Phoenix, near Sky Harbor International Airport, the zone will consist of an 80,000-square-foot multiuser structure for initial zone users in the 73-acre park.

Zone No. 76, Bridgeport, Connecticut

City of Bridgeport City Hall, 45 Lyon Terrace, Bridgeport, CT 06604

Tom Corso, (203) 576-7221

Zone in the City's Foreign-Trade Zone Industrial Park, covering 13 acres of city land bounded by Cedar Creek, Bostwick Avenue, and Stephens Road in southwestern Bridgeport. A 30,000-square-foot multipurpose building is planned for the 3-acre zone site to accommodate initial zone users.

Zone No. 77, Memphis Tennessee

Memphis and Shelby County Office of Planning and Development, City Hall, 125 North Main Street, Memphis, TN 38103

Charles Owen, (901) 528-3307

Dual-site zone with facilities in the 2,000-acre President's Island site, covering 22 acres at Port Street and Channel Avenue, with a 20,000-square-foot building for initial zone operations. The airport site covers 10 acres at Republican and Tchulahoma roads.

Zone No. 78 and Subzones 78A and 78B, Nashville, Tennessee

Metropolitan Nashville-Davidson County Port Authority, 601 Stahlman Building, Nashville, TN 37201

Ed. J. Johnson, (615) 259-6121

Public zone facility; will begin operations at a 2.5-acre site in the Cowan Industrial Park in downtown Nashville. A 65-acre parcel in the planned

2,000-acre Cockrill Bend industrial complex on the Cumberland River is to be developed in the project's second phase. Subzone 78A is at Nissan's truck manufacturing and assembly plant in Smyrna, TN. The 825-acre facility will employ 2,600 people and produce 160,000 light trucks, displacing about 60% of the trucks Nissan now imports from Japan. Subzone 78B is for Toshiba's color-television and microwave-oven manufacturing plant, located at 1420 Toshiba Drive, Lebanon, TN. The facility consists of a 315,000-square-foot plant located on a 102-acre site.

Zone No. 79, Tampa, Florida
Bureau of City Planning, 306 Jackson Street, City Hall Plaza, 8th Floor, East Wing, Tampa, FL 33602
Steve Michelini, (813) 223-8401
General-purpose zone in 3 phases, with sites in the port area, at the airport, and in an industrial park. The first phase involves a 29-acre site at the Tampa International Center, adjacent to the Port of Tampa. The second phase involves an undeveloped 33-acre site at Tampa International Airport. The third phase involves a 50-acre standby site at the 127-acre Tampa Industrial Park at M. McKinley Drive and Fowler Avenue.

Zone No. 80, San Antonio, Texas
City of San Antonio, P.O. Box 9066, San Antonio, TX 78285
Kenneth W. Daly, (512) 299-8080
Zone totaling 556 acres on 3 separate parcels. Site 1 is a 52-acre parcel in an industrial area on Coliseum Road at Interstate 35 in San Antonio. Site 2 covers 4 acres at 315 Medina Street adjacent to the downtown business district with 174,000 square feet of warehouse space. Site 3 is located in the Southwest Industrial Center on Quintana Road and Interstate 35 in Bexar County. Covering 500 acres, this site will be used to accommodate firms requiring their own facilities and to provide standby space for future zone development.

Zone No. 81 and Subzone 81A, Portsmouth, New Hampshire
New Hampshire State Port Authority, 555 Market Street, Box 506, Portsmouth, NH 03801
George Smith, (603) 436-8500
Zone covering 10 acres in the Port Authority's deep water port facility on Portsmouth Harbor. Two multipurpose buildings totaling 50,000 square feet are available for warehousing and display and processing operations. The subzone sites are at Nashua Corporation's facility, which covers 14 acres at 44 Franklin Street, Nashua, and in Merrimack, about 5 miles away, on a 101-acre parcel on Daniel Webster Highway; both being used for processing and international distribution.

Zone No. 82, Mobile Alabama
City of Mobile, Office of Economic Development, P.O. Box 1827, Mobile, AL 36608
Lee H. Covey, (205) 438-7433
Zone in the Brookley Industrial Complex, a 115-acre municipally owned facility at Brookley Airport on Mobile Bay. Zone covers 13 acres west of Brookley runway 18-36 and immediately South of Avenue G.; sponsored by the City of Mobile.

Zone No. 83, Huntsville, Alabama

Huntsville-Madison County Airport Authority, P.O. Box 6006, Huntsville, AL 35806
J.E. Mitchell, Jr., (205) 772-9395
Zone involves about 1,300 acres in the 3,000-acre in the Huntsville-Madison County Airport and industrial complex. An existing 50,000-square-foot warehouse is available for initial zone operations; sponsored by the Huntsville-Madison County Airport Authority.

Zone No., 84, Harris County, Texas

Port of Houston Authority, P.O. Box 2562, Houston, TX 77001
Richard P. Leach, (713) 225-0671
Zone project involves 33 noncontiguous sites, covering 1,700 acres, most of which are on or near the Houston ship channel. The Category A sites consist of 5 separate public-use facilities, covering 924 acres owned by the Port Authority. The remaining sites involve a mix of privately owned sites, some of which will be used only by the site owner; sponsored by the Port of Houston Authority.

Zone No., 85, Everett, Washington

Economic Development Council of Puget Sound, 1900 Seattle Tower, 1218 Third Avenue, Seattle, WA 98101
William P. Jeske, (206) 622-2730
Zone is at the Port of Everett's north terminal, located at East Norton Avenue and 21st Street. A 36,000-square-foot warehouse is available for initial zone activities; sponsored by the Puget Sound Foreign-Trade Zones Association.

Zone No. 86, Tacoma, Washington

Economic Development Council of Puget Sound, 1900 Seattle Tower, 1218 Third Avenue, Seattle, WA 98101
William P. Jeske, (206) 622-2730
Zone involves 16 acres within the 2,700-acre Port of Tacoma. A 151,000-square-foot building will be used for initial zone-related warehousing and manipulation operations; sponsored by the Puget Sound Foreign-Trade Zones Association.

Zone No. 87, Lake Charles, Louisiana

Port of Lake Charles, Lake Charles Harbor & Terminal District, P.O. Box AAA, Lake Charles, LA 70602
James E. Sudduth, (318) 439-3661
Zone covers 2 sites totaling 870 acres along the Calcasieu River and Ship Channel and the Industrial Canal in Lake Charles and Calcasieu Parish; sponsored by the Board of Commissioners of the Lake Charles Harbor and Terminal District.

Applications Pending

Las Vegas, Nevada

Nevada Development Authority, McCarran International Airport, P.O. Box 11128, Las Vegas, NV 89111
Al Dague, (702) 739-8222
This application has been amended. The new applicant is Nevada Development

Authority. The project will cover 54 acres and include 2 exhibition centers, a warehouse, and an industrial park site in Las Vegas and Clark County, NV.

Sterling Heights, Michigan
Greater Detroit Foreign-Trade Zone, Inc., 100 Renaissance Center, Suite 1370, Detroit, MI 48243
J.T. Auwers, (313) 259-8077
Proposal calls for a subzone for the new Sterling Heights plant of Volkswagen of America, Inc., located on 103 acres in the 283-acre facility, recently purchased by Volkswagen.

City of Industry, California
National Engineering Co., 255 N. Hacienda Blvd., City of Industry, CA 91744
Ira R. Snyder, (213) 333-1291
The proposal will cover 120 acres south of Valley Boulevard between Fairway Drive and Lemon Avenue. Zone will be the focal point of a 200-acre international-trade complex known as the Industry Distribution and Commerce Center, Foreign-Trade Zone/Freeport.

Cincinnati, Ohio
120 West Fifth Street, Cincinnati, OH 45202
Joe Kramer, (513) 579-3143
Grantee of Foreign-Trade Zone No. 46 requests subzone status for the Huffy Corporation's bicycle manufacturing plant (39 acres), located at Lake and Haverman Roads in Celina, OH. The facility produces about 2.5-million children's lightweight bicycles and a number of bicycle parts; employs 1,900 people.

Great Falls, Montana
Economic Growth Council of Great Falls, P.O. Box 1273, Great Falls, MT 59403
Joseph C. Mudd, (406) 761-5036
Proposed zone will cover 35,000 squre feet in the 2,000-acre Great Falls International Airport complex. An exisiting 7,500-square-foot building will be made available for initial zone operations.

Detroit, Michigan
Greater Detroit Foreign-Trade Zone, Inc., 100 Renaissance Center, Suite 1370, Detroit, MI 48243
J.T. Auwers, (313) 259-8077
Proposal calls for a subzone at Ford Motor Corp.'s Wixom assembly plant, located at 500 Grand River Expressway in Wixom. The recently renovated 320-acre facility produces about 77,000 of the company's new and lighter Lincoln-model automobiles annually.

Lawrence, Massachusetts
Massport, 99 High Street, Boston, MA 02110
Carolyn Wong, (617) 482-2930
Proposal calls for a subzone at Lawrence Textile's 2.5-acre plant, located at 516 Broadway, Lawrence, MA. The company performs a variety of services for foreign and domestic textile mills and textile product users, primarily for wool and wool-blend materials.

Onondaga, New York
Greater Syracuse Foreign Trade Zone, 1 Lincoln Center, Syracuse, NY 13202
N. Earle Evans, (315) 422-0121
Proposed zone will cover 21 acres in the 1,300 acre Woodward Industrial
Park on Steelway Boulevard, in the Town of Clay, about 5 miles from the
Syracuse-Hancock International Airport. An existing 64,000-square-foot
warehouse is available for initial general-purpose zone operations; spon-
sored by the County of Onondaga, NY.

Newport, Vermont
Northeastern Vermont Development Association, 44 Main Street, St. Johns-
bury, VT 05819
Henry W. Merrill, Jr., (802) 748-5181
Proposed foreign-trade zone will cover 16 acres in the 22-acre Newport
Industrial Park on Prouty Drive. It owns the property and has plans to
construct a 10,000-square-foot building for general-purpose zone use.

Harrison County, Mississippi
Mississippi Research & Development Center, P.O. Drawer 2470, Jackson,
MI 39205
Noel Guthrie, (601) 982-6606
Proposed zone covers 228 acres on 4 sites in Harrison County. Site 1 is
located in the Port of Gulfport on Highway 90. It involves a 55,000-square-
foot warehouse and 4 acres of open space. Site 2 covers 99 acres on 3 parcels
at Gulfport/Biloxi Regional Airport in Gulfport; to be used for air-cargo
related zone activities and as standby space for future development. Site 3
involves 97 acres in the 1,500-acre Bernard Bayou Industrial District,
located on Interstate 10 at Lorraine Road in Harrison County. Site 4
involves a 27-acre parcel in the 520-acre Long Beach Industrial Park on
Espy Avenue, Long Beach; sponsored by the Greater Gulfport/Biloxi Foreign Trade Zone, Inc.

Wilmington, Delaware
State of Delaware, Delaware Development Office, Dover, DE 19901
Arnold Sisco, (302) 736-4271
Proposed zone will involve 2 separate sites totaling 660 acres. Site 1 will
encompass the 615-acre Port of Wilmington, which is owned and operated by
the City of Wilmington. A 144,000-square-foot building near the terminal
area will be made available for initial zone activity. Site 2 involves an industrial area covering 45 acres on Southern Boulevard in and adjacent to the
Town of Wyoming, Kent County. An existing 30,000-square-foot structure is
currently being renovated as a refrigerated warehouse to be used by Quality
Kitchen for storage of orange juice concentrate.

Detroit, Michigan
Greater Detroit Foreign-Trade Zone, Inc., 100 Renaissance Center, Suite
1370, Detroit, MI 48243
J.T. Auwers, (313) 259-8077
Grantee of Foreign-Trade Zone 70 requests subzone status for Ford Motor
Corp.'s Dearborn plant, which covers 72 acres at 3001 Miller Road in Dear-
born, MI, about 12 miles from downtown Detroit.

Research Triangle Park, North Carolina
Triangle J Council of Governments, 100 Park Drive, P.O. Box 12276, Research Triangle Park, NC 27709
Lee H. Capps, (919) 549-0551
Proposed zone covers 387 acres at 3 sites in the Raleigh/Durham metropolitan area. All sites would be operated by International Ventures Ltd., a subsidiary of Davidson and Jones Development Co. The primary site, Site 1, involves the Imperial Center, a planned industrial park of 250 acres at New Page Road and I-40, adjoining the Research Triangle Park in Durham County. This facility is 4 miles from Raleigh/Durham Airport. Site 2 involves the Northside Distribution Center Industrial Park, covering 27 acres at Front Street and Industrial Drive, near U.S. 1/U.S. 64, in Raleigh. Site 3 is at the Woodland Industrial Park, covering 110 acres at Highway 56 and I-85, Granville County.

Birmingham, Alabama
Birmingham Area Chamber of Commerce, 2027 First Avenue, Birmingham, AL 35202
Robert Douglass, (205) 323-5461
The proposed zone will be located at the City's Airport Industrial Park, which covers 116 acres on Lake Boulevard and Birmingham Street, adjoining the 1,600-acre Birmingham Municipal Airport complex. A general-purpose building is planned to accommodate initial zone activity.

Colebrook, Massachusetts
New Hampshire Port Authority, 555 Market Street, Box 506, Portsmouth, NH 03801
George Smith, (603) 436-8500
Grantee of Foreign-Trade Zone 81 requests subzone status for Manchester Manufacturing, Inc's 180,000-square-foot manufacturing and warehousing facility, located on a 15-acre site in the Colebrook Industrial Park.

Battle Creek, Michigan
BC/CAL/KAL Inland Port Authority of South Central Michigan Development Corp., P.O. Box 1438, Battle Creek, MI 49016
Marilyn E. Parks, (616) 968-8197
BC/CAL/KAL, on behalf of the City of Battle Creek, grantee of Foreign-Trade Zone 43, and the Louisville and Jefferson County Port Authority, grantee of Foreign-Trade Zone 29, request subzone status for the forklift truck manufacturing and distribution facilities of Clark Equipment Co. in Springfield and Oshtemo, MI, and in Georgetown, KY. The Battle Creek plant covers 194 acres at 525 N. 24th Street, Springfield, MI, and produces lift-mast assemblies. Finished products are prepared for export at the 23-acre Oshtemo facility, located at 6677 Beatrice Drive, Oshtemo, MI. The Georgetown plant, which covers 97 acres at Delaplain Road and I-75, Georgetown, KY, is Clark's forklift truck production and final assembly operation.

Quincy, Massachusetts
Massport, 99 High Street, Boston, MA 02110
Carolyn Wong, (617) 482-2930
Grantee of Foreign-Trade Zone 27 requests subzone status for General Dynamics Corp.'s shipbuilding facility in Quincy, MA. It is located on the west bank of the Weymouth Fore River and covers 158 acres, including 27 acres on the water.

Dayton, Ohio
Greater Dayton Foreign-Trade Zone, Inc., 1980 Winters Bank Tower, Dayton, OH 45423
Harry R. Wise, (513) 226-1444
The proposed zone will cover 452 acres at the Dayton International Airport, a city-owned commercial, industrial, and transportation complex totaling about 3,200 acres. A 52,000-square-foot general-purpose building will be used for initial zone activity.

Clinton County, Ohio
F.P. Neuenschwander & Associates, 2066 Henderson Road, Columbus, OH 43220
Fred P. Neuenschwander, (614) 459-4000
The proposed zone will cover 1.1 acres in the Airborne Air Park, a 490-acre industrial park and airport complex at the former Clinton County Air Force Base near Wilmington, OH, about 30 miles southeast of Dayton.

St. Louis County, Missouri
St. Louis County Port Authority, 130 South Bemiston, Clayton, MO 63105
Wayne Weidemann, (314) 721-0900
The proposed zone covers 180,000 square feet in an underground warehouse facility, located on the west bank of the Mississippi River, 5000 Bussen Road, St. Louis County, about 8 miles south of downtown St. Louis.

Toledo, Ohio
Toledo-Lucas County Port Authority, 3332 St. Lawrence Drive, Toledo, OH 43605
Frank E. Miller, (419) 698-8026
Grantee of Foreign-Trade Zone 8 requests subzone status for Jeep Corp.'s 2 manufacturing facilities in Toledo. One plant covers 108 acres at 940 North Cove Boulevard, and the other 230 acres at 4000 Stickney Avenue. The plants produce 4-wheel drive passenger vehicles.

Providence, Rhode Island
Rhode Island Port Authority and Economic Development Corp., Seven Jackson Walkway, Providence, RI 02903
Norton L. Berman, (401) 277-2601
The proposed zone will involve 2 sites totaling 812 acres. Site 1 will cover 12 acres in the Port of Providence, a 185-acre commercial and industrial intermodal facility owned by the City of Providence. The marine terminal building will be used for initial zone activity. Site 2 will cover 800 acres in the Economic Development Corp.'s 2000-acre Quonset Point/Davisville Industrial Park, North Kingston, RI, about 20 miles south of Providence.

San Jose, California
City of San Jose, 801 North First Street, San Jose, CA 95110
Ted Daigle, (408) 277-4744
Grantee of Foreign-Trade Zone 18 requests authority to permanently reorganize the zone project to relocate the general-purpose zone facility and establish 2 zone annexes. Public zone operations will be transferred from the International Business Park site to a facility covering 5 acres at 535 Brennan Avenue, within the Rincon de los Esteros Industrial Redevelopment Project, San Jose.

Laredo, Texas
Laredo Development Foundation, P.O. Box 1435, Laredo, TX 78040
(512) 722-0563
Proposed zone involves 3 sites totaling 221 acres. Sites 1 and 2 are at the Laredo International Airport, a 1,600-acre industrial and transportation complex owned by the city. Site 1 covers 42 acres in the 100-acre Laredo International Airport Industrial Park at Naranjo Avenue and Bustamante Street. This facility has 18,000 square feet of existing warehouse space for initial zone activity. Site 2 involves 100 acres at the site of a future airport industrial park expansion on the east side of the Airport. Site 3 covers 80 acres in the proposed 300-acre Texas Mexican Railway Industrial Park on Highway 359 in Webb County.

Starr County, Texas
Starr County Industrial Foundation, P.O. Drawer H, Rio Grande City, TX 78582
Sam Vale, (512) 487-5606
Proposed zone covers 42 acres on 3 sites. Site 1, located on U.S. Highway 83 east of Roma in Starr County, has 8.6 acres of space available for firms needing separate zone facilities. Site 2 covers 3 acres at 1401 North U.S. Highway 83 in Roma. An existing 20,000-square-foot warehouse is available at this site for initial zone activity. Site 3 is a standby area for future zone development, covering 30 acres in the 45-acre Santa Cruz International Park off U.S. Highway 83 in Starr County.

Eagle Pass, Texas
P.O. Box C, City Manager's Office, Eagle Pass, TX 78852
Roberto Barrientos, (512) 773-1111
Proposed zone involves 5 sites totaling 1,380 acres. Site 1 is at the Eagle Pass Industrial Park, covering 188 acres at Industrial Boulevard and Brown Street in Eagle Pass. Site 2 involves the city's Mini Industrial Park, covering 17 acres at Industrial Boulevard and Adams Street, Eagle Pass. Site 3 is a standby area for heavy manufacturing, involving 1,100 acres at the Maverick County Airport, U.S. Highway 277 in Maverick County. Site 4, covering 55 acres on State Highway 1588 near Highway 277 in Maverick County, and Site 5, covering 17 acres on Highway 277 in northern Eagle Pass, are standby areas for future zone development.

Del Rio, Texas
City Manager's Office, City of Del Rio, P.O. Drawer DD, Del Rio, TX 78840
Jim Miceli, (512) 774-2781
Proposed zone covers 4 separate sites. Site 1 involves the Del Rio Industrial Park, covering 151 acres on Cienegas Road and Johnson Boulevard, in the extraterritorial limits of Del Rio. Site 2 is a city-owned industrial park, covering 220 acres at 10th Street and Johnson Boulevard, in the Del Rio International Airport complex. Site 3 is an existing public warehousing facility on 1.5 acres at 100 Jasper Road in Del Rio, to be used for initial zone activity. Site 4 involves 50 acres near Amistad Dam in Val Verde County to be used as standby space for future zone development.

Newark/Elizabeth, New Jersey
One World Trade Center, Room 64 West, New York, NY 10048
Catherine Durda, (212) 466-7985
Grantee of Foreign-Trade Zone 49 requests subzone status for Ford Motor

Corp.'s automobile assembly plant in Edison, New Jersey. Subzone will cover 77 acres on U.S. Highway 1, Edison, Middlesex County, NJ, about 18 miles from Newark.

LaGrange, Georgia
Georgia Foreign Trade Zone, Inc., 1200 Commerce Building, Atlanta, GA 30335
James Steele, (404) 524-8481
Grantee of Foreign-Trade Zone 26 requests subzone status for the gasket manufacturing facility of Goetze Gasket Company. Proposed subzone will involve Goetze's existing facility, covering 38 acres in the La Grange Industrial Park, La Grange, GA.

Wilmington, Delaware
State of Delaware, Delaware Development Office, Dover, DE 19901
Arnold Sisco, (302) 736-4271
Proposal calls for subzone status for the Wilmington Division of J. Schoeneman Company in Wilmington, DE. Proposed subzone for Schoeneman will involve 2 sites covering 5 acres in Wilmington. The first site is the company's main facility, covering 3 acres at 9 Vandever Avenue. The second location is a nearby annex, covering 2 acres at 1½ East 22nd Street. This subzone is a textile and apparel plant.

Milwaukee, Wisconsin
Foreign Trade Zone of Wisconsin, Ltd., 8512 West Bradley Road, Milwaukee, WI 53224
Vincent J. Boever, (414) 354-4404
Grantee of Foreign-Trade Zone 41 requests special-purpose subzone status for 3 related chemical manufacturing plants of the Aldrich Chemical Company, Inc. The proposed subzone for Aldrich will cover 113 acres at 3 locations in the Milwaukee area. The first site involves the company's main plant, covering 1.3 acres at 940 West St. Paul Avenue, Milwaukee. The second site is for the company's secondary plant, covering 2 acres at 230 South Emmber Lane, Milwaukee. The third site involves the company's hazardous products facility, covering 110 acres at Highway V and Trimberger Court, Sheboygan Falls, Wisconsin, 35 miles south of Milwaukee.

Louisville, Kentucky
Louisville and Jefferson County Riverport Authority, 6310 Cane Run Road, Louisville, KY 40258
James Kellow, (502) 935-6024
Grantee of Foreign-Trade Zone 29 requests subzone status for export operations at the sugar-processing plant of Southeastern Sweetners Distributing Co., Inc. in Louisville. The proposed subzone will be located at the existing facility of Southeastern Sweetners, covering 1 acre at 1900 South Seventh Street in Louisville. The plant is involved in receiving domestic liquid sugar and corn syrup, liquefying, blending, and repackaging the sweetners for domestic distribution.

Grand Forks, North Dakota
Grand Forks Development Foundation, Box 1177, 204 North 3rd, Grand Forks, ND 58201
Robert W. Nelson, (701) 772-7271
Proposed zone will involve 2 separate sites, totaling 48 acres in Grand Forks.

Site 1 will cover 6 acres at 5118 Gateway Drive (U.S. Highway 2), where 80,000 square feet of warehouse space is available. Site 2 will cover 42 acres adjoining a planned industrial park on South 48th Street, ½ mile south of Demers Avenue. This site has a 15,000-square-foot building for warehousing activity and open space for firms requiring separate facilities.

Oklahoma City, Oklahoma

Office of Research and Economic Development, City of Oklahoma City, 100 N. Walker, First Floor, Oklahoma City, OK 73102
Ed McGee, (405) 231-2285
Proposed zone will cover 640 acres in the 6,700-acre Will Rogers World Airport complex at Portland Avenue and S.W. 59th Street. The Airport Authority will construct a 60,000-square-foot multipurpose warehouse.

New Orleans, Louisiana

P.O. Box 60046, New Orleans, LA 70160
Robert Dee, (504) 897-0189
Grantee of Foreign-Trade Zone 2 requests authority to relocate its zone to include industrial park space in New Orleans. The new site will cover 76 acres in the Almonaster-Michoud Industrial District, the city's 12,000-acre industrial-development project, located at the intersection of the Inner Harbor Navigation Canal and Mississippi River-Gulf Outlet in eastern New Orleans.

McAllen, Texas

6401 South 33rd Street, McAllen, TX 78501
Frank Birkhead, (512) 682-4306
Grantee of Foreign-Trade Zone 12 requests authority to expand its zone project in McAllen, Texas. Expanded area will cover 40 acres immediately south of existing approved zone area. A 50,000-square-foot multiusers building will be constructed, and tracts will be available for tenants requiring their own facilities.

Appendix C
Average Hours and Earnings of Production Workers by State

Source: U.S. Department of Labor, Bureau of Labor Statistics, *Employment and Earnings*, (May 1984):142–146

Average hours and earnings of production workers on manufacturing payrolls in States and selected areas

State and area	Average weekly hours			Average hourly earnings			Average weekly earnings		
	1981	1982	1983	1981	1982	1983	1981	1982	1983
Alabama	39.9	38.5	40.7	$7.01	$7.33	$7.58	$279.70	$282.20	$308.51
Birmingham	39.8	37.8	40.1	7.90	8.05	7.92	314.42	304.29	344.21
Mobile	40.9	39.3	41.4	8.89	9.44	9.69	363.60	370.99	401.17
Alaska	40.0	38.6	36.2	11.42	11.74	12.34	456.80	453.16	446.71
Arizona	39.6	38.9	40.5	8.02	8.73	8.99	317.59	339.60	364.10
Arkansas	39.4	38.6	40.1	6.26	6.69	7.05	246.64	258.23	282.71
Fayetteville–Springdale	39.5	38.6	40.0	5.69	6.12	6.41	224.76	236.23	256.40
Fort Smith	38.6	37.3	39.8	6.40	6.77	7.18	247.04	252.52	285.76
Little Rock–North Little Rock	39.5	39.0	40.7	7.13	7.76	8.13	281.64	302.64	330.89
Pine Bluff	41.6	40.8	41.4	7.77	8.66	9.24	323.23	353.33	382.54
California	39.6	39.2	40.0	8.56	9.24	9.52	338.98	362.21	380.80
Colorado	39.8	39.2	39.9	8.28	8.63	8.97	329.54	338.30	357.90
Denver–Boulder	39.7	39.2	40.1	8.27	8.82	9.32	328.32	345.74	373.73
Connecticut	41.6	40.5	41.3	7.67	8.23	8.76	319.07	333.32	361.79
Bridgeport	42.7	41.1	41.7	7.88	8.46	9.22	336.48	347.71	384.47
Hartford	41.3	40.7	41.1	8.14	8.81	9.41	336.18	358.57	386.75
New Britain	42.1	40.5	41.1	7.81	8.36	9.04	328.80	338.58	371.54
New Haven–West Haven	39.8	39.1	39.3	7.45	8.04	8.67	296.51	314.36	340.90
Stamford	41.0	39.9	39.8	7.18	7.74	8.57	294.38	308.83	341.09
Waterbury	41.7	40.4	42.6	6.48	6.89	7.45	270.22	278.36	317.37
Delaware	40.3	39.2	40.5	8.28	8.64	9.13	333.68	338.69	369.77
Wilmington	40.1	39.0	40.7	9.57	10.08	10.58	383.76	393.12	430.61
District of Columbia:									
Washington SMSA	39.2	38.4	38.6	8.88	9.37	9.75	348.10	359.81	376.35
Florida	40.6	39.9	40.7	6.53	7.02	7.33	265.12	280.10	298.33
Fort Lauderdale–Hollywood	40.7	40.3	41.7	6.17	6.64	7.00	251.12	267.59	291.90
Jacksonville	41.9	38.7	40.5	7.53	8.01	8.02	315.51	309.99	324.81
Lakeland–Winter Haven	43.2	41.2	40.2	6.94	7.23	7.29	299.81	297.88	293.06
Miami	41.1	39.1	38.7	5.65	5.88	6.13	232.22	229.91	237.23
Orlando	42.5	41.3	42.0	6.85	7.32	7.61	291.13	302.32	319.62
Pensacola	42.5	41.0	42.4	7.79	8.19	8.84	331.08	335.79	374.82
Tampa–St. Petersburg	40.5	40.1	41.2	6.55	6.92	7.30	265.28	277.49	300.76
West Palm Beach–Boca Raton	41.4	40.9	41.6	7.02	7.24	7.72	290.63	296.12	321.15
Georgia	40.1	38.6	41.1	6.37	6.75	7.13	255.44	260.55	293.04
Atlanta	39.7	37.9	40.6	7.60	8.11	8.49	301.72	307.37	344.69
Savannah	43.9	43.1	43.8	8.17	8.69	9.25	358.66	374.54	405.15
Hawaii	38.5	37.9	38.6	7.53	7.97	8.23	289.90	302.06	317.68
Honolulu	37.5	37.6	38.3	7.49	7.99	8.31	280.88	300.42	318.27
Idaho	37.8	36.7	37.4	8.23	8.62	8.49	311.09	316.35	317.53
Illinois	40.0	39.2	40.6	8.91	9.31	9.70	356.23	364.86	393.59
Bloomington–Normal	38.5	37.9	40.8	8.20	8.70	9.17	315.46	329.38	374.16
Champaign–Urbana–Rantoul	38.2	38.1	38.1	8.07	8.83	9.28	308.39	336.16	353.50
Chicago SMSA	39.5	38.6	40.4	8.23	8.83	9.55	324.92	341.22	385.71
Davenport–Rock Island–Moline	39.5	35.9	39.3	10.93	11.75	12.15	431.90	422.29	477.90
Decatur	39.2	39.0	40.5	10.55	11.64	12.38	413.48	454.08	501.76
Kankakee	37.8	37.9	39.0	7.79	8.34	8.36	294.47	316.25	326.05
Peoria	39.3	38.0	39.9	11.73	12.37	11.79	460.68	469.54	470.77
Rockford	40.5	39.6	41.5	8.90	9.38	9.61	360.54	371.15	398.59
Springfield	40.1	40.6	42.2	9.62	10.54	11.08	385.66	428.01	467.19
Indiana	40.1	39.2	41.0	9.37	9.79	10.10	375.74	383.77	414.10
Gary–Hammond–East Chicago	40.5	38.6	(')	12.49	13.19	(')	505.85	509.13	(')
Indianapolis	40.6	40.0	(')	9.26	9.69	(')	375.96	387.60	(')

See footnotes at end of table.

State and area	Average weekly hours			Average hourly earnings			Average weekly earnings		
	1981	1982	1983	1981	1982	1983	1981	1982	1983
Iowa	39.5	38.7	39.7	$9.60	$10.01	$10.09	$379.20	$387.39	$400.57
Cedar Rapids	39.9	40.4	40.9	9.52	10.38	10.60	379.85	419.35	433.54
Des Moines	38.7	38.8	38.8	10.01	10.86	11.56	387.39	421.37	448.53
Dubuque	39.1	38.4	38.7	10.77	10.94	10.52	421.11	420.10	407.12
Sioux City	39.6	39.7	39.8	8.01	8.76	8.87	317.20	347.77	353.03
Waterloo–Cedar Falls	39.2	37.8	39.1	12.68	13.02	12.67	497.06	492.16	495.40
Kansas	40.4	39.2	39.1	8.05	8.80	9.28	325.22	344.96	362.85
Topeka	39.6	37.8	37.8	8.65	8.65	9.22	342.54	326.97	348.52
Wichita	41.5	40.1	40.5	8.74	9.58	10.15	362.71	384.16	411.08
Kentucky	39.3	38.4	39.2	7.86	8.38	8.79	308.90	321.79	344.57
Lexington–Fayette	39.0	38.9	39.6	8.12	8.80	9.42	316.68	342.32	373.03
Louisville	39.8	38.8	40.3	9.22	9.66	10.10	366.96	374.81	407.03
Louisiana	42.2	41.0	40.0	8.58	9.38	9.79	362.08	384.58	391.60
Baton Rouge	42.3	40.8	41.9	10.68	11.40	11.52	451.76	465.12	482.69
New Orleans	41.1	38.7	38.7	8.48	9.23	9.08	348.53	357.20	351.40
Shreveport	41.4	39.0	39.8	7.67	8.36	9.48	317.54	326.04	377.30
Maine	40.4	40.0	39.9	6.66	7.22	7.61	269.06	288.80	303.64
Lewiston–Auburn	38.0	37.8	39.4	5.58	5.96	6.16	212.04	225.29	242.70
Portland	38.8	38.8	37.8	6.49	7.19	7.67	251.81	278.97	289.93
Maryland	39.9	39.2	40.0	8.39	8.78	9.02	334.76	344.18	360.80
Baltimore	40.4	39.9	40.5	8.76	9.23	9.48	353.90	368.28	383.94
Massachusetts	40.0	39.2	39.9	7.01	7.58	8.01	280.40	297.14	319.60
Boston	40.3	39.3	39.5	7.58	8.12	8.69	305.47	319.17	343.31
Brockton	39.4	37.6	38.2	5.72	6.26	6.46	225.37	235.38	246.75
Fall River	37.8	35.8	36.4	5.61	5.88	6.44	212.06	210.50	234.42
Lawrence–Haverhill	40.2	39.3	39.6	7.21	7.67	8.02	289.84	301.43	317.59
Lowell	39.7	38.4	39.3	6.45	6.88	7.39	256.07	264.19	290.25
New Bedford	37.5	37.4	37.1	6.24	6.81	7.23	234.00	254.69	268.23
Springfield–Chicopee–Holyoke	41.0	40.5	40.7	6.94	7.54	8.06	284.54	305.37	328.04
Worcester	39.7	38.8	39.6	7.23	7.83	8.30	287.03	303.80	328.68
Michigan	40.5	40.2	42.5	10.53	11.18	11.62	426.27	449.33	494.00
Ann Arbor	42.2	41.6	43.2	11.14	11.61	11.94	470.58	482.35	515.97
Battle Creek	40.9	39.4	41.1	10.36	11.49	11.95	423.38	452.89	490.90
Bay City	40.7	40.2	42.3	9.31	9.67	10.21	378.54	388.32	431.45
Detroit	41.0	41.2	42.8	11.15	11.85	12.29	457.16	488.68	526.53
Flint	40.6	39.6	44.6	12.14	13.10	13.33	492.59	519.09	594.76
Grand Rapids	39.8	38.9	41.3	8.73	9.37	9.97	347.83	364.49	411.20
Jackson	43.0	40.8	41.5	9.27	9.80	9.74	399.24	399.25	404.22
Kalamazoo–Portage	40.3	39.5	41.6	9.97	10.20	10.90	401.50	402.68	453.57
Lansing–East Lansing	39.0	39.1	43.4	12.07	12.24	13.13	470.22	478.19	570.26
Muskegon–Norton Shores–Muskegon Heights	40.3	38.3	40.0	8.95	9.69	10.41	360.32	371.07	416.07
Saginaw	40.4	39.3	42.7	12.31	12.80	13.61	497.31	502.65	581.57
Minnesota	39.4	39.1	39.7	8.40	9.11	9.56	330.96	356.20	379.53
Duluth–Superior	39.6	37.2	37.6	8.39	8.76	10.02	332.24	325.87	376.75
Minneapolis–St. Paul	39.4	39.1	39.8	8.85	9.60	10.11	348.69	375.36	402.38
St. Cloud	35.7	35.6	36.6	6.95	7.92	8.43	248.12	281.95	308.54
Mississippi	39.3	38.1	40.1	6.01	6.41	6.70	236.19	244.22	268.67
Jackson	40.2	38.6	40.6	6.47	6.95	7.59	260.09	268.27	308.15
Missouri	40.3	38.6	39.9	7.90	8.46	8.89	318.37	326.56	354.71
Kansas City	39.8	39.0	40.5	8.94	9.56	9.94	355.81	372.84	402.57
St. Joseph	38.9	38.3	38.8	7.35	7.89	8.26	285.92	302.19	320.49
St. Louis	39.4	39.0	40.3	8.98	9.63	10.11	353.81	375.57	407.43
Springfield	40.1	39.8	40.0	7.42	7.52	8.10	297.54	299.30	324.00
Montana	41.0	39.3	39.7	9.09	9.86	10.42	372.69	387.50	413.67
Nebraska	40.3	39.9	40.3	8.01	8.47	8.75	322.80	337.95	352.63
Lincoln	38.3	38.2	39.2	7.80	8.41	8.94	298.74	321.26	350.45
Omaha	39.6	38.8	39.8	8.26	8.74	9.10	327.10	339.11	362.18

See footnotes at end of table.

State and area	Average weekly hours			Average hourly earnings			Average weekly earnings		
	1981	1982	1983	1981	1982	1983	1981	1982	1983
Nevada	38.6	37.3	38.8	$8.42	$8.80	$9.02	$325.01	$328.24	$349.98
Las Vegas	39.8	39.2	39.4	10.49	10.74	10.91	417.50	418.66	429.85
New Hampshire	39.9	39.6	40.2	6.41	6.94	7.38	255.76	274.82	296.68
Manchester	39.0	39.3	39.3	6.08	6.58	7.11	237.12	258.59	279.42
Nashua	39.9	39.6	40.9	7.13	8.00	8.71	284.49	316.80	356.24
New Jersey	40.6	40.1	(¹)	8.05	8.70	(¹)	327.16	348.73	(¹)
Atlantic City	38.9	38.8	(¹)	6.70	6.99	(¹)	260.68	271.20	(¹)
Camden	39.3	41.8	(¹)	8.19	9.10	(¹)	321.62	380.20	(¹)
Hackensack	40.8	39.9	(¹)	7.09	7.69	(¹)	289.14	306.80	(¹)
Jersey City	40.6	40.2	(¹)	7.56	8.18	(¹)	307.40	328.98	(¹)
New Brunswick–Perth Amboy–Sayreville	42.1	40.5	(¹)	8.99	9.71	(¹)	378.28	393.42	(¹)
Newark	40.8	40.7	(¹)	8.12	8.81	(¹)	331.58	358.24	(¹)
Paterson–Clifton–Passaic	41.6	40.3	(¹)	7.62	8.23	(¹)	316.85	331.44	(¹)
Trenton	39.0	39.4	(¹)	8.33	8.75	(¹)	324.95	345.20	(¹)
New Mexico	39.5	39.2	39.6	6.54	7.22	7.62	258.33	283.02	301.75
Albuquerque	40.1	38.9	39.4	6.63	7.72	7.49	265.86	300.31	295.11
New York	39.4	38.8	39.3	7.84	8.35	8.84	308.90	323.98	347.41
Albany–Schenectady–Troy	40.2	39.5	40.4	8.18	8.65	9.13	328.84	341.68	368.85
Binghamton	41.3	40.3	40.4	7.10	7.29	7.92	293.23	293.79	319.97
Buffalo	40.2	39.7	41.0	10.09	10.63	11.15	405.62	422.01	457.15
Elmira	40.4	39.9	39.7	7.71	8.45	8.90	311.48	337.16	353.33
Glens Falls	(¹)	(¹)	39.7	(¹)	(¹)	8.77	(¹)	(¹)	330.63
Monroe County	41.4	40.9	41.5	10.18	10.85	11.64	421.45	443.77	483.06
Nassau–Suffolk	40.1	39.5	40.0	7.43	8.10	8.71	297.94	319.95	348.40
Newburgh–Middletown	(¹)	(¹)	38.6	(¹)	(¹)	6.53	(¹)	(¹)	252.06
New York–Northeastern New Jersey	39.6	38.6	38.9	7.45	8.05	8.62	295.42	310.73	335.32
New York and Nassau–Suffolk	38.0	37.4	37.7	7.06	7.64	8.19	268.28	285.74	308.76
New York SMSA	37.4	36.8	36.9	6.95	7.50	8.01	259.93	276.00	295.57
New York City	37.1	36.5	36.7	6.90	7.45	7.92	255.99	271.93	290.66
Poughkeepsie	43.0	42.2	42.9	7.55	7.96	8.68	324.65	335.91	372.37
Rochester	41.2	40.7	41.3	9.58	10.26	10.91	394.70	417.58	450.58
Rockland County	40.2	39.1	40.0	7.50	8.37	8.84	301.50	327.27	353.60
Syracuse	40.8	40.0	40.7	8.35	8.89	9.65	340.68	355.60	392.76
Utica–Rome	40.1	39.0	40.0	7.35	7.82	8.23	294.74	304.98	329.20
Westchester County	39.9	(¹)	38.2	7.31	(¹)	8.59	291.67	(¹)	328.14
North Carolina	39.1	37.3	40.0	5.94	6.35	6.68	232.25	236.86	267.20
Asheville	39.5	38.3	39.9	5.78	6.14	6.55	228.31	235.16	261.35
Charlotte–Gastonia	40.2	38.0	41.4	5.96	6.37	6.69	239.59	242.06	276.97
Greensboro–Winston–Salem–High Point	38.9	36.7	38.8	6.57	7.04	7.32	255.57	258.37	284.02
Raleigh–Durham	39.4	38.2	40.7	6.78	7.39	7.91	267.13	282.30	321.94
North Dakota	38.1	37.6	38.0	7.12	7.50	7.74	271.27	282.00	294.12
Fargo–Moorhead	38.1	38.6	37.8	7.57	7.69	8.05	288.42	296.83	304.29
Ohio	40.9	40.1	41.4	9.53	10.07	10.56	389.78	403.81	437.18
Akron	41.8	41.0	43.1	9.50	9.83	10.49	397.10	403.03	452.12
Canton	40.0	38.6	39.6	9.76	10.22	10.66	390.40	394.49	422.14
Cincinnati	41.1	40.5	41.1	8.78	9.57	10.11	360.86	387.59	415.52
Cleveland	41.1	39.9	40.9	9.62	10.10	10.45	395.38	402.99	427.41
Columbus	40.0	39.8	40.7	8.67	9.31	9.97	346.80	370.54	405.78
Dayton	41.4	40.0	41.9	9.61	10.02	10.61	397.85	400.80	444.56
Toledo	40.9	41.1	42.9	9.93	10.89	11.28	406.14	447.58	483.91
Youngstown–Warren	40.8	39.3	42.1	11.62	11.72	12.38	474.10	460.60	521.20
Oklahoma	40.1	39.5	40.5	8.20	8.69	9.21	328.82	343.26	373.01
Oklahoma City	39.8	39.3	40.6	8.64	9.00	9.75	343.87	353.70	395.85
Tulsa	40.8	39.3	40.2	8.67	9.45	9.96	353.74	371.39	400.39
Oregon	37.5	37.9	38.9	9.47	10.02	10.24	355.13	379.76	398.34
Eugene–Springfield	38.2	38.3	39.5	9.77	10.38	10.55	373.21	397.55	416.73
Medford	37.4	38.2	39.1	9.11	9.48	9.69	340.71	362.14	378.88
Portland	38.1	38.0	39.5	9.52	10.16	10.40	362.71	386.08	410.80
Salem	35.1	35.7	36.7	8.83	8.82	8.82	309.93	314.87	323.69

See footnotes at end of table.

State and area	Average weekly hours			Average hourly earnings			Average weekly earnings		
	1981	1982	1983	1981	1982	1983	1981	1982	1983
Pennsylvania	39.2	38.4	39.2	$8.30	$8.63	$8.95	$325.36	$331.39	$350.84
Allentown–Bethlehem–Easton	38.6	37.8	38.0	8.63	8.87	9.20	333.12	335.29	349.60
Altoona	38.5	38.4	38.5	7.15	7.27	7.81	275.28	279.17	300.69
Delaware Valley	39.8	38.7	39.3	8.37	8.89	9.33	333.13	344.04	366.67
Erie	41.1	39.9	40.6	8.52	9.04	9.56	350.17	360.70	388.14
Harrisburg	39.9	38.7	39.6	7.74	8.34	8.52	308.83	322.76	337.39
Johnstown	37.3	35.4	36.1	8.80	8.70	8.13	328.24	307.98	293.49
Lancaster	39.2	38.4	39.3	7.22	7.82	8.32	283.02	300.29	326.98
Northeast Pennsylvania	36.7	36.4	37.3	6.38	6.86	7.37	234.15	249.70	274.90
Philadelphia SMSA	40.0	38.9	39.4	8.32	8.88	9.37	332.80	345.43	369.18
Pittsburgh	40.4	38.2	39.6	10.00	10.66	10.83	404.00	407.21	428.87
Reading	39.6	38.5	40.0	7.77	8.17	8.80	307.69	314.55	352.00
Williamsport	39.6	39.4	38.9	7.67	7.98	7.98	303.73	314.41	310.42
York	40.8	40.0	40.8	7.45	7.84	8.12	303.96	313.60	331.30
Rhode Island	39.3	38.6	39.0	6.10	6.61	6.92	239.73	255.16	169.88
Providence–Warwick–Pawtucket	39.4	38.6	39.1	6.06	6.53	6.85	238.76	252.06	267.83
South Carolina	40.4	38.2	40.6	6.18	6.68	7.03	249.67	255.18	285.30
Charleston–North Charleston	39.5	42.2	41.6	6.89	7.80	8.42	272.16	329.16	350.27
Columbia	39.7	37.7	39.8	6.05	6.46	6.81	240.18	243.54	271.04
Greenville–Spartanburg	40.3	37.9	40.5	6.08	6.10	6.72	245.02	245.21	272.16
South Dakota	41.6	41.1	41.2	7.12	7.36	7.28	296.19	302.50	299.94
Sioux Falls	46.8	45.3	45.4	8.99	8.37	7.66	420.73	379.16	347.76
Tennessee	39.9	38.6	40.5	6.72	7.16	7.49	268.13	276.38	303.34
Chattanooga	40.7	38.7	41.5	6.52	7.05	7.14	265.36	272.84	296.31
Knoxville	39.7	38.6	40.3	7.47	8.40	8.89	296.56	324.24	358.27
Memphis	40.3	39.9	41.1	7.50	7.80	7.90	302.25	311.22	324.69
Nashville–Davidson	40.6	39.1	40.9	7.34	7.87	8.28	298.00	307.72	338.65
Texas	41.3	40.0	40.9	7.95	8.60	8.88	328.34	344.00	363.19
Dallas–Fort Worth	40.8	39.6	40.9	7.58	8.29	8.76	309.26	328.28	358.28
Houston	43.6	41.5	41.5	9.63	10.28	10.77	419.87	426.62	446.96
San Antonio	40.7	39.5	41.2	5.80	6.29	6.61	236.06	248.46	272.33
Utah	39.7	38.5	39.4	7.74	8.40	8.71	307.28	323.40	343.17
Salt Lake City–Ogden	40.2	39.2	40.0	7.41	8.25	8.61	297.88	323.40	344.40
Vermont	40.0	39.0	40.0	6.79	7.35	7.66	271.60	286.65	306.40
Burlington	41.6	40.8	42.0	7.21	7.99	8.57	299.94	325.99	359.94
Springfield	40.9	39.4	39.6	7.55	7.78	7.94	308.80	306.53	314.42
Virginia	39.7	38.4	39.7	6.84	7.37	7.78	271.55	283.01	308.87
Bristol	37.7	37.1	39.3	6.05	6.40	6.50	228.09	237.44	255.45
Charlottesville	(¹)	38.1	39.5	(¹)	6.26	6.61	(¹)	238.51	261.10
Danville	(¹)	38.9	40.8	(¹)	6.75	7.15	(¹)	262.58	291.72
Lynchburg	40.4	37.3	38.6	6.71	6.95	7.32	271.08	259.24	282.55
Norfolk–Virginia Beach–Portsmouth	41.1	40.8	42.1	7.15	7.69	8.12	293.87	313.75	341.85
Northern Virginia	40.2	39.6	40.4	7.38	7.89	8.49	296.68	312.44	343.00
Petersburg–Colonial Heights–Hopewell	39.2	38.9	39.8	8.55	9.50	9.96	335.16	369.55	396.41
Richmond	40.1	38.6	39.3	8.81	9.30	10.24	353.28	358.98	402.43
Roanoke	39.6	38.7	40.1	6.36	6.70	6.97	251.86	259.29	279.50
Washington	38.8	38.5	38.9	10.44	11.23	11.41	405.07	432.36	443.85
West Virginia	39.4	38.8	39.6	8.80	9.40	9.74	346.72	364.72	385.70
Charleston	42.5	41.9	42.5	9.87	10.60	11.27	419.48	444.14	478.98
Huntington–Ashland	39.6	37.2	38.4	9.94	10.73	11.05	393.62	399.16	424.32
Parkersburg–Marietta	41.1	40.5	41.0	9.21	10.11	10.75	378.53	409.46	440.75
Wheeling	39.1	38.5	39.4	9.95	10.36	10.99	389.05	398.86	133.01

See footnotes at end of table.

State and area	Average weekly hours			Average hourly earnings			Average weekly earnings		
	1981	1982	1983	1981	1982	1983	1981	1982	1983
Wisconsin	40.1	39.6	40.7	$8.80	$9.37	$9.78	$352.55	$370.87	$398.05
Appleton–Oshkosh	41.9	41.0	42.2	8.43	8.94	9.41	353.08	366.13	397.10
Eau Claire	40.9	40.4	41.0	8.38	8.88	9.37	342.72	358.83	384.17
Green Bay	41.7	41.8	41.5	8.91	9.64	10.28	371.31	402.93	426.62
Janesville–Beloit	39.6	39.5	42.2	9.22	9.51	10.82	364.55	375.51	456.60
Kenosha	39.6	40.3	40.9	10.07	11.41	11.76	398.76	459.88	480.98
La Crosse	40.2	38.8	39.4	7.71	8.56	8.83	310.13	332.25	347.90
Madison	39.2	39.2	39.9	8.59	9.31	9.33	336.75	364.74	372.27
Milwaukee	40.0	39.5	40.6	9.71	10.44	10.86	388.09	412.03	440.92
Racine	39.7	39.3	40.3	9.44	9.90	10.15	375.16	388.94	409.04
Sheboygan	(¹)	(¹)	39.2	(¹)	(¹)	9.28	(¹)	(¹)	363.78
Wausau	(¹)	(¹)	41.6	(¹)	(¹)	9.08	(¹)	(¹)	377.73
Wyoming	40.0	38.2	36.9	7.89	8.62	8.72	315.60	329.28	321.77
Puerto Rico	38.2	37.5	38.9	4.39	4.64	4.82	167.77	174.00	187.50
Virgin Islands	42.3	42.3	41.4	8.50	9.76	10.35	359.55	412.85	428.49

¹ Not available.

NOTE: Area definitions are published annually in the May issue of this publication. All State and area data have been adjusted to March 1983 benchmarks except Gary–Hammond–East Chicago and Indianapolis Indiana; New Jersey; New York–Northeastern New Jersey, New York; and Wisconsin.

Appendix D
Tax Rates of Major Countries

Direct taxes of non-financial corporate and quasi-corporate enterprises as a percentage of net operating surplus

	United States[a]	Japan	Germany[b]	France	United Kingdom	Finland	Sweden
1962	39.3		33.8	22.9		34.3	19.2
1963	37.5		32.9	22.3		35.9	21.3
1964	35.9		31.1	21.1		39.6	24.0
1965	34.8		28.4	20.2		38.8	24.9
1966	34.6		26.6	19.2		37.9	26.1
1967	35.1		25.4	18.3		34.1	28.2
1968	35.2		24.3	18.1		30.7	27.2
1969	34.8		22.9	18.2		26.0	25.6
1970	34.7		21.4	18.2	22.3	22.6	23.8
1971	34.1		20.2	19.1	21.8	21.3	21.1
1972	34.1	24.1	18.5	21.3	24.8	20.1	18.9
1973	33.2	26.3	16.7	22.2	25.2	20.7	16.8
1974	33.3	27.0	16.6	25.3	24.5	23.3	17.6
1975	33.2	28.4	17.8	27.5	24.6	24.8	39.5
1976	32.8	28.7	18.5	28.3	24.6	24.7	47.9
1977	31.6	27.1	19.2	28.1	22.7	24.7	48.0
1978	31.4	26.7	20.1	29.2	23.4	22.9	49.7
1979	29.8	27.9	19.3	29.6	28.2	19.8	48.5
1980	26.9	28.9		30.4		18.0	27.9

a) The yearly data underlying the centred five-year moving average are: 1979: 30.9; 1980: 30.0; 1981: 24.6; 1982: 17.3; 1983: 18.2. This last datum is an estimate based on the U.S. National Income and Product Accounts.

b) Because of different national accounts conventions, figures for Germany consistent with those for the other countries could not be obtained. The Secretariat has developed a proxy measure whose level is indicative only. Its movements should be reliable.

Note: Centred five-year moving averages.
Source: OECD *National Accounts.*

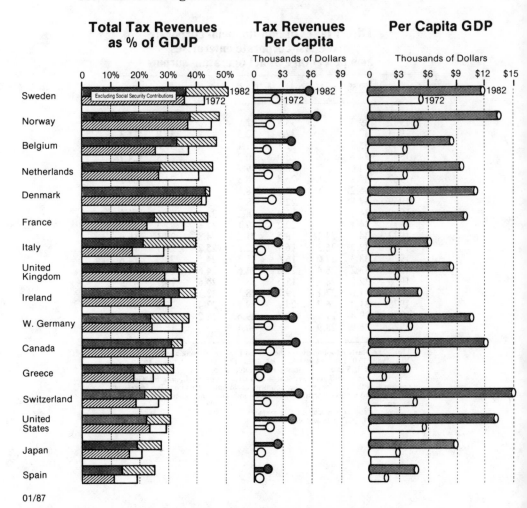

Total Tax Revenues as % of GDJP

Tax Revenues Per Capita
Thousands of Dollars

Per Capita GDP
Thousands of Dollars

01/87

SOURCE: The Conference Board, *Economic Road Map*, December 1984.

Taxes in Industrial Countries

Appendix E
State Taxes

Source: All States Tax Handbook, 1986 Edition (Englewood Cliffs, NJ: Prentice-Hall, 1986), ¶222.

CORPORATION INCOME—RATES, RETURNS, PAYMENTS

¶222 **How much and when.** This chart gives the income tax rates on business corporations, due dates and filing extensions, and to whom paid.

Col. A RATES and MINIMUM TAX	Col. B RETURN & PAY DATES (1, 8)	Col. C INSTALLMENTS DUE (2)	Col. D TO WHOM
ALA. 5%	Mar.15 (14, 31)		Dept. Rev.
ALASKA 1%, 1st 9,000; 2%, $10-$20M; $20-$30M, 3%; $30-$40M, 4%; $40-$50M, 5%; $50-$60M, 6%; $60-$70M, 7%; $70-$80M; 8%; $80-$90M, 9%; over $90M 9.4% (11, 37)	Mar. 15(34)		Dept. Rev.
ARIZ. 2.5% 1st $1M; 4% 2nd $1M; 5% 3rd $1M; 6.5% 4th $1M; 8% 5th $1M; 9% 6th $1M; 10.5% over $6M (43).	Apr. 15 (14, 31)		Dept. Rev.
*ARK. 1% 1st $3M; 2% 2nd $3M; 3% next $5M; 5% next $14M; 6% over $25M (37)	May 15 (14, 32)		Dir. Fin. & Admin.
CALIF. 9.6%. Min. $200 (3, 37)	Mar. 15 (3)		Franch. Tax Bd.
COLO. 5% (annual rate reduction see (16)) (37)	Apr. 15 (31)		Dept. Rev.
CONN. 11.5% (17, 30)	Mar. 31 (32)		Comr. Rev. Serv.
DEL. 8.7%	Apr. 1 (14)		Div. Rev.
D.C. 10% + 5% surtax eff for tax year or part starting after 9-30-84 Min. $100. (37)	Mar. 15 (31)		Dept. Fin. & Rev.
FLA. 5.5%	Apr. 1 (4, 14, 31)		Dept. Rev.
GA. 6%	Apr. 15 (14, 31)		Comr. Rev.
HAWAII 5.85% 1st $25M; 6.435% bal. (24,37)	Apr. 20 (31, 33)		Tax. Dist. or Dept. Tax.
IDAHO 7.7% (22, 37)	Apr. 15 (31)		Tax Comn.
ILL. 4%	Mar. 15 (14, 27)		Dept. Rev.
IND. 3% (10)	Apr. 15 (14)		Dept. Rev.
IOWA 6% 1st $25M; 8% next $75M; between $100M to 10%; over $250M and over 12% (38)	Apr. 30 (33)		Dept. Rev.
*KANS. 4.5% + 2.25% surtax on over $25M (37)	Apr. 15 (14, 31)		Dir. Tax.
*KY. 3% on 1st 25M; 4% on 2nd $25M; 5% on next $50M; 6% on next $150M; 7.25% over $250M(18)	Apr. 15 (31)		Rev. Cabinet
LA. 4% 1st $25M; 5% 2nd $25M;	May 15 (14, 31)		Dept. Rev.

Col. A RATES and MINIMUM TAX	Col. B RETURN & PAY DATES (1, 8)	Col. C INSTALLMENTS DUE (2)	Col. D TO WHOM
6% next $50M; 7% next $100M; 8% over $200M			& Tax.
ME. 3.5% on 1st $25M; 7.93%, $25M-$75M; 8.33%, $75M-$250M; 8.93% over $250M	Mar. 15 (1, 14, 32)		State Tax Assr.
MD. 7%	Mar. 15 (31)		State Comptr.
MASS. *Excise:* $2.60 per $M on tan- gible values or net worth + 9.5% (incl. 14% surtax) of net income; $228 min. *Income:* 5%	Mar. 15 (32)		Comr. Rev.
*MICH. 2.35% (13, 37)	Apr. 30 (14)		Dept. Treas.
MINN. 6% on 1st $25M; 12% on bal. (36, 37)	Mar. 15 (31, 33)	(28)	Comr. Rev.
MISS. 3% 1st $5M; 4% next $5M; 5% on bal	Mar. 15 (14, 32)		Tax Comn.
*MO. 5% (37)	Apr. 15 (14, 31)		Dir. Rev.
MONT. 6.75%. Min. $50 (9, 37)	May 15 (33)		Dept. Rev.
NEBR. 4.75% 1st $50M; 6.65% over $50M (25)	Mar. 15 (31, 33)		Dept. Rev.
N.H. 8.25% (eff 7-1-85; 8% eff 7-1-87(6)	Mar. 15 (26, 32)		Dept. Rev. Admn.
N.J. 9% (15)	Apr. 15 (31, 33)		Div. Tax.
N.MEX. 4.8% on 1st $1 million; $48M plus 6% on 2nd $1 million; $108M plus 7.2% over $2 million	Mar. 15 (14, 31)		Rev. Div.
*N.Y. 10%. Min. $250 (17, 23)	Mar. 15 (33)		Tax Comn.
N.C. 6%	Mar. 15 (33)	(5)	Sec'y. Rev.
N.DAK. 3% on 1st $3M; 4.5%, next $5M; 6%, next $12M; 7.5%, next $10M; 9%, next $20M; $10.5% over $50M (37)	Apr. 15 (14, 48)		Tax Comr.
*OHIO. 5.1% on 1st $25M plus- 9.2% over $25M, see (19). Min. $50.	Mar. 30 (14, 31)		State Treas.
OKLA. 5% (eff for tax years begun after 1984; *was* 4%)	March 15 (14, 31)		Tax Comn.
*OREG. 7.5%. Min. $10 (37)	Apr. 15 (14, 31)		Dept. Rev.
*PA. 9.5% (eff for calendar and fiscal years starting 1985 and later; was 10.5%)	Apr. 15 (31)		Dept. Rev.
R.I. 8% (17, 29) Min. $100.	Mar. 15 (31, 33)		Tax Admr.
S.C. 6%	Mar. 15 (32)		Tax Comn.
TENN. 6%	Apr. 1 (32)		Dept. Rev.

Col. A RATES and MINIMUM TAX	Col. B RETURN & PAY DATES (1, 8)	Col. C INSTALLMENTS DUE (2)	Col. D TO WHOM
UTAH. 5%. Min. $100 (21, 37)	Apr. 15 (31, 33)		Tax Comn.
VT. 6% on 1st $10M; 7.2% on next $15M; 8.4% next $225M; 9% over $250M min. $75 ($50)(44)	Mar. 15 (14, 32)	(7)	Comr. Taxes
VA. 6% (40)	Apr. 15 (14, 31)		Dept. Tax
W.VA. 6% on 1st $50M; 7%, over $50M (flat tax of 9.75% eff 7-1-87) (42)	Mar. 15 (14, 31)		Tax Dept.
WIS. 7.9% (39)	Mar. 15 (14, 31)		Dept. Rev.

Appendix F
The Implications of a Strong Dollar

A Strong Dollar:

Modifies relative international prices and costs. (It increases relative U.S. prices and costs, and reduces relative European and Japanese costs.)

Affects international competitiveness. (It reduces U.S. competitiveness, but increases foreign competitiveness.)

Changes flow of international trade and investment. (U.S. foreign trade balance deteriorates. U.S. DFI increases. European and Japanese trade balance improves and their DFI declines.)

Modifies international profitability and corporate finance. (Affects profitability of international operation and borrowing of foreign funds. More borrowing occurs in foreign currencies that have comparatively low interests rate, such as the Swiss franc and German mark.)

Impact on U.S. MNCs:

Expands investment financed domestically and from parent. Investment is inexpensive; operation is not too costly.

Expands export shipments to the U.S., exploiting increased competitive advantage.

Reduces profit and remittances. (Profit is worth less for the parent when consolidated; profitability levels in local exchange may remain unchanged.)

Increases domestic borrowing or borrowing of foreign currencies, which is less costly.

Impact on European and Japanese MNCs:

Reduces DFI activity. (It becomes too costly to invest and operate abroad.)

Expands purchases from home markets. (Investors take advantage of lower prices at home.)

Increases profit and remittances. (Profit made is worth more for parent companies when consolidated, but profitability in local exchange remains constant.)

Increases borrowing in national currencies.

Further Assessment of Specific Implications

Relative International Prices and Cost Effects

The sharp appreciation of the dollar since the end of 1980 has modified relative international prices and costs. The changes in relative prices and costs make it more expensive for foreign buyers to purchase goods in the U.S. and for foreign MNCs to operate here.

International Competitiveness

U.S. MNCs operate in Europe and Japan as domestic firms, and are subject to those nations' conditions and environment. Hence, they are subject to the same international competition as European and Japanese firms.

Flow of International Trade and DFI

Patterns and directions of trade and investment are modified by substantial currency movement. With a strong dollar, export of U.S. industrial goods will decline, while imports will increase. Consequently, the trade balance will deteriorate. The Europeans and Japanese will experience an opposite case.

Direct foreign investment in the U.S. may decline because: (1) it is too costly to operate in the United States; (2) it is too costly in terms of the exchange rate to invest or acquire companies; and (3) it is more attractive to export to the U.S. than to produce here.

U.S. investment abroad is expected to expand because: (1) acquiring abroad is relatively inexpensive; and (2) direct export is too difficult and must to some degree be replaced by local production abroad.

MNCs are likely to modify their international sourcing (producing parts of a product around the world and assembling it in one location and expand intercompany transactions. Foreign subsidiaries of U.S. MNCs are likely to become supply sources for U.S. markets.

European and Japanese MNCs are likely to reassess their strategies, reducing direct production overseas and increasing exports from home markets.

International Corporate Finance

Borrowing in the Eurocurrency market is always sensitive to shifts in the exchange rate and interest rate. If the dollar remains strong, MNCs will be attracted to borrowing currencies with low interest rates. However, since those markets are relatively thin, borrowers are bound to experience increased interest rates.

Appendix G
State Business Incentives

Source: Robert J. Reinshuttle, *Economic Development: A Survey of State Activities,* (Lexington, Kentucky: The Council of State Governments, 1983), pp. 10–11, 12, 18, 21, 31, and 32.

State Services To Business And Industry

| State | Information Services | | | | | Technical Services | | | | | Labor Services | |
	General Information Service	Keeps Inventories	Issues Directories	Makes Special Community or Economic Studies	"One Stop" Business Permitting	Mapping	Statistical	Legal	Engineering	Architectural	Recruit Labor	Train Labor
Alabama	•	•	•	•	•		•				•	•
Alaska	•	•	•	•	•						•	•
Arizona				•								
Arkansas	•	•	•	•	•	•	•				•	•
California	•	•	•	•	•	•	•				•	•
Colorado	•	•	•	•	•	•	•				•	•
Connecticut	•	•	•	•	•	•	•				•	•
Delaware	•	•	•	•	•	•	•				•	•
Florida	•	•	•	•	•		•				•	
Georgia	•	•	•	•	•	•	•				•	•
Hawaii	•	•	•	•	•	•	•				•	
Idaho	•	•	•	•	•	•	•				•	•
Illinois	•	•	•	•	•		•	•			•	•
Indiana	•	•	•	•	•	•	•	•			•	•
Iowa	•	•	•	•	•		•				•	
Kansas	•	•	•	•	•	•	•				•	•
Kentucky	•	•	•	•	•	•	•				•	•
Louisiana	•	•	•	•	•	•	•				•	•
Maine	•	•	•	•	•		•				•	•
Maryland	•	•	•	•	•	•	•	•	•	•	•	•
Massachusetts	•	•	•	•	•	•	•	•	•	•	•	•
Michigan	•	•	•	•	•	•	•				•	•
Minnesota	•	•	•	•	•	•	•	•			•	•
Mississippi	•	•	•	•	•	•	•				•	•
Missouri	•	•	•	•	•		•				•	•
Montana	•	•	•	•	•	•	•				•	•
Nebraska	•	•	•	•	•	•	•				•	•
Nevada	•	•	•	•	•		•				•	•
New Hampshire	•	•	•	•	•	•	•		•		•	•
New Jersey	•	•	•	•	•	•	•				•	•
New Mexico	•	•	•	•	•	•	•		•		•	•
New York	•	•	•	•	•	•	•		•	•	•	•
North Carolina	•	•	•	•	•	•	•				•	•

North Dakota
Ohio
Oklahoma
Oregon
Pennsylvania
Rhode Island
South Carolina
South Dakota
Tennessee
Texas
Utah
Vermont
Virginia
Washington
West Virginia
Wisconsin
Wyoming
Puerto Rico

State Industrial Plant and Location Assistance Services

State	Industrial Site Selection Service	Industrial Parks State				Industrial Plants State			
		Plans	Develops	Operates	Leases	Builds	Operates	Leases	Sells
Alabama	•								
Alaska	•								
Arizona	•								
Arkansas	•								
California	•								•
Colorado	•								
Connecticut	•	•	•						
Delaware	•	•	•						
Florida	•								
Georgia	•								
Hawaii	•		•		•				
Idaho	•								
Illinois	•	•							
Indiana	•								
Iowa	•								
Kansas	•								
Kentucky	•		•[1]			•[1]		•[2]	•[3]
Louisiana	•								
Maine	•		•			•		•	•
Maryland	•	•	•						
Massachusetts	•								
Michigan	•	•	•						
Minnesota	•	•	•						
Mississippi	•	•	•						

Missouri
Montana
Nebraska
Nevada
New Hampshire
New Jersey
New Mexico
New York
North Carolina
North Dakota
Ohio
Oklahoma
Oregon
Pennsylvania
Rhode Island
South Carolina
South Dakota
Tennessee
Texas
Utah
Vermont
Virginia
Washington
West Virginia
Wisconsin
Wyoming

1. Finances
2. Foreclosures
3. Assists in marketing
4. State mill and elevator

State Financial Assistance Services For Industrial Development

State	Statewide Development Credit Corporation	State Industrial Finance Authority	State Tax Incentives[1]	Local Tax Incentives[1]	State "Enterprise Zone" Legislation
Alabama					
Alaska					
Arizona					
Arkansas					
California	P	•			P
Colorado	P		•	•	P
Connecticut	•	•	•		•
Delaware		•			P
Florida	•	•	•	•	•
Georgia			•	•	
Hawaii			•	•	
Idaho					
Illinois	•	•	P	•	P
Indiana	•	•	•	•	•
Iowa		•	•	•	
Kansas			•	•	•
Kentucky	P	•	•	•	•
Louisiana			•	•	•
Maine	•	•	•	•	
Maryland	•	•	•	•	•
Massachusetts	•	•	•	•	P
Michigan	•	•	•	•	P
Minnesota	P	•		•	•
Mississippi		•	•		P
Missouri	P	•	•	•	•
Montana		P	•	•	

Nebraska

Nevada

New Hampshire

New Jersey

New Mexico

New York

North Carolina

North Dakota

Ohio

Oklahoma

Oregon

Pennsylvania

Rhode Island

South Carolina

South Dakota[2]

Tennessee

Texas

Utah

Vermont

Virginia

Washington

West Virginia

Wisconsin

Wyoming

Puerto Rico

1. Not including "free port" legislation.
2. No state corporation tax.
P = Pending

Foreign Offices to Promote Industrial Development and Trade

State	Regional Focus	Number of Employees											Office Changes in Last Five Years	Planned Changes in 1983
		Japan	Belgium	West Germany	England	China	Canada	Mexico	Brazil	Switzerland	Netherlands	France		
Alabama	Yes except Japan	4		1	2					2			Expand	None
Connecticut	Yes			2									None	None
Florida	Yes	*		2									Expand	None
Georgia	Yes	3	3				1						Expand	None
Illinois	Yes	1	7			2			5				Expand	Japan open 1/83
Indiana	Yes	1	2										None	None
Iowa	Yes			2									None	None
Kansas	...			*	*									
Louisiana	Yes			1									Reduction from 2 to 1	None
Maryland	Yes	2	3										Expand	Expand
Massachusetts	...	*	*											
Michigan	Yes except Japan	2	5.5										None	None
Missouri	Yes	2		3		1						1	Expand	Expand
Nebraska	Yes	*	*										Expand	None
New York	Yes except Japan /Canada	2		2	2		4						Expand	None
North Carolina	Yes	2		2									Expand, Japan opened	None
Ohio	Yes	3	4										W. Ger. replaced by Belg.	Expand
Pennsylvania	Yes	*		*	*				*			*	Expand	None
South Carolina	Yes		2										None	None
Texas	No							2					None	None
Vermont	No					2.5							None	None
Virginia	Yes	6	8										Expand	None
Washington				3 contract staff									Reduction	None

* Consultant on contract.

State Industrial Finance Authorities: Funding Limitations

State	Source of Funds	How Funds Are Held	Maximum Total Amount Permitted for Loans & Loan Guarantees	Maximum for Percent of Project Covered	Maximum Length of Amortization
California	LA	In	$350,000	80% direct; 90% guarantees	25 yrs. direct; 7 yrs. guarantees
Connecticut	LA, GO	Rev, In, Treas	$850,000	90%	25 yrs.
Hawaii	RB		No limit	100%	40 yrs.
Illinois	LA	Rev, In	No legal limit	Usually under 30%, no legal limit	25 yrs.
Indiana	LA	Rev, In	$2,000,000 per project	90% real estate; 75% equipment	25 yrs.
Kentucky	LA, GO	Rev, In	$1,000,000	50%	Match first mortgage lender
Maine	RB		$5,000,000	100%	
Maryland				100%	25 yrs.
Michigan	LA, RB	Rev, In	$1,000,000 unless waived by ⅔ vote	50%	Working capital not to exceed 5 yrs.; other up to life of assets
Minnesota	LA	Rev, Treas			25 yrs.
Mississippi[1]	LA	Rev, In, Treas	$250,000	25% Indian; 20% other	
Missouri	LA, RB	Rev, In	$5,000,000 total for direct; $1,000,000 per project guarantees	Board determines direct; 90% guarantees	30 yrs. direct; Board determines guarantees
Nebraska[2]	RB				
New Hampshire	RB		$18,000,000	50%	25 yrs.
New Jersey	LA	Rev	$1,000,000 guarantees; $250,000 dir.	100% direct; 90% guarantees	10 yrs.
New York[3]	GO, RB	Rev, In	$300,000,000 guarantees	40%	20 yrs.
Ohio	LA		$5,000,000 guarantees; 30% fixed assets for direct	90% guarantees; 30% fixed assets for direct	25 yrs.
Oklahoma	GO, RB	Rev, In, Treas	$1,000,000	25% of land, bldg., heavy equipment	15 yrs.
Pennsylvania	LA, GO	Rev, In, Treas	$1,000,000 per firm	79%	15 yrs.
Rhode Island	LA, GO		$5,000,000	90%	25 yrs.
South Dakota[4]			NA	40%	Commission determines
Texas	LA	Treas	$35,000,000 guarantees; $8,500,000 direct to local devel. $10,000,000 direct to private ind.	100% guarantees; 100% direct to local devel. corp. 40% direct to private ind.	25 yrs. direct to local devel. corp. 5 yrs. direct to local devel. corp. 20 yrs. direct to private industry
Vermont	LA	Rev, In			
West Virginia	LA, RB	Rev, In	$500,000 per project	50%	25 yrs. real estate; 10 yrs. equipment

LA — Legislative Appropriation
GO — General Obligation Bonds
RB — Revenue Bonds
NA — Not applicable

Rev — Revolving Fund
In — Invested
Treas — Held in State Treasury

1. Mississippi indicates there is a limit on the maximum total amount permitted for loans and loan guarantees but does not specify amount.
2. Nebraska's Development Finance Fund is newly formed and only authorized to issue industrial revenue bonds for industrial and commercial projects in blighted areas.
3. New York's figures are for loan guarantees made to local development corporations by the Job Development Authority.
4. South Dakota's Economic Development Finance Authority was newly authorized by legislation in 1982.

Industrial Promotion: Field Representatives and Out-of-State Information Offices
(Does not include tourism and vacation travel)

State	Distribution of Field Representatives				Out-of-State Information Centers in United States
	Within State	Outside State Within U.S.	Outside U.S.	No Geographic Boundaries	
Alabama¹			3		No
Alaska					No
Arizona					No
Arkansas					
California	0	0	0	0	No
Colorado	0	0	0	0	No
Connecticut	0	0	2	12	No
Delaware	8	0	0	8	No
Florida	11	2	6	0	
Georgia	6	11	7	0	
Hawaii					
Idaho	1	0	0	0	Washington, DC
Illinois	16	1	10	0	Washington, DC
Indiana	7	3		8	No
Iowa	4	0	2	7	No
Kansas	0	0	0	0	
Kentucky	2	1	0	5	New York, NY
Louisiana	3		1	6	No
Maine	0	0	0	3	No
Maryland	6	0	3	10	
Massachusetts	10	0	0	4	Washington, DC and New York, NY
Michigan	15	0	5	21	No
Minnesota	3	0	0	0	No
Mississippi	7	6	2	6	Washington, DC

State				
Missouri	10	0	3	7	No
Montana	7			3	No
Nebraska	0	0		5	No
Nevada	0	0	0	0	No
New Hampshire				6	
New Jersey					
New Mexico[2]	0	0	0		No
New York	70	0	5	20	No
North Carolina	5	0	2	15	No
North Dakota	0	0	0	11	No
Ohio	6	0	7	0	Washington, DC
Oklahoma	0	0	0	4	No
Oregon	4	0	0	4	No
Pennsylvania[3]	0	0	4	13	U.S. government trade centers
Rhode Island				6	No
South Carolina	15	15	1	15	No
South Dakota				7	No
Tennessee[4]	14	0	0	4	No
Texas	0	0	1		No
Utah				4	
Vermont				4	No
Virginia	5	0	3	8	No
Washington	0	0	1	11	No
West Virginia	11	11	0	11	No
Wisconsin				7	No
Wyoming	0	0	0	0	No

1. Alabama has a regular staff of industrial developers who work both within the state and in other states.
2. New Mexico's industrial representatives travel in and out of state extensively.
3. Pennsylvania uses 13 agency employees with no geographic boundaries.
4. Using Tennessee as home base, 10 staff members recruit in the United States and 4 recruit internationally.

Appendix H
Foreign Investment in U.S.
Manufacturing Industries

Source: The Conference Board

A/S Niro Atomizer, Denmark
Tennessee
The Crossvile Ceramics Co., a subsidiary of A/S Niro is planning to construct a new ceramics plant in the Crossville Cumberland County Industrial Park. Employment: 100 people.

AB Bofors, Sweden
Connecticut
Bofors acquired Weda Pump, a producer of drainage pumps and swimming pool cleaners.

Access Engineering, United Kingdom
North Carolina
Access Engineering Co. U.S.A., a subsidiary of an English company, established a $5 million plant at Charlotte, NC to produce wood scaffolding. Employment: 20 people.

Adelaide Brighton Cement Ltd., Australia
Florida
Adelaide has purchased Stresscon from Lonestar Industries. Stresscon is in the pre-stressed and pre-cast concrete business. A partnership between Lonestar and Adelaide, Adelaide Brighton Cement (Florida) Inc., will run the company.

Ajinomoto, Japan
Iowa
Ajinomoto will build a $25 million plant at Eddyville to produce Lysine for hog and poultry feed.

Akzo, The Netherlands
Illinois
Akzo acquired Landchem, a producer of specialty coating and printing-ink resins.

Akzo, The Netherlands
South Carolina
American Enka Co., a unit of Akzo, has begun expanding its carpet yarn plant.

Akzo, The Netherlands
Texas
Akzo Chemie America Ketjen Catalysts Division, a subsidiary of Akzona, Inc. which in turn is a unit of Akzo, will spend $40 million on a new plant for fluid cracking catalysts.

Akzo Coating NV, The Netherlands
California
Akzo plans to buy Bostik West's paint production division located in Torrance, CA. Akzo is a paint manufacturer also.

Alcan Aluminum Ltd., Canada
Georgia
Alcan Aluminum Corp. has formed Alcan Recycle and will also expand its recycling plant in Greensboro, GA.

Alcan Aluminum Ltd., Canada
Kentucky
Alcan bought the Kentucky and southern Indiana operations of Arco Metals Co. The plants employ 3,000 people and produce aluminum foil and other aluminum products.

Alcan Aluminum Ltd., Canada
North Carolina
Alcan Building Specialties, a division of Alcan Aluminum Corp., has begun construction of a $3.5 million aluminum building Employment: will increase from 61 to 79 in the near future.

Alcan Aluminum Ltd., Canada
Pennsylvania
Alcan Cable Co. plans a $7 million expansion of its clad and unclad aluminum industrial cable plant.

Nestle Alimenta SA, Switzerland
Georgia
Alimenta has started production at its new $4.7 million peanut processing plant. It is located in Camilla, GA. Employment: 130 workers.

Alpine Electronics Inc., Japan
California
Alpine has established an automotive security equipment subsidiary in Torrance, CA.

Alsthom-Atlantique, France
Texas
A-A has purchased an 80% interest in Subsea Technology Inc. The firm, renamed ACB-Subsea Technology International Inc., will manufacture underwater oil exploration mechanical structures.

AMCA International Corp., Canada
Tennessee
A $6 million expansion of Varco-Pruden Metal Building Systems plant (a division of AMCA) will enable Varco-Pruden to produce windows, roof sheets, and doors in addition to the production of the main frame structure for a pre-engineered building. Employment: will expand from 75 to 225 persons.

Anchemia Chemicals Ltd., Canada
New York
Anchemia Chemicals Inc., a subsidiary of Anchemia, will spend $1 million to expand its inorganic chemicals facility. Employment: 15 workers.

APV Holdings, United Kingdom
Illinois
Anderson Brothers, dairy products machinery manufacturer, has been acquired by APV for $7 million (L5m).

Armitage Shanks Group Ltd., United Kingdom
North Carolina
Armitage will build a 200,000 sq. ft. plant at Mooresville, North Carolina to produce ceramic bathroom fixtures. Initial employment will be 130 people.

ASEA AB, Sweden
Texas
ASEA, Inc. plans to construct a new manufacturing facility to produce hydraulic motors.

ASEA AB, Sweden
Wisconsin
ASEA Robotics, Inc., a subsidiary of ASEA, Inc. will expand its manufacturing capacity by 50%. The company plans to ship more than 370 electric robots this year.

Associated British Foods Ltd., United Kingdom
North Carolina
R. Twining & Co. Ltd., a wholly-owned subsidiary of Associated plans to expand its Greensboro plant by adding 55,000 sq. ft. to its facilities. Employment: Approximately 40 jobs will be created.

Astro Dairy Products Ltd., Canada
New York
Astro plans to acquire a fluid milk facility located in NY. The acquisition will cost about $1.5 million and should provide an additional 40 or more jobs.

Atochem S.A., France
Pennsylvania
Rilsan (subsidiary of Atochem) will be expanding its Rilsan Industries, Inc. plant. There will be a 40% increase in polymerization capacity, textile hot-melt adhesives as well as other materials. The expansion will take place during the fall months of 1985.

Avon Industrial Polymers Ltd., United Kingdom
Mississippi
Bell Avon Inc., a joint venture of Avon Industrial and Bell Aerospace Textron, is constructing a new plant at Picayune to produce skirts and maintain air-supported craft.

Baader, West Germany
Massachusetts
Baader North America will produce fish processing equipment in a plant purchased in New Bedford.

Barthelmess GmbH & Co., West Germany
New York
Barcana Inc., a subsidiary of Barthelmess has invested $3 million for the acquisition of an artificial flower plant facility. 100 jobs will be provided.

BASF A.G., West Germany
Louisiana
BASF Wyandotte Corp. is expanding its capacity of acetylene chemicals by building two new plants.

BASF A.G., West Germany
Texas
Badische Corp., subsidiary of BASF will build a new plant in Freeport, Texas to produce acrylic acid. The annual acrylic acid capacity should be 300 million.

BASF A.G., West Germany
West Virginia
BASF Wyandotte, a subsidiary of BASF A.G., will invest between $15 and $20 million over the next five years to renovate their Huntington, W. Virginia plant in which to produce alkali blue and C-amine. Production capacity will increase 40% with the installation of new equipment and debottlenecking.

BAT Industries PLC, United Kingdom
Ohio
Appleton Papers Inc., a subsidiary of BAT, will purchase P.H. Glatfeller Co.'s paper milling facility in West Carrollton, OH for $83 million.

BAT Industries PLC, United Kingdom
Wisconsin
Appleton Papers Inc., a subsidiary of Batus, is planning an expansion project of its Locks Mill. Plans include the building of a new pulp warehouse.

Bayer A.G., West Germany
New Jersey
Haarman & Reimar, a subsidiary of Bayer, is constructing a $3 million 30,000 sq. ft. facility at Branchburg, NJ to produce flavors, fragrances and aroma chemicals. The use of computerized blending equipment for major perfume ingredients will be employed.

Bayer A.G., West Germany
Texas
Mobay Chemical Corp., a wholly-owned subsidiary of Bayer will be expanding its aliphatic polyisocyanate manufacturing facilities at Baytown, Texas. This will be the first facility in the U.S. to produce the isocyanurate of HDI (hexamethylene diisocyanate).

Beecham Group PLC, United Kingdom
California
Beecham Group will take the control of Roberts Consolidated Industries Inc. (USA), a maker of glue products. Cost of the transaction: $85 million.

Bell Canada Enterprises, Canada
New York
Bell acquired Case-Moyt, a Rochester producer of printed material. Case-Moyt has sales of roughly $50 million and employs about 1,000 people.

Berg Industries, West Germany
Tennessee
Berg will produce furniture, framing and architectural components in a plant at Morristown. Over 80 people will be employed.

Bespak PLC, United Kingdom
North Carolina
Bespak, an aerosol valve supplier, is planning the construction of a U.S. subsidiary to be located in Cary, NC. Employment: 80 persons.

Boehringer Ingleheim Health CareOrg, West Germany
Ohio
Roxanne Laboratories Inc., owned by Boehringer, will consolidate the five production plants that are dispersed around Columbus. The pharmaceuticals manufacturer will add 74 new jobs to the present number of 267.

Boiseries Crotone Inc., Canada
New York
Cronte Lumber Mill, a subsidiary of Boiseries, has acquired a wood products plant in Essex County, Westport, NY. Employment: 6+ workers.

Bonnier Group, Sweden
Washington
The Bonnier Group, the largest Swedish publisher, has acquired a 50 percent interest in the Washington Dossier magazine.

Bowater Corp. PLC, United Kingdom
Tennessee
Camvac International Inc., a subsidiary of Bowater will produce metallized paper in an $18 million plant at Morristown. Employment will reach 150 by 1986.

Bowater Corp. PLC, United Kingdom
South Carolina
Bowater, Inc. is planning a $341 million expansion of its mill at Catawba, South Carolina. Involved in the expansion will be the addition of a paper production machine as well as equipment for refiner pulping, coating and finishing. The project will be completed by 1986. 200 new jobs will be created.

Braun Melsungen, West Germany
Pennsylvania
Burron Medical Products Inc., a division of B. Braun of America Co., Inc. has begun construction of its $3 million facility. The manufacturing/distribution will produce plastic medical devices. Employment: 500 new employees by the 1990's.

Brent Chemicals Intl, United Kingdom
California
Brent will acquire Leeder Chemicals Inc., a specialty chemicals manufacturer for $3.5 million. Leeder is located in La Mirada, CA.

Bridon PLC, Noranda Mines, United Kingdom
New Jersey, Indiana
Bridon American, a joint venture of the two companies, purchased the wire rope and strand manufacturing facilities of U.S. Steel.

Brink/Molyn Group, The Netherlands
Louisiana
Brink/Molyn Group, a manufacturer of paints and coatings, acquired a majority interest in Bywater Coatings Co., a supplier of coating materials.

British Petroleum, United Kingdom
Michigan
Sovonics Solar Systems, a partnership formed by Standard Oil Co. (Ohio), a unit of BP, and Energy Conversion Devices Inc., is planning to spend $6 million on two solar cell plants.

British Petroleum, United Kingdom
North Carolina
Chase Brass & Copper Co., a unit of Sohio Chemicals and Industrial Products Co. which is a unit of Standard Oil Co. (Ohio), will build a $40 million copper strip plant.

British Printing & Comm. Corp. PLC, United Kingdom
North Carolina
Providence Gravure and The British Printing & Communications Corp. PLC of London has formed a joint venture, Compucolor International, and will build a printing/transmission plant in North Carolina for $5 million. Employment: 40 persons by the end of 1985.

Buehrmann, The Netherlands
New Jersey
Acquired Astro-Packaging, a New Jersey based producer of envelopes and air-cushion folders. Astro has six U.S. plants and annual sales of about $17 million.

Burda GmbH, West Germany
Arizona
Burda through its joint venture with U.S. Meredith Corp. of Des Moines, Iowa will build a $90 million printing plant in Casa Grande, Arizona.

Business Accessories Ltd., Canada
New York
Business Accessories has leased a plant at Amherst and will produce office items such as wastebaskets, letter trays, etc. Twelve people will be employed.

Cadbury Schweppes USA, Inc., United Kingdom
Pennsylvania
Peter Paul Cadbury, Inc., the maker of chocolate candies and confectioneries, plans a $9.54 million expansion of its plant in the Humboldt Industrial Park in Pennsylvania. Employment: 162 employees within three years.

Central Tobacco Co. Ltd., Canada
New York
Clinton Tube Inc., a subsidiary of Central Tobacco, has invested $1.25 million in an expansion project of its paper mill facility. Location: Plattsburgh, NY; employment: over 40 jobs.

Centrale Suikermaatschappij N.V., The Netherlands
Connecticut
CS has purchased a division of Ingredient Technology Corp. (Breddo Division) for an undisclosed amount. Both CS and Breddo manufacture products for the food industry.

Chemie Linz, Austria
Tennessee
Chemie Linz acquired a 50% interest in Gilmore Chemicals of Memphis for about $4.5 million. The two companies will produce chemicals to protect plants at facilities near Kansas City, MO.

Chromatics, Inc., Sweden
Connecticut
Chromatics will build a 20,000 sq. ft. plant located in Brookfield, Connecticut to produce colorants used in wire and cable coatings. About 35 people will be employed.

Ciba-Geigy, Switzerland
Delaware
Ciba-Geigy Corporation, the U.S. subsidiary of C-G, will spend SFrs. 50 million to acquire a pigments line from Du Pont de Nemours & Co. and a pigments facility located in Newport, DE.

Ciba-Geigy, Switzerland
New Jersey
Will spend over $100 million on a 3-year project at its 30-building complex in New Jersey. Plans include a facility in which to manufacture active ingredients for pharmaceuticals.

Coates Bros (Inks) Ltd., United Kingdom
New Jersey
Coates has purchased for $10.1 million, Colonial Printing Inks, a maker of silk-screen inks. Coates manufactures litho printer ink.

Coats & Clark Ltd., United Kingdom
New York
Gries/Dynast Co., a subsidiary of C&C Ltd., is building a highly-automated plant along with corporate headquarters. The facility will use microprocessor-controlled machines and materials-handling procedures that are ultra-sophisticated.

Combined Technologies Corp. PLC, United Kingdom
New Jersey
Laserstore, a U.S. subsidiary, will build a plant to produce optical tape drives.

Computer and Systems Engineering, United Kingdom
Maryland
CASE has purchased Rixon, a subsidiary of Schlumberger and a data communications company. The acquisition cost: $27 million. Rixon had sales of $35 million in 1983.

Conalco, Australia
Washington
Conalco plans to buy an ingot smelter located in Goldendale, WA from Martin Marietta Corp.

Concentric Overseas Ltd., United Kingdom
North Carolina
Concentric plans to construct a manufacturing facility in North Raleigh, NC. The production of diesel engines will be continued there.

Consolidated Gold Fields PLC, United Kingdom
Tennessee
Knoxville Iron Co., a subsidiary of Consolidated will spend $14 million to modernize its facilities producing products for the construction and mining industries.

Cookson Group PLC, United Kingdom
New Jersey
Alpha Metals Inc. has been acquired by a supplier of electronic materials, Cookson Group PLC. The transaction cost about $20 million.

Courtaulds PLC, United Kingdom
Alabama
Courtaulds North America, Inc. will improve the quality of fibers produced at the viscose rayon plant via a $10 million investment in this expansion project.

Courtaulds PLC, United Kingdom
Kentucky
Betts Packaging Inc., a unit of Courtaulds, will lease a plant in Kenton County and produce laminated tubes for toothpaste.

Courtaulds PLC, United Kingdom
New Jersey
The Newark unit of Georgia-Pacific Corp. that produces cast-acetate film has been acquired by Courtaulds.

D Lazzaroni & Co., Italy
New York
Lazzaroni Saronno, Ltd. will invest $500,000 to add 10,000 sq. ft. to its cookie manufacturing plant in Congers, Rockland County, NY. Jobs should increase by 30 or more.

Dai-Ichi Seiko Co., Japan
Georgia
Will build a facility near Atlanta to produce video cassettes.

Davidson Group, Ltd., United Kingdom
Massachusetts
American Davidson, an affiliate of Davidson, plans to purchase Westinghouse Sturtevant's industrial fan business. 350 people are employed at the 600,000 sq. ft. plant.

Dawson International PLC, United Kingdom
Pennsylvania
Dawson acquired J.E. Morgan Knitting Mills Inc., a maker of thermal underwear and blankets, for $42.5 million.

DCC Mfg. Co., Ltd., Japan
New Jersey
Dainichiseika Colour & Chemicals Mfg. Co., Ltd. has established a color pigment processing facility in Clifton, NJ. Future plans include the production of pigments for the automotive industry.

DDS Group, Denmark
Illinois
Novenco, Inc., a subsidiary of DDS, spent $1 million to expand its heating and ventilating fan production facility at Springfield, Illinois. Employment will increase by 15.

Delas Weir, France
Combustion Engineering and Delas Weir have formed a joint venture, C-E/Delas Weir Inc. to manufacture parts for nuclear power plants located in the U.S.

Dhul Corp., Spain
California
Dhul, a maker of flan, a custard-like dessert, plans to open a plant in Sacramento.

Didier-Werke AG, West Germany
Ohio
Didier Taylor Refractories Corp., a unit of Didier-Werke, plans to undertake an expansion project which includes the construction of a new refractory cement facility. Employment: 135–150 persons.

Diesel Kiki Co., Japan
California
Setting up a joint venture with Wynn's International Inc. of Fullerton, California based in Texas to produce heat exchangers, a major component of automobile air conditioners.

Distillers Co. PLC, United Kingdom
Kentucky
Acquired Old Fitzgerald Distillery, a Shively, Kentucky producer of bourbon and other products. Old Fitzgerald employs 150–175 people.

Dolomitwerke GmbH, West Germany
Pennsylvania
Wulfrath Refractories Inc., a subsidiary of Dolomitwerke, will purchase a factory in Tarentum that produces refractory bricks, mortars and plastics for the steel and cement industries. Cost was not disclosed.

Domtar Inc., Canada
Michigan
Domtar Industries Inc. will spend $3.8 million to reopen a gypsum wallboard plant at Grand Rapids, Michigan. New machinery will be installed and 80 people will be employed.

Domtar Inc., Canada
New York
Domtar has acquired another specialty papers industry, Upson Co., located in Lockport, NY. Terms were not disclosed.

Dunlop Tire & Rubber Co., United Kingdom
New York
Dunlop is engaging in a $15 million expansion and adding 110,000 sq. ft. to its plant in Tonawanda, NY. They will produce radial tires for light and medium-sized trucks.

Dynamit Nobel AG, West Germany
North Carolina
Dynamit Nobel will build a $35 million plant at Research Triangle Park, North Carolina to produce silicon wafers. Over 200 people will be employed.

Dynamit Nobel AG, West Germany
Illinois
Dynamit Nobel of America, Inc. will increase its production capacity of cross-linked polyolefin foam by 40% at its South Holland, Illinois plant. The foam is used mainly by the sports industry in the production of athletic shoes, linings and protective paddings.

Dyno Industrier A.S., Norway
Utah
Has acquired IRECO Chemicals of Salt Lake City, Utah which produced slurry explosives. The name will be changed to IRECO, Inc. and will operate as a subsidiary of DYNO.

Ebara, Japan
California
Acquired Cyrodynamics Pumps for about Yen 1,500 million. Cyrodynamics has annual sales of about $75 million and an estimated 1/3 share of the world market for cyrogenic pumps. Cyrogenics was formerly a unit of Worthington Pump.

Electrolux Group AB, Sweden
Texas
National Union Electric Co., a subsidiary of Electrolux will use a $2.5 million industrial revenue bond issue to add 62,500 sq. ft. to the already existing 120,000 sq. ft. Employment: 40 additional persons.

Elf Aquitane, France
Virginia
Texasgulf, a mining unit of Elf, bought a plant that produces defluorinated phosphate. Some renovations will be made.

Ellis & Everard, United Kingdom
Virginia
Ellis will acquire the Prillaman Group, a manufacturer of industrial chemicals. The acquisition cost $6.5 million.

Epson Corp., Japan
Oregon
Epson is planning to build a plant for production of matrix printers for personal computers. Initial employment of 500 people.

Express Dairy Foods Ltd., Ireland
California
Carberry Milk Products, sub of EDF, plans to build a $60 million cheese processing plant in California.

Fairey Holdings Ltd., United Kingdom
Pennsylvania
Fairey acquired Red Lion Controls, a producer of micro-electronic devices.

Ferranti PLC, United Kingdom
Texas
Ferranti acquired TRW Controls Corporation, a producer of control systems for the gas, electricity and oil distribution industries.

Ferruzzi S.P.A., Italy
Louisiana
Citrus Lands of Louisiana, Inc., a wholly-owned subsidiary is planning to build a $90 million alcohol distillery. Grain will be supplied by the nearby-located Mississippi River Grain Elevator. 40 million gallons of ethanol will be supplied a year. Employment: 100 persons; completion date: 1986.

Fichtel & Sachs Industries, AG, West Germany
North Carolina
Gas Spring Corp. a subsidiary of FSI, will build a $7.7 million plant to assemble springs which keep extended hatch-backs and other types of doors open. Employment will be increased by 245.

Fisher Gauge Works Ltd., Canada
New York
Fisher Gage Inc., subsidiary of FGW will engage in an expansion project by adding new equipment to the existing stock. Fisher is a nonferrous founding firm.

Fisons PLC, United Kingdom
Fisons PLC bought Scimed International Co. and Curtiss Matheson Scientific Co. - both subsidiaries of Coulter Electronics. Cost of transaction: $50 million.

Fisons PLC, United Kingdom
Massachusetts
Fisons, for $2.5 million, has acquired United Diagnostics, a diagnostic reagent maker.

Fletcher's Ltd., Canada
Washington
Fletcher's has acquired General Meats and Provisions, Inc. from Sea Galley Stores, Inc. When the plant reopens as Fletcher's Fine Foods, Inc., it will operate as a local bacon-and-ham slicing facility.

Formosa Plastics Corp., Taiwan
Louisiana
Formosa will make a $20 million expansion. Their vinyl chloride production capacity will be increased. 100 construction jobs will be created.

Foseco Minsep PLC, United Kingdom
Ohio
Foseco, a maker of specialty chemicals, will acquire Gibson-Homans Co., a manufacturer of protective coatings, for $46.6 million.

Franz Group, West Germany
Virginia
The Franz Group, a window manufacturer, plans to construct a 21,000 sq. ft. building in the Oyster Point Industrial Park. Employment: 24 plus 16 in sales and installation.

Fuji Koki Mfg. Co., Ltd., Japan
Fuji Koki has purchased the remaining 50% interest in Pace Products Inc., a joint venture with Virginia Chemical Co. of the United States. Pace, which will be renamed Fuji Koki America Co., produces valves for automobile air conditioners.

Fujikura Ltd., Japan
South Carolina
Alcoa Conductor Products Co., a subsidiary of Alcoa, and Fujikura, have formed a $15 million joint venture. The venture will manufacture telecommunications products.

Fujitsu Ltd., Japan
Oregon
Will build two plants in Oregon for $170 million which will manufacture disk drives and semiconductors. Each plant will employ 500 people.

Fujitsu Ltd., Japan
Texas
Fujitsu is building a yen 1 billion facility in Dallas to produce cellular mobile phones.

Geka Brush, West Germany
Vermont
Geka Bridgeport Manufacturing, a joint venture between Bridgeport Metals Good and Geka Brush, is beginning its operations to produce cosmetic and pharmaceutical brushes and other products. Employment: 50–75 persons.

Genitel Electronique Inc., Canada
New York
Aubut Electronic Corp., sub. of Genitel, will acquire a plant that produces electronic components. This plant is located in Willsboro, Essex County, NY and will increase the number of jobs by five or more.

Gold Star, Korea
Alabama
Gold Star of America, Inc. is constructing a new (its third) manufacturing facility to produce up to 500,000 microwave ovens a year at its Huntsville-Madison County Airport complex. The facility is set for completion during the summer months of 1985.

Grandmet, United Kingdom
Alabama
Diversified Products Corp. will use $8 million to build an addition to its home exercise equipment facility. Employment: will increase from 2800 to 3100.

H. Weidman, Switzerland
Vermont
The French and Bean Building has been purchased by EHV-Weidman Industries, the manufacturer of electrical insulation and fiberboard products. Total manufacturing space is now 247,000 sq. ft.

Hall Holdings, United Kingdom
Ohio
Hall acquired an Austin Tool & Mine Co. plant in Cleveland, Ohio to produce mining equipment.

Hans W. Barbe Chemische Erzeugnisse, West Germany
Georgia
HWB Chemische plans to construct a $1 million plant (Hall County, GA) to produce specialty coated clays.

Hanson Trust PLC, United Kingdom
Connecticut
Hanson acquired U.S. Industries, a Stamford-based firm producing a wide range of products including office and residential furniture, industrial products, chemicals and business equipment. U.S. Industries has sales of roughly $970 million.

Harlequin Enterprises, Ltd., Canada
New York
Harlequin has purchased from Simon & Schuster the Silhouette Publishing Co. for the amount of $10 million. They will also be receiving a share of Simon & Schuster's earnings over the next seven years.

Hawker-Siddeley, United Kingdom
Washington
The Dosco Corporation is building a plant in Washington County for the production of tunnel supports which will be supplied to the mining and civil engineering industries. Employment: 30–40 people.

Hellige GmbH, West Germany
Massachusetts
Hellige-a West German subsidiary of Lilton Industries-has taken a majority control in Datamedix Inc. (USA). Hellige produces electronic medical systems.

Helly-Hansen, Inc., Norway
Washington
Helly-Hansen will build a $3 million manufacturing and distribution facility at Redmond to produce raingear and sportswear.

Hermann Schoepp GmbH & Co., West Germany
North Carolina
Schoepp Velours of America Ltd., a manufacturer of pile velours and a subsidiary of Hermann Schoepp, will spend $5 million to build a 50,000 sq. ft. facility. Employment: 70 people.

Hille-Mueller GmbH, West Germany
Connecticut
Rafferty Brown Steel Co., a unit of Hille-Mueller will acquire a 35-acre tract on which to construct a 50,000 sq. ft. plant to produce low-carbon, flat-rolled steel.

Hitachi Chemical Co. Ltd., Japan
Georgia
Will build a $13 million plant in Dekalb County, Georgia to build wired circuit boards for computers. Eighty people will be employed.

Hitachi Ltd., Japan
Texas
Plans to expand its semiconductor operations in the U.S. by constructing a wafer fabrication facility. Will build the plant in Irving, Texas, near its existing operations plant, with a capital expenditure of about $45 million.

Hitachi Metals International Ltd., Japan
Michigan
Hitachi Magnetics Corp. will engage in a $9 million expansion of its metal alloy facility. Employment: 70 additional employees.

Hitachi Metals Ltd., Japan
California
Hitachi acquired Systems Magnetic Co., an Anaheim producer of voice coil motors for magnetic heads and other parts for computer peripherals. Systems has annual sales of about $13 million.

Hoechst A.G., West Germany
South Carolina
American Hoechst Corp., a subsidiary of Hoechst, is planning a $55 million expansion of its polyester film plant. 20 million pounds of film will be produced a year. 100 new jobs will be created.

Honda Motor Co., Japan
Ohio
The U.S. production subsidiary, Honda of America Mfg., Inc. plans to build a $42 million plastics injection molding facility in Marysville. Employment: 140 persons.

Honda Motor Co., Japan
Ohio
Honda and four other Japanese firms will build a $30 million plant near Dayton, Ohio to produce fuel tanks and other parts for automobiles.

Honda of America Inc., Japan
Ohio
Bellemar Parts Industries Inc., a division of Honda is planning to construct a new plant at Russells Point, Ohio for the manufacture of exhaust pipes and other automotive parts. Employment: 40 people.

Hyundai, Korea
California
Modern Electrosystems Inc., a subsidiary of Hyundai, is building a $10 million plant at San Jose to produce semiconductor chips.

Imperial Chemical Industries PLC, United Kingdom
Illinois
Imperial has agreed to buy Beatrice Cos.' chemical business for $750 million. This chemical business produces composite materials used in the aerospace industry and other products.

Imperial Chemical Industries PLC, United Kingdom
Illinois
ICI is acquiring closely held Coe Laboratories Inc., a maker of dental materials and services.

Interstate Meat Co. Ltd., Canada
New York
Interstate plans to acquire a meat packing plant located in Champlain, NY. The project will cost approximately $1 million and increase jobs by 70.

Iseki Polytech Inc., Japan
Alabama
Iseki will build a plant in Montgomery, Alabama. It will produce underground and tunneling machinery. Employment: 250–300 jobs.

Japan Digital Laboratory, Japan
California
Plans to set up a wholly-owned company in the U.S. The unit which will act as a supplier of color printers for local firms will be based in Westlake Village, California.

KabiVitrum AB, Sweden
KabiVitrum will buy the parenteral nutrition product line and part of a plant in Clayton along with 675 employees from the Cutter Group of Miles Laboratories Inc.

Kanto Seiki Co. Ltd., Japan
Tennessee
Will build a $12 million plant at Lewisburg, Tennessee to produce plastic parts for Nissan trucks.

Kaufman Footwear Industries Ltd., Canada
New York
Kaufman's subsidiary, Kaufman Footwear Inc., has expanded its women's footwear business resulting in a job change of 30+ workers at the Batavia, NY location.

Kawasaki Steel Corp., Japan
California
Kawasaki (25%), Companhia Vale do Rio Doce Ltd. (25%), and a Long Beach businessman (50%) have formed a venture, Pacific Steel, which will buy an idle steel mill from Kaiser Steel Corp. Employment: 450 jobs.

KemaNord Inc., Sweden
Mississippi
KemaNord plans to expand its Columbus, Mississippi sodium chlorate plant. Plans include the construction of a building in which to put new cells.

Kibun, Japan
North Carolina
Kibun Corp. of America has established a plant at Raleigh, North Carolina to produce fish cakes.

Kikkoman, Japan
Wisconsin
Kikkoman Foods Inc., a subsidiary of Kikkoman, will invest $7 million to expand soy sauce production.

Kirin Brewery Co. Ltd., Japan
KB Co. Ltd. and Amgen (NASDQ-AMGN) have formed a 50-50 joint venture, Kirin-Amgen Inc. The venture firm will make erythropoietin, a male hormone produced using genetic engineering techniques.

Koemmerling/Germany, West Germany
New Jersey
Koemmerling/Germany bought a 19,800 sq. ft. building in Hackensack and will build a 14,750 addition to produce vinyl windows.

Kohkoko, Japan
Washington
Kohkoko USA, Inc.'s new manufacturing plant to produce polyvinyl chloride film and sheeting, will be financed through a $6.5 million industrial revenue bond issue. About 25 people will be employed.

Koito, Westfalische, Japan, Germany
Illinois
North American Lighting, a joint venture of Koito and Westfalische, will expand facilities for production of automotive lighting at Flora, Illinois.

Kosmos Export GmbH, West Germany
Ohio
Kosmos and Cafaro Co. of West Germany plan to build a brewery in Youngstown, Ohio. The plant will cost over $20 million. Employment: Initially 135 persons.

Kostka S.A., France
North Carolina
Kostka, a lamp manufacturer, plans to locate American operations in Greensboro, NC. Employment: 20 people over a 2-year period.

Kuraray Co., Ltd., Japan
Texas
Eval Co. of America, a 50-50 joint venture of Kuraray and Northern Petroleum Co., will build a plant near Houston, TX, to produce ethylene vinyl alcohol copolymer resins.

Kyocera Corp., Japan
Washington
Will build a $30 mill plant and research facility at Vancouver Washington to produce ceramic products. Employment of manufacturing workers is expected to reach 250 by 1985.

L'Air Liquide, France
Florida
Liquid Air Corporation will build a $14 million plant at Orlando to produce liquid oxygen, nitrogen and argon. The plant is expected to be operational in October, 1985 and will employ 30.

Laporte Industries, United Kingdom
Laporte has purchased Ohio Sealants Inc., a maker of building industry chemicals.

Laporte Industries, United Kingdom
Georgia
Laporte has purchased Chemical Specialties, a maker of chemical products for wood treatment. The chemical facility is located in Valdosta, GA.

Laporte Industries, United Kingdom
Wisconsin
Laporte has purchased Great Lakes Biochemical Co., a maker of chemical products and bio-chemical water treatment.

Legrand, France
New York
Legrand will acquire Pass and Seymour Inc., a Syracuse manufacturer of electrical wiring devices. All 750 employees will be retained.

Legris France SA, France
New York
Legris Inc. will add 12,000 sq. ft. to its plant in Rochester, NY. Legris is a producer of valves and pipe fittings. Project cost: over $858,000. Employment: more than 18 new jobs.

Levy Industries Ltd., Canada
New York
Levy will spend $1.5 million for the acquisition of a Niagara Falls automotive parts facility. Employment: 150 workers.

Lin-Pac Flexible Packaging Ltd., United Kingdom
Tennessee
Lin-Pac (England) is planning to construct a facility for the production of corrugated board and packaging. Initial employment: 50 persons.

Linde, West Germany
South Carolina
Baker Material Handling Corp. plans to construct a 200,000 sq. ft. plant. The company makes fork lift trucks. Employment: 200 persons.

Liquid Air Corp., France
Illinois
Cardox Corp., a division of LAC will build, at a cost of $15.3 million, three carbon dioxide plants. The locations are: Auburn, Maine; South Point, Ohio; Jasper, Tennessee. Employment-more than 40 persons per plant.

LM Ericsson Telephone, Sweden
New Hampshire
LM Ericsson, a communications company, has acquired Facit Inc. of Nashua.

Lumonics Research Inc., Canada
California
Lumonics, a supplier of laser equipment, has acquired for $4.3 million, Laser Identification Inc. located in a Los Angeles suburb.

Makita Electric Works Ltd., Japan
Georgia
Makita Electric Works Ltd., has selected a suburb of Atlanta as the site for its first U.S. electric-tool factory.

Maple Leaf Shoe Co. Ltd., Canada
New York
Maple Leaf will spend over $700,000 for the acquisition of a footwear facility in Plattsburgh, NY. Employment: 40+ workers.

Marquardt GmbH, West Germany
New York
Marquardt Switches Inc. will build a 24,000 sq. ft. plant to produce switches. Up to 120 people will be employed.

Maruyasu Kogyo Ltd., Japan
California
Maruyasu Industries Co. (sub of Maruyasu Kogyo) and Curtis Products Inc. have formed a 50-50 joint venture. The joint venture firm will manufacture automobile tubing.

Mazda Motor Corp., Japan
Michigan
Mazda will acquire an idle foundry from Ford Motor Co. in Flat Rock and construct a new yen 110 billion plant to start building compact cars late in 1987.

MGM Textile Industries Inc., Canada
New York
MGM Technologies will spend $1 million for the acquisition of a knit fabric facility located in St. Johnsville, Montgomery County, NY. Employment: over 100 workers.

Michelin, France
South Carolina
Michelin Tire Corp. plans to expand its truck tire plant in Spartanburg, SC. It will be used for the production and marketing of an experimental radial aircraft tire.

Mineba Co., Ltd., Japan
California
Mineba has acquired Universal Magnetics, Inc., a maker of direct-current motors for printers that are high speed. Universal is located in Chatsworth, CA. Cost: $5 million. Mineba is a manufacturer of precision ball bearings.

Minerals & Resources Corp. Ltd., Canada
Iowa
Terra Chemicals International Inc., a subsidiary of Minerals & Resources Corp. Ltd. and Hudson Bay Mining and Smelting Co. Ltd. will construct a dry flowable formulation facility. Employment: 50 persons.

Mitsubishi Chemical Industries Ltd., Japan
Alabama
Is joining Celanese Corp. to produce and market a high-grade fertilizer in the US. The plant will be built in Bucks, Ala. by next year that would produce 20,000 tons of the compound fertilizer, called IBDU. 50% owned by NY-based Celanese; 35% by Mitsubishi Chem.; 15% by Mitsubishi Corp. (chem unit parent co.)

Mitsubishi Corp., Japan
Alabama
Mitsubishi International Corp. plans to construct a $5 million steel fabrication plant. Employment: 35 persons.

Mitsubishi Corp., Japan
Alabama
Mitsubishi plans to build a $5 million facility in Athens to produce electronic components. Employment: 40 workers.

Mitsui Bussan, Japan
Texas
Alumax, Inc., a joint venture of Amax of the U.S. (50%) and three Japanese companies including Mitsui Bussan (50%), plans to construct an aluminum plant that will produce rolled aluminum. The cost of the plant is $50 million. Employment: 300 persons.

Mizuno Corp., Japan
Georgia
Mizuno Golf Co., a subsidiary of Mizuno Corp., will assemble golf clubs at its Gwinett County facility. During the first year 100,000 golf clubs should be assembled.

Monier Ltd., Australia
Florida
Monier Company expanded production facilities at Lakeland and will triple output of concrete roof tiles to 280,000 squares a year.

Morgan Crucible Company, United Kingdom
Illinois
Morgan Refractories, Inc., a subsidiary of Morgan Crucible, purchased the assets of Thermal Ceramics Industries, Inc. The acquisition cost $1.3 million.

Mori Seiki Co., Ltd., Japan
Texas
Mori Seiki will construct a machine tool assembly plant. Completion date: 1986.

Muller Manufacturing Ltd., Canada
New York
Muller has recently opened a plant to manufacture packaging devices for wrapping industrial pallets. The new plant is located in DeWitt. Employment: 20 persons.

Musashi Seimitsu Kogyo K.K., Japan
Michigan
Will build a plant in Battle Creek to produce camshafts, gears and other automobile parts.

N.V. Philips, The Netherlands
California
Control Data Corp. (Minn.) and N.V. Philips have formed a joint venture, Optical Storage International. The new firm will make computer data storage devices that are laser-based.

NEC Corp., Japan
Oregon
NEC America, Inc., subsidiary of NEC Corp., has plans to construct a new fiber-optics communications equipment plant for a cost of $67 million.

NEC Corporation, Japan
Georgia
NEC Home Electronics (USA) Inc. will build an $8.3 million plant in Henry County, Georgia to produce color television sets. Initial employment will be 110 people; plant opening is scheduled for summer, 1985.

Neoplan Worldwide, West Germany
Pennsylvania
Neoplan plans to set up a new bus production plant which will be located in Honeybrook, Chester County. Employment: 400 workers.

Nestle S.A., Switzerland
California
Nestle acquired Hills Bros. Coffee, a San Francisco-based producer of coffee products.

Nestle S.A., Switzerland
California
Alcon Laboratories, a subsidiary of Nestle, has paid $503 million for CooperVision Inc., a manufacturer of soft contact lenses.

Nestle S.A., Switzerland
Illinois
Nestle has acquired the assets of a major chocolate manufacturer, Paul F. Beich Co.

Nihon Plast Ltd., Japan
Ohio
Will build a $2.5 million plant in Preble County, Ohio to produce steering wheels and other parts for automobiles.

Nippon Densan Corp. (NIDEC), Japan
Connecticut
Nippon Densan acquired the axial tube fan line and the Torrington, Connecticut plant of Clevepak Corporation. The plant will be expanded at a cost of $3–$5 million.

Nippon Kokan K.K., Japan
Pennsylvania
Nippon Kokan paid $292 million to acquire an interest in National Steel Corp. National has plants in Michigan, Illinois and Indiana.

Nippon Oil Seal, Japan
Georgia
NOS, U.S. affiliate of Nippon, will spend about $10 million to expand its oil seal production plant at Lagrange, Georgia. 15 new jobs have been added to the 270-person work force.

Nippon Pigment Co., Ltd., Japan
Texas
Nippon Pigment plans to construct a $4 million facility in Houston to produce color pigments. The pigments will be used in the automotive and electric machinery industries.

Nippon Sheet Glass Co., Japan
New Jersey
NSG will build a plant in New Jersey to begin production of Selfoc Micro Lens. The Selfoc lens can split, gather and receive light.

Nippondenso Co., Japan
Michigan
Nippondenso Co., a Japan-based auto parts maker, said it will build a $50 million plant to make automotive parts in Battle Creek, Michigan.

Nissan Motor Co., Japan
Tennessee
Plans to spend $85 million in order to begin the production of Sentra passenger cars in Smyrna, TN. Employment: 1000 workers.

Nisshin Steel Co., Japan
West Virginia
Nisshin Steel Co. & Wheeling-Pittsburgh Steel Corp. formed a venture to

build a $50 million steel-sheet plant at Wheeling-Pittsburgh's W.VA works to produce 150,000 tons of steel sheets annually. Will be owned 35% by Nisshin, 15% by Mitsubishi Corp. and 50% by Wheeling.

Nissho-Iwai, Japan
New York
Nissho-Iwai and Kawasaki Heavy Industries will lease 150,000 sq. ft. of industrial space at Yonkers to build railroad cars. 150 jobs will be created.

Nord Bitumi, Italy
Georgia
Nord Bitumi, a maker of Poly 4, a membrane-type roofing material, has leased a 45,000 sq. ft. building in Macon to continue this product line. Initial employment: 15 persons.

North American Lighting Inc. (NAL), Japan
Illinois
NAL, a maker of lighting equipment, will set up a new facility in Flora, IL, in order to meet the increasing demands from Nissan and other automotive manufacturers.

North American Philips Corp., The Netherlands
Indiana
Magnavox Government and Industrial Electronics, a subsidiary of North American, will build a new plant to continue production of government and industrial electronics equipment. Employment: 250–300 persons.

Northern Telecom Ltd., Canada
Georgia
Northern Telecom Inc. will spend $42 million to expand its telecommunications production plant at Stone Mountain. The 800 person workforce will increase by 400.

Northern Telecom Ltd., Canada
Tennessee
The U.S. subsidiary, Northern Telecom, Inc., is planning to build three new facilities outside of Research Triangle Park, NC. An additional 1000 employees will be hired.

Novo Industri A/S, Denmark
North Carolina
Novo Laboratories, Inc. a subsidiary of Novo, will be expanding its enzyme producing subsidiary, Novo Biochemicals, Inc.

NTN Toyo Bearing Co., Ltd., Japan
Illinois
NTN Toyo will construct a facility to take care of tapered roller bearing production. The facility will be located at NTN Toyo's subsidiary, NTN Elgin Corp. Operational date: March 1985.

Oak-Mitsui Inc., Japan
New York
Mitsui Mining & Smelting Co. Ltd. is engaged in a $20 million expansion project. This metal foil plant is located in Hoosick Falls, Rensselaer County, NY.

Okamoto Machine Tool Works Ltd., Japan
Illinois
Okamoto Corp., a subsidiary of Okamoto Machine, plans to construct a facility in which to assemble medium-size grinding machines.

Omi Kenshi Co. Ltd., Japan
Georgia
Omi Georgia, a joint venture firm owned by Omi Kenshi and Nissho Iwai Corp., are engaged in a $1.5 million expansion of its yarn-spinning business. The project includes construction of a 17,500 sq. ft. warehouse. Employment: an additional 20–25 new employees.

Opto Electronics Co., Japan
New York
Plans to construct a facility to manufacture bar-code reader assembly kits in the U.S. Employment: 40–50 workers.

Opto Electronics Co. Ltd., Japan
New York
Opticon Inc., sub of O-E has acquired a new semiconductor facility in Orangeburg, Rockland county, NY.

Paul Hettich GmbH, West Germany
North Carolina
Furntek Hettich Corp., a producer of furniture fittings, acquired Richard Heinze America Ltd., a producer of fittings and a U.S. subsidiary of a German firm.

Pechiney Ugine Kuhlman Corp., France
Michigan
Howmet Turbine Components Corp., a subsidiary of Pechiney, will spend $5 million to expand production of coatings used to protect turbine components at its facilities in Whitehall, MI.

Pechiney Ugine Kuhlman Corp., France
Pennsylvania
Mill Products Division, a division of Howmet Aluminum Corp. (sub. of Pechiney), is working on an $18 million 15,000 sq. ft. expansion of its plant. The Mill Products Division converts aluminum ingots into finished coils. Employment: 1,150 persons.

Petitjean SA, France
Pennsylvania
Petitjean acquired plants producing tubular products from Union Metal Mfg. Co.

Petrofina, Belgium
Texas
Cosden Oil & Chemical, a subsidiary of Petrofina, purchased a 470 million
1b/year polypropylene facility from Arco Chemical.

Philips, The Netherlands
Maine
Philips Elmet Corp., a unit of Philips, is planning an expansion of its
tungsten facility. Employment: will add approximately 400 jobs to the
already existing 310.

Phoenix, West Germany
Pennsylvania
Will build a 43,000 sq. ft. plant at Lower Swatara township in Pennsylvania
to produce electronic components. Over 100 people will be employed.

PLM AB, Sweden
Georgia
PLM AB, Metal Box Plc (UK) and Dorsey Corp. (U.S.) have formed a joint
venture in Atlanta to produce a new kind of plastic container for soft drinks.
The venture will go under the name of Petainer Development Co.

PRB Group, Belgium
New York
Recticel Foam Corp., a producer of plastic products and a subsidiary of PRB,
will invest $2.2 million to expand production capacity. Ten jobs will be
created.

Precision Service & Engineering Ltd., Canada
Georgia
Will produce equipment for the forest product industry in a plant at Macon,
Georgia. About 10 people will be employed.

Reckitt and Colman, United Kingdom
Airwick, a maker of air freshner and a unit of Ciba-Geigy, has been purchased for L165m by Reckitt. Reckitt produces house-hold products and
foods.

Reed International, United Kingdom
California
Acquired Frazee Paint and Wallcoverings, a San Diego, California producer
and distributor of wall paper and paints. Frazee has sales of about $60
million.

Rheon Automatic Machinery Co., Japan
California
Rheon, a maker of food processing machinery, plans to construct a baking
facility in Irvine, CA. The plant will make croissants and other pastries.

Rhone Poulenc S.A., France
Colorado
Rhone Poulenc Inc., in agreement with Brown Disc Manufacturing will acquire 73.5 percent of Brown's outstanding shares. Brown is a manufacturer of floppy discs.

Ringier Print, Switzerland
North Carolina
Ringier Print US Inc., a subsidiary of Ringier, plans to open its new plant in Charlotte. The US firm will make color separations for the printing industry. Employment: 15 people initially.

Rohm GmbH, West Germany
Arkansas
CY/RO Industries, a company formed via a partnership of American Cyanamid Co. and Rohm GmbH of West Germany, plans to construct a $20-25 million plant which will manufacture acrylite FF. Employment: 100 persons.

Royal Packaging Industries, United Kingdom
Alabama
Keyes Fibre Co., a unit of RPI, announced plans for a $3 million expansion of its paper goods facility.

Sadolin and Hohnblad Ltd., Denmark
North Carolina
Sadolin Technology U.S.A. (unit of SHL) will open a new chemical coating facility. Employment: 6 persons initially.

Saint-Gobain Pont-A-Mousson, France
Texas
Cameron Wholesale Division, a unit of Certain-Teed Corp. (sub. of Saint-Gobain), is planning to build a new $2 million 70,000 sq. ft. plant in Alvarado, TX to produce interior and exterior door units. Initial employment: 40 persons.

Sait Overseas Technical and Trading, Italy
Connecticut
Sait has acquired Kendall Co. Under Sait ownership the facility will manufacture industrial abrasive products.

Salzgitter Stahl GmbH, West Germany
Pennsylvania
Feralloy Corp., a processor of steel coils for use in building materials and a subsidiary of Salzgitter, will receive a $2 million industrial development bond from the Contra Costa County Board of Supervisors. The bond will enable Feralloy to expand.

Samsung Group, South Korea
California
Tristar Semiconductor, a firm funded by the Samsung Group, has put to use a facility at Santa Clara, CA for the production of 64K dynamic RAMS.

Sanofi, France
Wisconsin
Sanofi Inc., a subsidiary of Sanofi, will acquire Dairyland Food Laboratories Inc., a producer of ingredients for the dairy and food industries. DFL had sales of $14 million in 1983.

Sanoh Industrial Co., Ltd., Japan
California
Sanoh Manufacturing Corp., formed by Sanoh Industrial and Sanyo Electric Co., Ltd. in a joint venture, plans to set up a plant to produce refrigerator parts.

Sante Fe International Corp., Kuwait
Sante Fe, based in Alhambra, California and owned by Kuwaiti government's Kuwait Petroleum Company has acquired Occidental Geothermal Inc. from Occidental Petroleum Corp. for $350 million including $325 million in cash.

Scandinavian Transport Products, Norway
Minnesota
Scandinavian is planning to locate a snowplow and dump truck facility in MN. Employment: 30–50 new jobs.

Scanner Industries, Canada
New York
Scanner will build television receiving dishes in a plant at Massena, N.Y. Employment will be 25–30 people.

Scapa Group, United Kingdom
Louisiana
Kern Rubber Co., a subsidiary of Scapa Group, plans to build a 35,000 to 40,000 sq. ft. facility for a cost of $5 million. The plant will employ up to 30 persons and will produce rubber-covered rolls for production machinery.

Sesame Ltd., Canada
New York
Sesame's subsidiary, Sesame Industries Inc., plans to expand its plant that manufactures paper coating and glazing. Employment will increase by 10 people at the Plattsburgh, NY facility.

Settsu Paperboard Mfg. Co., Japan
California
Settsu and Consolidated Fibers Inc. have formed a 50–50 joint venture. The joint venture company, Settsu Consolidated Fibers will operate as a paper production business.

SGS-ATES, Italy
Arizona
SGS-ATES, owned by the Italian holding company Instituto per la Ricostruzione Industriale, plans to construct a new facility to produce semiconductors. The facility will be located in Phoenix.

Shachihata, Japan
New Jersey
Shachihata Inc. (U.S.A.) will build a 30,000 sq. ft. manufacturing distribution facility at Lakewood, New Jersey. Shachihata produces preinked rubber stamp products.

Shell, The Netherlands
Illinois
Shell Oil Co. has begun a $100 million expansion project at its Wood River Refinery (Illinois). The catalytic cracking units will be modernized.

Shikishima Baking Co., Japan
California
Pasco Corporation of America, a subsidiary of Shikishima, plans to market 100 kinds of breads using highly automated equipment. Employment: 15 people.

Shin-Etsu Chemical Co. Ltd., Japan
Texas
Shintech Inc., a subsidiary of Shin-Etsu, is engaging in an expansion of its polyvinyl chloride capacity.

Shinko Electric America, Japan
California
Shinko, a supplier of lead-frames plans to enlarge its plant located in Manteca, Industrial Park. The project will cost $4.5 million and includes the building of new offices and the installation of equipment. Employment: an additional 76 workers.

Shiseido Co. Ltd., Japan
New Jersey
Shiseido, a cosmetic manufacturer is planning to build a cosmetic facility to produce skin creams and makeup. The plant will be located in Auckland, NJ.

SICPA S.A., Switzerland
Virginia
SICPA plans to build another (its third) printing ink facility in Springfield, VA. Initial employment: 60 workers; over 100 after the first year.

Siemens A.G., West Germany
Colorado
Siemens Components, Inc. (sub) which designs and sells metal oxide semiconductor field effect transistor (MOSFET) semiconductors will add a highly automated production line at its facility at Broomfield, CO. The plant will now also produce MOSFET chips. Employment: 100 persons in the next few years.

Siemens A.G., West Germany
Massachusetts
Siemens-Allis, Inc. and Siemens Capital Corporation, both units of Siemens A.G., will acquire Challenger Electronic Controls, a maker of programmable controllers. Challenger's business will be integrated with Siemens-Allis Automation, Inc., a newly formed company in Waltham, MA.

Siemens A.G., West Germany
New York
Osram Corp., a subsidiary of Siemens will begin production of a new line of energy-efficient compact fluorescent lamps. Initial employment: 60 people.

Societe de Mecanique Magnetique, France
Virginia
Societe and Inland Motor Specialty Products Division of Kollmorgen Corporation (U.S.A.) have formed a joint venture, Magnetic Bearings, Inc. to manufacture magnetic bearings.

Societe des Ciments Francais, France
Kentucky
SCF, through its subsidiary Coplay Cement Company, has acquired Louisville Cement Company for $112 million. Louisville Cement has 495 employees, two plants in Indiana.

Societe Nationale Elf Aquitaine, France
Alabama
M&T Chemicals, Inc., a unit of SNEA will engage in a joint venture with Mitsubishi Rayon Co. to manufacture additives used to produce plastics.

Societe Nationale Elf Aquitaine, France
New Jersey
M&T Chemicals, Inc., a unit of SNEA plans a $10 million expansion of its chemical complex. Employment: 13 people.

Solvay & Cie, Belgium
Texas
Interox America, owned by both Solvay & Cie and Laport Industries will expand its plant that produces hydrogen peroxide.

Solvay et Cie., SA, Belgium
Acquired the Nutrition & Health Division of T H Agriculture & Nutrition Co., Inc. of Kansas City, Kansas. The Division makes products for the animal feed industry and pharmaceuticals for humans, and was formerly a unit of North American Philips.

Sony Corp., Japan
Indiana
The U.S. subsidiary, Sony Corp. of America, plans to construct a plant that will produce laser video discs at Terre Haute, IN for a cost between $15-$20 million. Initial employment—100 persons; will increase to 250 within two or three years.

St. Lawrence Cement, Inc., Canada
New York
St. Lawrence bought a cement plant and distribution system located in the Catskill, NY area from Lone Star Industries. The purchase cost $30 million plus an unspecified amount for inventories.

Standard Microsystems, Inc., Philippine Islands
California
International Assemblies, a joint venture of Standard and other firms has begun operations at its Milpitas facility for the production of plastic IC packages. Initial employment: 70 persons.

Staroba Plastics & Metal Products, Canada
New York
Staroba Plastic & Metal Products of NY Inc. has acquired a Lackawanna plastics facility.

Stettner, West Germany
Tennessee
Acquired a facility at Chattanooga, Tennessee and will produce components for communication devices and appliances. About 10 people will be employed initially.

Stora Kopparbergs Bergslags AB, Sweden
Acquired Newton Falls Paper Mill Inc. from the American Broadcasting Companies and McGraw-Hill Inc.

Sumitomo Corp., Japan
Mississippi
Sumitomo will build a plant at Vicksburg to process Japanese steel into shapes and lengths. Up to 20 people will be employed.

Sumitomo Electric Industries Ltd., Japan
North Carolina
Will build a plant at Raleigh, North Carolina to produce fiber optic cables. Initial employment will be 200 people.

Sumitomo Metal Industries, Ltd., Japan
Arkansas
Western Tube & Conduit Corp., an (80% owned) subsidiary of Sumitomo Metal Ind. will build a new factory in Little Rock, Arkansas to manufacture conduit tubes and other welded tubes. Will employ 150 workers.

Sumitomo Metal Industries, Ltd., Japan
Texas
Sumitomo Metal has purchased a U.S. steel pipe threading company and has formed a joint venture with Sumitomo Corp. and Vallourec S.A. (France). The facilities and staff of Premium Threading Service have been taken over by the venture firm, VAM PTS Co.

Sumitomo Metal Mining Co., Japan
California
Sumitomo plans to build a facility in Fremont, CA for the production of lead frames for integrated circuits.

Suntory International, Japan
California
Suntory, the leading maker and importer/exporter of alcoholic beverages plans to acquire Chateau St. Jean, a winery located in Sonoma County, California. It plans to spend more than $40 million for the winery.

Superfos, Denmark
Virginia, Florida
Superfos acquired Roster, a producer of phosphates, from Universal Leaf Tobacco for roughly $100 million.

Swedish Match, Sweden
Tennessee
Harris-Tarkett, U.S. subsidiary of Swedish Match, will build an $8 million hardwood-flooring plant at Johnson City. Production is expected to begin in 1985 and 60 workers will be employed initially.

Swiss Aluminum (Alusuisse), Switzerland
New Jersey
Alusuisse will construct a $4.9 million facility to produce aluminum aerosol cans.

Tabuchi Electric Co., Ltd., Japan
Tennessee
Plans to spend $1.2 million in an effort to increase the capacity of the Jackson, TN transformer plant.

Tama Chemical Industries, Ltd., Japan
Washington
Tama has begun work on a new plant to manufacture high purity solutions used by the electronic and fiber optics industries. Initial employment: 8 persons.

Tarkett AB, Sweden
New York
Floor Products Division, a subsidiary of Tarkett, plans to spend $4.5 million in an expansion project. The floor tile manufacturer is located in Vails Gate, Orange County, NY.

Tarmac P.L.C., United Kingdom
Florida
Tarmac has agreed to purchase for about $80 million aggregates, ready-mix and concrete block plants in Florida from Lone Star Industries.

Tate and Lyle PLC, United Kingdom
Pacific Molasses, a subsidiary of Tate and Lyle, will buy Agriproducts, a division of Beatrice Inc. Amount of the transaction: $43.2 million. Revenue of Agriproducts in 1984: about $122 million.

Telemecanique, France
Telemecanique announced negotiations to acquire industrial controls division of Gould Inc. The division has about $70 million in sales; 1000 employees.

The Fleeting Organization Ltd., United Kingdom
Florida
Fleeting is spending $1.5 million on facilities at Tampa to produce beer. Initial employment will be 7 people.

Thomson-CSF, France
California
Passive Components Division, a unit of Thomson, plans to build a capacitor manufacturing plant in Canoga Park, CA.

Thyssen-Bornemiza, The Netherlands
California
T-B is planning to acquire Torr Vacuum Products, Inc., a maker of diffusion pump systems. 100 persons are employed there.

Tiense Suiker International, The Netherlands
Illinois
TSI and Chappel Armand International, an investment firm, has acquired the Joan of Arc Co. located in Peoria, IL. Joan of Arc processes vegetables.

Tokai Seiki Co. Ltd., Japan
Georgia
Tokai Seiki acquired Scripto, Inc., an Atlanta-based producer of writing instruments, from Allegheny International.

Tokyo Electric, Japan
California
Tokyo Electric Co. Ltd. will set up a software development center for point-of-sale systems in Los Angeles, CA.

Topy Industries, Ltd., Japan
Kentucky
Topy Industries, Inc., a wholly-owned subsidiary of the Japanese firm to be set up early in 1985 to manufacture wheels for Japanese and other automakers in the U.S. capitalized at US$10,000,000. Plant to cost yen 6 billion, to turn out 350,000 wheels monthly starting in June 1986.

Toshiba Corp., Japan
Tennessee
Toshiba plans to spend $2.1 million to expand its microwave oven production facility located in Lebanon, TN. Capacity should increase 40 percent.

Toshiba Corp., Japan
New York
Toshiba formed a joint venture with Westinghouse Electric and will produce television tubes in a formerly vacant Westinghouse plant at Horsehead. Total investment will be $100 mill. and employment will be between 600 and 800 people.

Toyo Giken Co., Ltd., Japan
Toyo Giken and American Cal Enterprise have formed a joint venture, American Tool & Forging Co., to manufacture socket wrenches.

Toyo Suisan Kaisha, Ltd., Japan
California
Maruchan, Inc., a subsidiary of Toyo, will spend $3 million for the expansion of its noodle plant.

Toyoda Machinery Works, Ltd., Japan
Illinois
Toyoda Machinery USA, Inc. located at Schaumburg, Illinois will begin full-scale assembly of its machine tools. The facility is designed for assembly and manufacturing operations.

Triple Crown Electronics Ltd., Canada
Florida
Plans to build a 35,000 sq. ft. facility in Deerfield Beach to produce equipment for the cable and satellite television industries. Employment: About 200 workers within three years; 75 initially.

Tsuzuki Spinning Co., Ltd., Japan
Alabama
TNS Inc., a subsidiary of Tsuzuki, has acquired Avondale Mills' Cowikee spinning plant. 150 people are employed there.

Unavailable, Canada
New York
Battat Inc., a manufacturer of children's games and toys plans to expand its facility by 12,500 sq. ft. Employment: Over 15 more workers. The plant is located in Champlain, NY.

Unavailable, Canada
New York
Berlin & Associates Inc. has acquired an advertising display manufacturing facility. An additional 10 persons will be employed.

Unavailable, Canada
New York
Clinton Tube Inc., a subsidiary of a Canadian firm has acquired a paper mill located in Plattsburgh, NY. The acquisition cost $1.25 million.

Unavailable, Canada
New York
Cyber Digital Inc., a manufacturer of radio and TV equipment plans to engage in a $8.5 million expansion project. Employment: 36+

Unavailable, Canada
New York
Darling Body Fashions, a subsidiary of a Canadian firm, is in the process of

acquiring a women's underwear facility located in Buffalo, NY. Employment: over 60 new workers.

Unavailable, Canada
New York
Elastometal Inc. will acquire a ball and roller-bearing facility located in Niagara Falls, NY. Employment: more than 20 additional workers.

Unavailable, Canada
New York
Independent Products Co., a subsidiary of a Canadian firm will expand its prepared meat plant. Employment: 25+; cost: $1 million. The plant is located in Champlain, NY.

Unavailable, Canada
New York
Technomin Inc. has acquired a prefabricated metal buildings plant for a cost of $40,000. The plant is located at Rouses Point, NY.

Unavailable, Canada
New York
Tiny Tots Knitting Mills is acquiring a new plant to manufacture children's outerwear. Employment: More than 100 workers.

Unavailable, Japan
New York
Izumi Corp. Industries Inc., a subsidiary of Japanese firm, has added new equipment to its automotive parts plant in an expansion project. Location: Yaphank, Suffolk County, NY.

Unavailable, Switzerland
New York
Stella Corp., a subsidiary of a Swiss firm has acquired a furniture facility located in Long Island City, Queens, NY.

Unavailable, United Kingdom
New York
Gemini Mannequins, a subsidiary of a UK firm has acquired a Kings County, Brooklyn, NY mannequin facility. The acquisition will provide an additional 10 jobs.

Unice S.A., Spain
Florida
Unice Florida, Inc., a subsidiary of Unice S.A. will open its new inflatable novelty ball plant located in Orlando. Initial employment: 30 persons.

Unitech PLC, United Kingdom
New York
Unitech acquired U.S. Components, a New York City-based producer of connectors for the electronic and military markets for $3 million.

United Biscuits (Holdings), U.S., Ltd., United Kingdom
Indiana
Keebler Co., a division of UB and a leading maker of cookies and crackers is

expanding its plant in Bluffton, IN. The expansion will provide additional production and warehouse space. Employment: 150 new jobs.
Vekaplast, West Germany
Pennsylvania
Vekaplast USA has established facilities at Cranberry Township Pennsylvania, and is producing vinyl window frames.

VMF Stork, The Netherlands
North Carolina
Stork Screens American Inc., a subsidiary of VMF Stork, will add 20,000 sq. ft. to its plant in Charlotte, North Carolina to continue in the production of metal perforated rotary printing screens. Employment will be increased by 25 to 30 persons.

Volkswagenwerk AG, West Germany
Pennsylvania
Volkswagen of America Inc. (subsidiary) is planning to retool its plant in New Stanton, PA. The project will cost $200 mill.

W.C. Heraeus GmbH Group, West Germany
Georgia
Heraeus-Amersil Inc., the wholly-owned subsidiary of W.C. Heraeus plans to build a wave guide quartz tubing plant in Buford, GA. Initial employment: 50 people.

W.C. Heraeus GmbH Group, West Germany
California
Heraeus-Volkert, Inc., a subsidiary of W.C. Heraeus, will establish a stamping facility for producing lead frames at a site to be selected in northern California.

Wacker Chemitronic, West Germany
Oregon
Wacker Siltronic, a subsidiary of Wacker Chemitronic, plans to construct an $80 million polysilicon plant at Portland. This will be the firm's first polysilicon facility in the U.S. Employment is expected to double from its present 860-person work force.

Wacoal Corp., Japan
Wacoal, a leading manufacturer of lingerie, plans to build a facility for the production of women's wear. Initial employment: 100 workers.

Wandel and Goltermann GmbH, West Germany
North Carolina
W&G Instruments, Inc., the U.S. unit of Wandel, is constructing a $6 million equipment testing facility in Research Triangle Park. Employment: 40 transfers from New Jersey; 60 additional workers.

Wolter Samson Group, The Netherlands
Connecticut
The Institute for Management Inc., a publishing firm located in Old Saybrook, has been acquired by WSG.

YKK, Japan
Georgia
YKK, U.S.A., will engage in a $100 million expansion of its zipper facility. Employment will be increased from 700 to 1000 persons.

Zahnradfabrik Friedrichshafen, West Germany
Ohio
ZF has purchased a division of Dana Corp., namely, the truck-transmission manufacturing unit. It will be operated as Z-F Spicer International.

Zeitler GmbH Packing, West Germany
New York
Zeitler's subsidiary, Glass and Frame Inc. plans to expand its wood frame business in Schenectady, NY. Employment: 47+ workers.

Notes

1. See John M. Stopford and John H. Dunning, *Multinationals: Company Performance and Global Trends* (London: Macmillan, 1983) and John M. Stopford, *The World Directory of Multinational Enterprises 1982-83* (Detroit: Gale Research Co., 1982).

2. U.S. Department of Commerce, Bureau of Economic Analysis (BEA), *Foreign Direct Investment in the United States,* Annual Survey Results, Preliminary 1982 Estimates, December 1984.

3. United Nations Center on Transnational Corporations, *Transnational Corporations in World Development, Third Survey* (New York, 1983). See also U.N. Center on Transnational Corporations, *The CTC Reporter*, 18 (Autumn 1984).

4. Ibid.

5. Ibid.

6. Ibid.

7. OECD, Committee on International Investment and Multinational Enterprises: *Trade Related Investment Measures and the International Investment Process* (Paris, 1984), *Detail Benchmark Definition of Foreign Direct Investment* (Paris, January 1983), and *Investment Incentives and International Investment Process* (Paris, 1983).

8. Richard Breadly and Stuart Mayers, *Principles of Corporate Finance,* 3d ed. (New York: McGraw-Hill, 1984).

9. David K. Eiteman and Arthur I. Stonehill, *Multinational Business Finance,* 3d ed. (Reading, Mass.: Addison-Wesley, 1982).

10. Group of Thirty, *Foreign Direct Investment 1973-87* (New York, 1984).

11. Eiteman and Stonehill, *op. cit.*

12. See Howard A. Stafford, *Principles of Industrial Location* (Atlanta: Conway Publications, 1979).

13. U.S. Department of Commerce, *The Multinational Corporation: Studies on U.S. Foreign Investment,* vol. 1 (1972), pp. 14-15.

14. Group of Thirty, *op. cit.*

15. Data in this section were obtained from the *Economic Report of the President* (Washington, D.C.: GPO) and U.S. Department of Commerce, BEA, *Survey of Current Business,* various issues.

16. U.S. Department of Commerce, Bureau of the Census, *Statistical Abstract of the United States, 1980.*

17. Ibid.

18. *Fortune*, August 1983 and August 1974.

19. U.S. Department of Commerce, BEA, *Foreign Direct Investment in the United States*, Annual Survey Results, Preliminary 1982 Estimates, December 1984; U.S. Department of Commerce, *Survey of Current Business* (October 1984).

20. Estimates by the author.

21. Estimates by the author.

22. Kenneth P. Johnson and Howard L. Friedenberg, "Regional and State Projections of Income, Employment, and Population to the Year 2000," *Survey of Current Business* (May 1985):39–63; Daniel H. Garnick, "Patterns of Growth of Metropolitan and Nonmetropolitan Areas: An Update," *Survey of Current Business* (May 1985):34–35.

23. *The Economic Report of the President* (Washington, D.C.: GPO, February 1985).

24. Statistics for this section come from U.S. Department of Commerce, Bureau of the Census, *Statistical Abstract of the United States, 1984*; *The Economic Report of the President, op. cit.*; International Monetary Fund, *Directions of Trade*, various issues, and U.S. Department of Commerce, International Trade Administration, *International Economic Indicators*, March 1985.

25. Ibid.

26. U.S. Department of Commerce, "U.S. Business Enterprises Acquired or Established by Foreign Investors in 1983," *Survey of Current Business*.

Index

About the Author

Harvey A. Poniachek is vice president and economist at Bank of America, North America Division, Economics and Marketing Research, and adjunct associate professor of economics and finance at New York University, College of Business and Public Administration. He has been with Bank of America since 1973—engaged in money and foreign exchange markets, strategic planning and banking studies, and monitoring the economies of Canada, Europe, the Middle East, and Africa. In 1979-80 he spent six months as a visiting economist at Bank of America's European headquarters in London.

Dr. Poniachek conducted major research studies on a broad spectrum of topics, including the Eurocurrency market and the foreign exchange system, international banking and the payments system, correspondent banking, the financial services industry and bank competition, regional economies, international trade finance, foreign direct investment, and financial management of U.S. MNCs. He has gained extensive expertise in the banking industry and was a member of the Hudson Institute study on the future of the financial services industry.

Harvey Poniachek received a Ph.D. degree in 1977 from the State University of New York at Albany where he specialized in econometrics, monetary economics, and international finance. He has published in professional journals and is the author of *Monetary Independence Under Flexible Exchange Rates* (1979); "The Financial Markets," chapter 18 of *Handbook of International Business*, edited by Ingo Walter (1982); and "Foreign Exchange Rate Determination," in *International Finance Handbook*, edited by A. George and I. Giddy (1982).

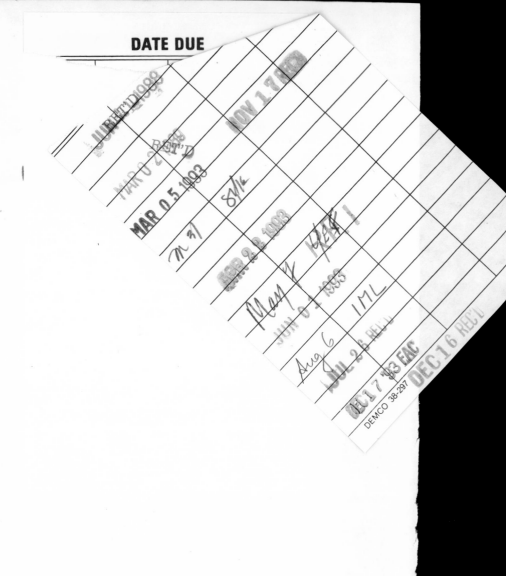